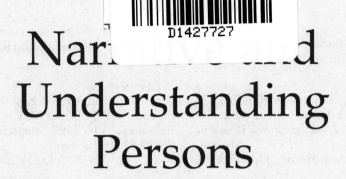

Narrative and Understanding Persons

ROYAL INSTITUTE OF PHILOSOPHY SUPPLEMENT: 60

EDITED BY

Daniel D. Hutto

CAMBRIDGE
UNIVERSITY PRESS

PUBLISHED BY THE PRESS SYNDICATE OF THE UNIVERSITY OF CAMBRIDGE
The Pitt Building, Trumpington Street, Cambridge, CB2 1RP,
United Kingdom

CAMBRIDGE UNIVERSITY PRESS
The Edinburgh Building, Cambridge CB2 8RU, United Kingdom
32 Avenue of the Americas, New York, NY 10013–2473, USA
477 Williamstown Road, Port Melbourne, VIC 3207, Australia
Ruiz de Alarcón 13, 28014 Madrid, Spain
Dock House, The Waterfront, Cape Town 8001, South Africa

© The Royal Institute of Philosophy and the contributors 2007

Printed in the United Kingdom at the University Press, Cambridge
Typeset by Michael Heath Ltd, Reigate, Surrey

Library of Congress Cataloguing-in-Publication Data applied for

Contents

List of Contributors

Kathy Behrendt, University of Oxford

Gregory Currie, University of Nottingham

Shaun Gallagher, University of Central Florida, USA

Peter Goldie, University of Manchester

Daniel Hutto, University of Hertfordshire

Peter Lamarque, University of York

Marya Schechtman, University of Illinois, Chicago, USA

Galen Strawson, City University of New York, USA, and University of Reading

Dan Zahavi, University of Copenhagen, Denmark

Notes on Contributors

Kathy Behrendt received a D.Phil from Oxford (under the supervision of Derek Parfit, Quassim Cassam, and Paul Snowdon) in 2000. She has held posts at New College and St. Catherine's College, University of Oxford. She has special interests in neo-Kantian approaches to personal identity and, more recently, in death. She has published works on personal identity and the self.

Gregory Currie teaches philosophy at the University of Nottingham where he is currently Dean of the Faculty of Arts. He is also an editor of *Mind and Language*. His most recent book is *Arts and Minds* (Oxford University Press, 2004) and he is completing a book on narrative. Related projects include work on points of view, on empathy, and on the anthropology of art and the aesthetic.

Shaun Gallagher is Professor of Philosophy and Cognitive Sciences at the University of Central Florida. He has been occasional Visiting Professor at the University of Copenhagen (2004–06) and Visiting Scientist at the Medical Research Council's Cognition and Brain Sciences Unit at Cambridge University (1994). He is co-editor of the interdisciplinary journal *Phenomenology and the Cognitive Sciences*. His research interests include phenomenology and philosophy of mind, cognitive sciences, hermeneutics, theories of the self and personal identity. His most recent book, *How the Body Shapes the Mind*, is published by Oxford University Press (2005). He is co-editor of *Does Consciousness Cause Behavior? An Investigation of the Nature of Volition* (MIT Press 2006). He is currently working on several projects, including a book co-authored with Dan Zahavi, *The Phenomenological Mind: Contemporary Issues in Philosophy of Mind and the Cognitive Sciences* (Routledge 2007). His previous books include: *Hermeneutics and Education* (1992) and *The Inordinance of Time* (1998).

Peter Goldie is The Samuel Hall Chair and Head of Philosophy at The University of Manchester. His main philosophical interests concern value and how the mind engages with value, and particularly with issues concerning the emotions, character, and narrative. He is the author of *The Emotions: A Philosophical Exploration* (Oxford: Clarendon Press, 2000), and *On Personality* (London: Routledge, 2004), editor of *Understanding Emotions:*

Notes on Contributors

Mind and Morals (Aldershot: Ashgate Publishing, 2002), and co-editor of *Philosophy and Conceptual Art* (Oxford: Oxford University Press, 2006).

Daniel D. Hutto is Professor of Philosophical Psychology at the University of Hertfordshire. His recent projects have focused on consciousness, intentionality and our everyday social understanding. He is author of *The Presence of Mind* (1999), *Beyond Physicalism* (2000), *Wittgenstein and the End of Philosophy* (2003/2006) and *Folk Psychological Narratives* (MIT Bradford Books, 2007) and a co-editor of *Folk Psychology Re-Assessed* (Springer, 2007).

Peter Lamarque is Professor of Philosophy at the University of York, UK. He is editor of the British *Journal of Aesthetics* and author of *Fictional Points of View* (Cornell, 1996), *Truth, Fiction, and Literature* (with Stein Haugom Olsen) (Oxford, 1994) and *Philosophy of Literature* (Blackwell, forthcoming). He edited *Philosophy and Fiction* (Pergamon, 1983), the *Concise Encyclopedia of Philosophy of Language* (Elsevier, 1997) and (with Stein Haugom Olsen) *Aesthetics and the Philosophy of Art: the Analytic Tradition: an Anthology* (Blackwell, 2003).

Marya Schechtman is Associate Professor of Philosophy at the University of Illinois at Chicago. She is the author of *The Constitution of Selves* and several articles on personal identity and the philosophy of psychology. Her current project is a manuscript exploring the relation between metaphysical and practical conceptions of personal identity.

Galen Strawson is Distinguished Professor of Philosophy at the CUNY Graduate Center, New York, and Professor of Philosophy at the University of Reading. He is the author of *Freedom and Belief* (1986), *The Secret Connexion: Realism, Causation and David Hume* (1989), *Mental Reality* (1994) and, with others, of *Consciousness and its Place in Nature* (2006).

Dan Zahavi (1967) is Professor of Philosophy and Director of the Danish National Research Foundation's Center for Subjectivity Research at the University of Copenhagen. He obtained his PhD from Katholieke Universiteit Leuven in 1994 and his D.Phil. from University of Copenhagen in 1999. Zahavi's systematic work has mainly focused on the notions of self-consciousness and intersubjectivity. Zahavi has been the recipient of the Ballard Prize in Phenomenology, and was awarded a prize by the Royal Danish Society of Sciences and Letters in 2000 for his research in phenomenology. He is currently serving as president of the Nordic Society for Phenomenology. Zahavi has published more than 100 articles on topics in philosophy of mind, phenomenology, and history of philosophy. His most important publications include *Husserl und die transzendentale Intersubjektivität* (Kluwer 1996), *Self-awareness and Alterity* (Northwestern University Press 1999), *Husserl's Phenomenology* (Stanford University Press 2003), and *Subjectivity and Selfhood* (MIT Press 2005).

Narrative and Understanding Persons

DANIEL D. HUTTO

Our world is replete with narratives—narratives of our making that are uniquely appreciated by us. This can hardly be denied, certainly if by 'narratives' we have in mind only those of the purely discursive variety—i.e. those complex representations that relate and describe the course of some unique series of events, however humble, in a coherent but selective arrangement.[1] Our capacity to create, enjoy and benefit from narratives so defined—be they factual or fictive—surely sets us apart from other creatures. Some, impressed by the prominence of this phenomenon in the traffic of human life, have been tempted to deploy that famous Aristotelian formula, holding that we are, *inter alia*, not just social or rational or political animals but that we are also rightly distinguished as *narrative* or *story-telling* animals.

This observation peaks philosophical interest in diverse ways. We might wonder: what, if anything, are the identifying features of narratives? What is the basis of our unique narrative capacities? Which cognitive and imaginative capacities enable us to produce and appreciate them? What roles or functions might narratives play in our lives? Although not exclusively, most of the papers collected

[1] This emphasis on the essentially discursive nature of narratives is consonant with a number of working definitions that have proposed to help us better understand the notion. See for example: G. Prince, *Narratology: The Form and Functioning of Narrative* (The Hague: Mouton, 1982), 4; J. Bruner, *Acts of Meaning* (Cambridge, MA: Harvard University Press, 1990), 43; P. Lamarque and S. Olsen, *Truth, Fiction and Literature* (Oxford: Oxford University Press, 1994), 225; N. Carroll, *Beyond Aesthetics* (Cambridge: Cambridge University Press, 2001), 126. Perhaps unsurprisingly, there is no agreed definition or criterion for sharply identifying narratives—and certainly none couched in terms of necessary and sufficient conditions. If it is thought that this is a serious concern about the philosophical usefulness of the notion then it must also be noted that we are no worse off in this regard than when we make free use of notions of such 'knowledge' or 'causation' (at least, as things stand). It seems we have little choice but to work with our pre-theoretic, unanalysed—ordinary—understanding of narratives. We can make clear enough what we mean by means of examples, if need be.

1

in this volume touch on this last question in one way or another (even if only by adopting a sceptical tone that urges caution about our expectations in this regard). The fact is that claims about what narratives 'do for us' range from the modest to the downright remarkable. The nine original contributions contained in this anthology divide into two types: those which clarify or warn against existing claims that have been made about the importance of narratives in our lives and those which advance new proposals on this topic. The first three papers fall into the latter category— advancing, in turn, distinct claims that narratives are implicated in, if not essential for: (a) enabling us to exercise our imaginations in unique ways; (b) developing our everyday understanding of actions performed for reasons; and (c) external reflection, evaluation and orientation in our understanding of the situations of ourselves and others.

In 'Framing Narratives', Gregory Currie considers how our engagements with fictional narratives—complex representational artefacts—allow us to exercise our imaginations, extending them to novel topics and in novel ways. He advances the view that apart from grasping an author's communicative intentions about the represented storied events, an important part of engaging with narratives involves the adoption of 'frameworks', for readers or listeners not only note what happens in stories, they are also 'encouraged to adopt a *way of engaging* imaginatively with those events' (Currie, this volume). This is quite distinct from the kind of imaginative demands required to apprehend a story's content—as detailed by its plot or *fabula*. Adopting a framework is instead to adopt a kind of attitudinal and emotional stance—in effect, it is to don a 'new persona' at the invitation of the narrative itself and the way it is constructed. Whether or not the invitation is issued by the author, it is our ability to engage with narratives in this sort of way that is responsible for their enabling us to see things in new ways (and not just to imagine new things).

Currie maintains that, so understood, the 'motives and mechanisms' that drive framework adoption are equally at work in other visceral and imaginative engagements; for example those that characterise joint attentional encounters. In both cases, subpersonal mechanisms for imitative and emotional responding are brought to bear.[2] Thus, even though consumers of narratives are not always in

[2] For this reason, he denies that the process is best understood in terms of developing a 'theory' (even if a not very explicit one) about the persona embedded in narrative.

the company of real others, both activities involve emotional and imaginative positionings. Often one harmoniously resonates with— even comes to identify with—another during joint attention. And the same can hold true of the way we engage with a given narrative. The important difference is that in the latter case even if one is not responding to another living human being one is still resonating with a personality (and never merely with a text), though the personality might not be that of the author. Importantly, we need not always identify with personas on offer; we can also react against or resist them. And this fact, Currie argues, sheds light on the problem of imaginative resistance, which is experienced when one is repelled by certain narratives. By distinguishing a narrative content from its framework, Currie offers a bifurcated account of the different kinds of imaginative abilities that must be employed when it comes to understanding and appreciating narratives. As a result, we can distinguish two importantly different varieties of imaginative dissonance that occur when we attempt to engage with some narratives—one being more intellectual than the other.

In his paper 'The Narrative Practice Hypothesis', Hutto identifies a quite different role that narratives might play in our lives—that of enabling us to use and develop our characteristic ability to make sense of intentional action as being performed for a reason. His proposal consists of two novel, complementary claims. The first is that our everyday understanding of intentional action is itself an essentially narrative practice—i.e. that 'folk psychological' understanding always takes the form of constructing narratives. The second is that children acquire the relevant interpretative skills for achieving this through repeated encounters with specific kinds of narratives, when they are appropriately supported by others. This is the normal route through which we become familiar with both the core principles of folk psychology and the norm-governed possibilities for wielding it in practice, i.e. knowing how and when to use it.

This goes against the received view that our everyday folk psychological abilities are a special kind of native cognitive endowment; one gifted to us by our evolutionary forefathers. Rather than supposing that this capacity depends upon or presupposes inherited 'theory of mind' abilities, Hutto argues, in contrast, that we each normally acquire a skilled understanding of basic folk psychology for the first time in ontogeny by engaging with narratives with a special subject matter—i.e. those which are about protagonists who act for reasons. In this, children must have the appropriate support of their carers, with whom these narratives, understood as complex representations, are objects of joint attention. Emphasizing this last point, Hutto takes a leaf out of Sellars' book and underlines the essentially intersubjective, socially scaffolded basis of our capacity to understand ourselves and others as those who act for reasons.

In 'Dramatic Irony, Narrative and the External Perspective' Peter Goldie emphasizes the important role that narratives play in enabling us to take up third-personal, but not impersonal, perspectives on the situations of others. This, he holds, is necessary if we are to engage with them properly. He contrasts this activity with that of perspective shifting of the sort in which one either imagines being in the shoes of the other or imagines being the other, taking on the relevant traits and dispositions oneself. On the supposition that in most cases we already have a reasonable grasp of the thoughts and feelings of others, Goldie's focus is on the question of 'how are we best to use the psychological resources at our disposal, including our imagination, to engage with these thoughts and feelings' (Goldie, this volume). In this context, echoing certain well-known criticisms of simulation theory, he worries that 'perspective shifting' accounts run the risk of leading us to *over*-identify with the other in ways that prevent or make it impossible to achieve an adequate appraisal or evaluation of their situation. Only in standing back, in grasping the wider details of the other's story—by appreciating dramatic ironies that are only visible from a distant, external stance—are we able to make the appropriate assessments.

Goldie's conclusion lends support to the popular idea that self-narratives are crucial vehicles for reflecting upon our lives and actions—that they make possible certain prominent kinds of our ethical and personal development. For example, autobiographical snippets, whether issued as remembrances of self-dialogue or in the natural course of conversing with others, serve as objects of reflection and review.[3] This sort of activity provides the fodder for steering and leading our lives in ways that other, less articulate creatures simply cannot.

---

[3] Autobiographical self-narratives, however short, reveal more than just the 'facts' about our situations (to the extent that they succeed even in that); their content and composition also reveals something about their authors—about their character and concerns. Something shows through in what one chooses to highlight about oneself and how this is done. It may be that these expressions are importantly influenced by our wider vision of ourselves. Bruner and Kalmar have explored this thought, framing it in

As such, 'the narratives we weave about our lives can profoundly affect how we respond to our past and how we lead our lives in the future'.[4] Only creatures capable of this kind of articulate self-scrutiny can make choices based on the higher-order reflection of first-order desires and tendencies.[5] Personal development based on such self-examination is neither thought to be straightforward nor easy, especially since what one is aiming at is not clearly defined in advance. In this respect it contrasts with the way we prosecute our more finite projects and it is for this reason that it has been frequently likened to embarking on a kind of medieval quest.[6] It goes without saying that if narratives did play any or all of these important roles, they would be phenomena of great philosophical significance.

Even so, these claims are comparatively modest. For some have taken a further step, holding that narrative activity is not only crucially important to human being in the sort of ways outlined above—they claim it is its *very core*. This view is enshrined in the idea that narratives are not just uniquely human creations of special importance but, as persons, we each and every one of us, are the unique creations of a special sort of narrative activity! Human selves just *are* narrative constructions. So seriously is that idea

---

the following way: "Typically, we tell ourselves about our own Self and about other Selves in the form of a story. These stories, however, seem to fall into narrative genres. Is this only a convention, or is it a necessary condition of self-telling?" (J. Bruner and D. A. Kalmar, 'Narrative and Metanarrative in the Construction of Self', *Self-awareness: Its Nature and Development*, M. Ferrari and R. J. Sternberg (eds.) (New York: Guilford, 1988), 308–331, 318). However, when we answer that question it seems clear that narrative expressions are a unique way of *manifesting* ourselves.

[4] P. Goldie, *On Personality* (London: Routledge, 2004), 117.

[5] For Taylor this equates to making 'strong evaluations', i.e. comparative judgements about our first-order desires, inclinations and choices. In doing this, he too holds that it is necessary to make use of an independent standard—one that we ought to acknowledge. C. Taylor, *Sources of the Self: The Making of Modern Identity* (Cambridge: Cambridge University Press, 1989), 4.

[6] See ibid., p. 48; A. MacIntyre, *After Virtue* (London: Duckworth, 1984), 219.

Daniel D. Hutto

entertained by some that it has even been proposed that 'we as a species might be appropriately named *Homo narrans* rather than *Homo sapiens*'.[7]

At first blush, such a re-designation and the claim about our nature upon which it is based may appear extravagant. Yet it would be difficult to overestimate the seductive attraction it holds for popular and scientific imaginations. I was reminded of this while taking a break from preparing this very introduction. I embarked on an expedition to the Science Museum in London in order to fulfil a promise to my eldest son, only to happen upon an exhibition entitled '100 years of psychology in Britain'. Serendipitously, there we saw the following words:

Telling Stories

Once upon a time, it was believed that stories merely recorded what happened in the world. But some modern psychologists have come to regard stories as having almost supernatural power. What we call 'human nature' is now thought by some to be created by language, by conversations, narratives, folk-tales, songs and poetry. We literally talk ourselves into existence.

This is headline grabbing stuff. If we take it seriously, the very idea naturally invites a host of questions. For example, we might wonder: How can *we* be the products of acts of narration, if in some sense we are responsible for the production of the relevant self-making narratives? This is an especially pressing question since proponents of the narrative self-constitution view are typically loathe to recognise the existence of narrative-transcendent selves— the kinds of selves that might play this logical role, acting as narrators. Instead, they have tended to attempt to make sense of the idea that human beings develop their ability to weave self-narratives slowly, over time. Additionally, it is often supposed that this process of development is socially mediated and scaffolded.[8] Through discrete stages human children gradually

---

[7] R. A. Neimeyer, 'Community and Coherence: Narrative Contributions to the Psychology of Conflict and Loss', *Narrative and Consciousness: Literature, Psychology and the Brain*, G. D. Fireman, T. E. McVay, and O. J. Flanagan (eds.) (Oxford: Oxford University Press, 2003), 167.

[8] For example, a major part of the notion I have of 'myself'—that is as a person exhibiting certain characteristics and fulfilling certain roles—is parasitic on my grasp of the canonical forms provided by my society. For example, the characters we encounter, both real and fictional, serve as models for my own self-understanding. Developmentally speaking, one

learn to form explicit self-narratives. Allegedly this enables them, not merely to describe and express themselves in new ways, but to become selves in the first place. These selves, as we know, become increasingly more elaborate and complex over time.

As a result, certainly in the early stages, 'we (unlike professional human storytellers) do not consciously and deliberately figure out what narratives to tell and how to tell them. Our tales are spun, but for the most part we don't spin them: they spin us'.[9] Accordingly, it is a mistake to think of your storyteller—the 'I'—as a self that exists independently, over and above the narratives that might be told about it. This is in line with the fact that it seems that the only way to characterise any such 'self'—the only way of giving it any substance—is to supply some sort of narrative or other about it.[10]

Reasoning of this sort is predicated upon the strong claim that 'our interpretation of ourselves is constitutive of what we are'.[11] The fashioning of any self worthy of the name is the outcome of a peculiar kind of hermeneutic activity. Consequently, personhood is not an automatic birthright of all human beings—and it looks like it may be forever denied to other species of animal. Schechtman makes explicit this consequence of the strong reading of the

---

learns to take up a 'story-telling' stance towards one's own actions just the way one learns to do so towards the actions of others.

[9] D. C. Dennett, *Consciousness Explained* (New York: Penguin Books, 1991), 418.

[10] Any substantive answer to the question 'Who am I?' requires an act of narrative self-expression (O. Flanagan, *Self Expressions: Mind, Morals and the Meaning of Life* (Oxford: Oxford University Press, 1996). Here we need more than a logical placeholder—a philosopher's 'I'. What we are after is a full-fledged 'me'. Being a 'me' requires having a persona (at least one!) that is tied to certain actions, reasons, projects, goals, and choices, which are only understood by looking both to the person's past and future. To be interested in this is to be concerned with the characterisation problem of personal identity and opposed to its more famous cousin the re-identification problem (the two are often confused or conflated, to no good effect).

[11] C. Taylor, 'Self-Interpreting Animals', *Human Agency and Language* (Cambridge: Cambridge University Press, 1985), 47.

narrative self-constitution view: 'Some, but not all, individuals weave stories of their lives, and it is their doing so that makes them persons'.[12]

This idea about what it is to be a person is frequently combined with the claim that this self-constituting narrative activity is necessary for ethical flourishing; i.e. it is the basis for the development of selves of the morally significant kind. Our self-narratives, it is held by some, are the means by which we navigate in moral space, orienting towards the good. It is usual that the scope of this activity is thought to be writ large: 'In many narratives the self seeks its identity on the scale of an entire life'.[13] Or, as Taylor famously remarks, 'as I project my life forward and endorse the existing direction and give it a new one, I project a future story, not just a state of the momentary future but a bent for my whole life to come'.[14]

These are very bold claims about the role and importance of narratives in our lives, and they invite philosophical critique. In his important piece 'Against Narrativity' Galen Strawson raised some serious challenges for those who assume that because some people have narrativizing tendencies when thinking about their lives, all do (a descriptive claim about human psychology). He also denounced as pernicious the (normative) claim that one must exhibit narrative tendencies in order to be truly ethical or lead a flourishing human life, defending instead the idea that there exists a range of possibilities for temporal self-experience. In this world, he claims, there are Episodics, Diachronics, non-Narratives and Narratives—each of whom enjoys distinct modes of self-experience. As the labels imply, only members of the latter class necessarily exhibit narrativizing tendencies of a non-trivial kind. If this is right, the narrativity thesis is false as an unrestricted claim about the character of human self-consciousness; not everyone tends to *experience* or *live* or *see* his or her life in a storied way. But more than this, Strawson has argued that none of these types can lay claim to ethical superiority.

---

[12] M. Schechtman, *The Constitution of Selves* (Ithaca: Cornell University Press, 1996), 94. The clear implication is that those unable to tell stories about themselves—those who cannot self-interpret, although immune from self-deception, buy this at the cost of being cut off from the possibility of self-knowledge and ethical development.

[13] P. Ricoeur, *Oneself as Another* (Chicago: Chicago University Press, 1992), 114–115.

[14] Ibid, p. 48.

Recapitulating and extending the latter critique in his contribution to this volume, 'Episodic Ethics', Strawson devotes himself to the task of undermining the claim that seeing one's life in narrative terms is an essential requirement of genuine human flourishing or moral being. His strategy is to demonstrate the falsity of this idea by establishing that living or experiencing life in an Episodic fashion—in which one does not regard one's self as something that persists in such a way that it was there in the (further) past and will be there in the (further) future—in no way impairs one's capacity to live an ethically and emotionally rich life. Consideration is given to the capacity of Episodics to experience negative moral emotions such as remorse, contrition, regret and guilt. These topics receive separate discussions in the essay.[15] Crucially, it is argued that having the morally relevant occurrent emotions and dispositions does not depend essentially on any particular mode of self-understanding or relating. We can be sure of this, he suggests, because the psychological mechanisms that inculcate and sustain moral behaviour—such as those of conscience and responsibility—are much more ancient than the Diachronic (let alone Narrative) modes of self-experience. On this point Strawson defends what he calls the Emotional Priority Thesis, in an attempt to ensure that the dependencies are understood the right way around. As a result, the content of moral experience and the focus of moral rebuke or praise should always be one's present dispositions—one's currently existing ethical virtues and vices. Accordingly we are told that, 'the heart of moral responsibility considered as psychological phenomenon is just a sort of instinctive responsiveness to things [and as such]... Moral responsibility in this fundamental sense is non-historical' (Strawson, this volume). The paper concludes by considering whether there are any other morally relevant traits—such as loyalty, gratitude, vengefulness, etc.—that are beyond the reach of Episodics. The verdict is that while certain temporal temperaments may be associated with certain traits more than others, nothing logically bars non-Narratives from exhibiting them in their own way—thus nothing prevents them from leading fully ethical lives.

Striking a similarly critical tone, Peter Lamarque emphasizes the important differences between literary narratives and those we find in the dialogues and conversations of everyday life. Against the popular narrativist trend, he warns of the serious dangers of

---

[15] For example, it is argued that guilt 'adds nothing to moral being' and that 'it is to be sure a chimpanzee thing' (this volume).

transposing (or more precisely, imposing) the former onto the latter; the risk of 'aestheticizing if not fictionalizing, real lives'. This happens, for example, when direct comparisons are made between a reader's life and that of some specific literary character or episode from literature. Such attempts operate on the supposition that art can—in important and illuminating ways—'hold up a mirror to life.' They are witnessed in the tendency to use literary examples as bases for influencing the direction of one's life or to inform activities of self-understanding and self-creation. Lamarque finds this especially worrisome. He maintains that any attempt to model our lives on those of literary figures is ill-founded because the degree of fit between the two is so poor. Such endeavours either involve taking over too much from art to life in a potentially dangerous way or, worse still, they promote a diminished understanding of what makes great literature great, i.e. by ignoring its unique qualities. Any successful attempt to treat literary characters as friends or as guiding exemplars would require us to bracket all of their specifically 'literary' properties.

In making this case, Lamarque cites five important principles that detail the precise ways in which literature is special. For example, we are reminded, *inter alia*, that the very existence of literary characters is entirely description-dependent; that their nature is determined by their being elements in a larger artistic canvas; and that every detail of a literary work admits of questions concerning its aesthetic significance with respect to the whole. In line with this, it is observed that the kind of explanation that is appropriate for making sense of literary actions and events differs sharply from the causal and rational varieties used in everyday life. Together these reflections underline a true gap between real-life and literary narratives. As a consequence it is concluded that insofar as accounts of narrative identity or self-constitution rely on making serious comparisons with literary characters or works, they are shown to be absurd and untenable.

In 'Reasons to be Fearful', Kathy Behrendt focuses on a topic—death—which she argues poses special challenges for both the Episodic view of the self promoted by Strawson and those narrativist accounts which model lives too directly on stories (i.e. those that, like conventional works of literature, have 'beginnings, middles and ends'). Strawson, as noted above, is of the view that there are many selves. Although they exist for variable duration, these are short-lived entities as compared with the human beings to whom they bear a special relation. This feature of Strawson's account is used to raise worries about the rational basis of his fearing death despite the fact that his self-experience is of the Episodic sort. The tension, Behrendt claims, is that he recognizes that his death must come after any future events in his life—i.e. it is an event which he, *qua* this present mental entity, will not undergo. Nevertheless, he holds that the threat of an infinitude of non-existence posed by death reasonably carries emotional import for him. Behrendt objects to this explanation on several grounds; her chief complaint is that if falls foul of the 'temporal fallacy' in that it wrongly treats death as an 'eternal state of affairs'—one that is directly comparable to what goes on in life. Moreover, Strawson's official reason for fearing death would give him equal reason to fear the infinity of non-existence that preceded his birth, by parity of reasoning. Consequently, she concludes, although it may be a fact that Strawson fears his death, there is no reason to do so in light of his episodic experiential tendencies. An illuminating comparison is then made between Strawson's anti-narrative views and traditional Epicurean offerings; both are ultimately regarded as debarring rational accommodation of this fear.

Even so, such a-rationalism may be superior to narrativist attempts to deal with this topic. For those who see lives in storied terms tend to think that we should not treat death per se as bad or regrettable, only premature death—i.e. the sort which interrupts a life before it has reached its 'proper' conclusion. But, Behrendt claims, this simply isn't the normal attitude that people—even those with narrativist tendencies—routinely take towards their own impending death. Moreover, she holds that it is not an attitude they can adopt unproblematically. For, to do so is to foreclose on life's possibilities in a restrictive and artificial way, and one which is at odds with the narrativist commitment to a view of life as fraught with possibilities and projecting towards a future. Also, once again, to hold this sort of view is to mistakenly treat death as 'an event in life'—as the concluding moment of each of our life-stories. Apart from misunderstanding the nature of death, this is problematic for the narrativist for other reasons too; for one's death is surely not an event that one can weave into a self-constituting narrative. Behrendt recognizes that some philosophers only seek to endorse the weaker view that narratives play a central role in shaping our lives without claiming that we in fact think of our lives in storied terms (or should do so). Yet she offers reasons for thinking that this softer rendering of the narrative account 'risks becoming a conceit'. In sum, it is concluded that our attitude towards death resists rational treatment by those with narrative and non-narrative tendencies alike.

Daniel D. Hutto

In the light of these criticisms, it seems desirable for those attracted to the narrative self-constitution view to seek to develop its more modest variants. One need not defend the view that the relevant narrative activity necessarily involves having an encompassing vision or story of one's life as a *whole* or that the narratives in question must be modelled on those of literature. For example, the self-narratives in question may be shorter than the shortest short story. In responding to MacIntyre on this very point, Cooper once convincingly argued that reason-giving explanations are in effect 'little narratives', designed to make our actions intelligible occasion by occasion. And, as he insisted, it 'would be illegitimate to extrapolate from the existence of these little narratives to a grand narrative of a life-as-a-whole'.[16] Others have recognised this too: 'Like plans, these narratives can be 'larger' or 'smaller', structured hierarchically, from a narrative about a whole life, right down the 'mini-narrative' that you might tell of this morning you got up, got dressed and had breakfast'.[17] This seems to highlight an important difference in the roles that shorter self-narratives and those of the meta-variety might play. This suggests a more modest rendering of the narrative self-constitution thesis: perhaps selves need not always be built from knitting together a series of mini-narratives in order to form an 'omnibus' edition. Indeed, for some, this latter activity may simply be impossible for various reasons.[18]

Obviously, what one says on this score matters to the content and assessment of the narrative self-constitution view. For example, it was noted above that Galen Strawson argues fiercely against the truth of the psychological narrativity thesis, descriptively construed. He holds that it is false in any *non-trivial* sense. But, crucially, he fashions his criterion of triviality with direct reference to Taylor. Thus Strawson allows that many everyday activities—his own example is that of coffee-making—might involve past appraisal and future planning of a quite *limited* scope—and to this extent he allows that they might be said to involve narration in an uninteresting sense.[19] Yet, it is arguable that, far from being trivial, these narratives ought to be at the centre of our attention in

---

[16] D. Cooper, 'Life and Narrative', *International Journal of Moral and Social Studies* 3, 1988, 161–172, 165.

[17] P. Goldie, op. cit. note 4, 116.

[18] Bruner and Kalmar focus on what 'impels and deters' from production of such meta-narratives, op. cit. note 4.

[19] See G. Strawson, 'Against Narrativity', *Ratio* 17 (2004), 428–542, reprinted in *The Self?*, G. Strawson (ed.) (Oxford: Blackwell, 2005), 73.

understanding certain self-directed activity as much as those of the more meta-variety. If so, this would presumably close the gap between the Espisodic, Diachronic and Narrative temperaments, which Strawson identifies.

This theme is picked up and developed by Schechtman in her contribution. In direct response to Strawson's worries, she sets out to clarify and refine her original narrative self-constitution thesis. Crucially, a useful taxonomy is provided by considering a range of possible answers to three important questions: What counts as a life narrative? What count as having a narrative? And, what are the practical implications of having (or failing to have) a narrative? Narrative views exist along a continuum precisely because any given one might advance stronger or weaker replies to each of these questions. Like Goldilocks (and baby bear), Schechtman prefers a moderate response every time. Locating her own account in the mid-range, while she denies that the construction of self-narratives can be understood as purely sub-personal activity, it is equally not something that need be an explicit project. So understood, 'there is no requirement that an identity constituting narrative have a unifying theme, or represent a quest or have a well defined plot that fits a distinct literary genera'.

More than this, she now identifies two distinct but inter-related strands within her position. These speak to different questions about personal identity that come into view when we distinguish 'selves' of the Strawsonian Episodic variety—i.e. psychological entities that are the subjects of experience—from 'persons'—whose existence implies longer term social relations, commitments and responsibilities. To be a person is to exist in such way as to be open to moral and legal accountability, and for it to make sense that one has concerns for one's future and continued survival. Selves, by way of contrast, are less public and less long-lasting. They are bound up with certain actions and experiences in a strong way that is affectively salient, thus only certain phases of our existence are identity-conferring with respect to selfhood. Accordingly, persons and selves are constituted by different kinds of self-narratives, in different ways; the life of a single person may be comprised of many distinct shorter narratives. Acknowledging this distinction yields a more nuanced and multi-faceted version of the narrative self-constitution view. A complete account of personal identity, Schechtman claims, requires attending to both aspects. Not only does this division of labour provide the basis for a more refined, two-tiered narrative account of personal identity, she claims that it is compatible with Strawson's observations in a way that defuses his primary objections. Nevertheless, disagreements are likely to remain—the paper concludes by considering those that are most likely and important.

Focusing on how to best understand the correct interface between phenomenology and hermeneutics, Dan Zahavi raises concerns about narrative accounts of the self from a different direction—and in a way that matters in the light of Schechtman's proposed refinements. After providing an extremely valuable short review of prominent positions in the literature, he stresses limits and potentially distorting effects of the narrative view of the self, if it is adopted as the only way of legitimately understanding selfhood. Specifically, he attempts to demonstrate that unqualified, extreme narrative approaches to the self are limited in two important respects. Fundamentally, they fail to recognize appropriately the existence of a core consciousness of the sort that is primitive and pre-reflective; one is bound up with non-discursive ways of being in the world—i.e. the kinds of consciousness that are associated with the having of a first person perspective, experiences of embodied ownership and the like. Since such experiences are phenomenologically salient, if Zahavi is right to claim that 'it doesn't make sense to speak of a first-person perspective without speaking of a self' then it seems we have little option but to acknowledge the existence of non-narrative selves. Relatedly, it is complained that this failure makes it impossible for proponents of exclusively narrative accounts of selfhood to make adequate sense of the experience of 'otherness' of the sort that has been highlighted by Sartre and Lévinas. To regard others as always completely accessible to us by means of some narrative or other is unfaithful to aspects of our phenomenology. Despite these criticisms, Zahavi makes it clear however that he sees a potential partnership between different treatments of core and narratively extended forms of consciousness, holding out hope that phenomenology and hermeneutics may yet prove to be complementary.

Gallagher's concluding contribution provides a good example of how this might be achieved. Recognizing that narratively constituted selves are not the *only* selves, he concentrates on explicating the underlying cognitive capacities that underpin our basic narrative competency—those which make it possible to enjoy the developmental opportunities that engaging in intersubjective, socially framed narrative practices provide. To benefit from these requires capacities not only for understanding narratives but also a basic kind of narrative understanding. Focusing on the capacity to generate coherent self-narratives, he distinguishes and discusses four non-negotiable pre-requisites. These comprise capacities for temporal ordering (constituting two sub-abilities that relate, on the one hand, to the objective ordering of events and, on the other, to the capacity to situate past and future happenings egocentrically); minimal self-reference; episodic and autobiographical memory; and metacognition. Each of these capacities is discussed in its own right, but so too are the complex dependencies and inter-dependencies between them.

Picking up on a familiar thread, Gallagher argues that the ultimate pay-off of exercising our narrative competencies in the right way and in the right conditions is the development of a narrative self. But, like Schechtman, he opts for a modest understanding of such selves, holding that 'The narrative self may be more than a simple abstract point of interesting narratives, but less than a unified product of a consistent narrative' (Gallagher, this volume). Indeed, he holds that narratively constituted selves will be more or less stable and unified and that they are always at serious risk of self-deception, confabulation and the like. This is illustrated in his concluding discussion of the deficits in narrative competency, as present in dysnarrativia and various forms of schizophrenia, which serve as powerful reminders of the value and importance of our capacity to form coherent and stable, if less than fully unified, self-narratives.

Framing Narratives

GREGORY CURRIE

Marianne Dashwood was well able to imagine circumstances both favourable and unfavourable to her. But for all her romantic sensibility she was not able to imagine these things from anything other than her own point of view. 'She expected from other people the same opinions and feelings as her own, and she judged of their motives by the immediate effect of their actions on herself.'[1] Unlike her sister, she could not see how the ill-crafted attentions of Mrs. Jennings could derive from a good nature. And when Elinor had to explain her troubles with Edward Ferrars, she knew that Marianne would feel it as a reminder of her own relations to Willoughby, judging Edward's behaviour as equivalent to that of Willoughby himself. Without the capacity to shift her point of view, Marianne can get no ironic distance from herself; she cannot see the unrealism of her later determination 'to live solely for my family'.

Simplifying a good deal, we can say that imaginative abilities vary on two dimensions. Imagination gives us the capacity to engage with things and events which are not (at least not yet) actual. Imagination also gives us ways of responding to things in the world, and to things that may be offered us to imagine in this first sense, from a perspective not our own. Marianna's excess of the one and lack of the other dramatically narrow her understanding; her's is a vividly imagined and highly egocentric world. Elinor's good sense derives from a balance of the two, and no act of imagining, however vivid and affecting, is allowed to dominate just because it claims the authority of her own perspective.

This essay explores some ways in which fictional narratives exercise these imaginative abilities together.

1 Narratives and their frameworks

Makers of narratives give us connected sequences of events, sometimes of their own invention, sometimes by way of an attempt to reconstruct the real past. The agent who merely conceives a series of events, however connected, has not yet made a narrative;

---

[1] J. Austen, *Sense and Sensibity*, Volume II, Chapter 9.

Gregory Currie

that requires a coherent representational vehicle—words, sounds, images—capable of making the events and their relations, or some of them, intelligible to an audience. A narrative is an artefact, wherein the maker seeks to make manifest his or her communicative intentions. When the audience grasp those intentions, they have a grip on what the events of the narrative are, and how they are related.

In communicating these events, the maker may do more; he or she may convey a *framework* which the reader is encouraged to adopt, a way of engaging imaginatively with those events. Adopting this framework helps us 'to notice and respond to the network of associations that make up the mood or emotional tone of a work.'[2] The maker represents the events of the story, and by representing them, expresses certain evaluations of and responses to those events. By the operation of mechanisms I'll discuss later, this translates into our feeling a pull, often a substantial one, in the direction of just those responses. Sometimes that way of responding is one we easily and comfortably adopt. But some narratives frame their events in ways that do not come naturally to us, and good narratives often challenge us to see events in unfamiliar ways.[3]

I should say something about the idea that narratives *represent* their stories, and are *expressive* of their frameworks, for the distinction I intend is not readable from the common (and varied) meanings these terms have. I treat representation and expression as different ways in which something can function for us as an *indicator*.[4] In my terms, a narrative counts as a representation of its story because it indicates to us what its story is in a communicative way—via uptake of utterer's intentions. Makers of narratives tell their stories by getting us to see what their story-telling intentions are. And a narrative is expressive of its framework in so far as that framework is indicated to us, not via our recognition of the maker's

---

[2] R. Moran, 'The Expression of Feeling in Imagination', *Philosophical Review* 103, 1994, 75–106, 86. I am indebted to Moran's account of the distinction between imagining something, and approaching something in an imaginative way.

[3] See W. Booth's *The Company We Keep: An Ethics of Fiction* (Chicago: Chicago University Press, 1988) for a perceptive account of our relations with 'our best narrative friends.'

[4] For an account of the relations between indication and representation see F. Dretske, *Explaining Behaviour* (Cambridge, Mass.: MIT Press, 1988), Chapter 3.

intention but by less reasoned, more affectively driven and perhaps more automatic processes, some of which I shall describe further on.

Note, however, that the representation/expression distinction as I make it maps imperfectly onto the story/framework distinction. Narrative makers will occasionally represent some of the evaluations and responses that go to make up the framework, engaging in explicit communication about how we should engage with the work; Trollop is fond of telling us what he thinks of his characters and, taking on a tiresome narrative persona, will even relate his reactions on having met them. Still, framework goes better, more naturally with expression than with representation; narrative makers do not need to make explicit statements in order to guide our responses, and often succeed better when they don't. And explicit statement has a fragile status in determining a framework; what is merely expressed will dominate if there is a clash, with the explicit statement now labelled 'unreliable narration'. Importantly, what is expressed need not be intended. Our story-telling often gives people reason to draw conclusions about our own frameworks, conclusions that we did not intend them to draw and which we might not be aware of, just as our facial expressions and postures express our feelings. With the canonical works of literature, drama and film, we do often find a narrative constructed with the intention that it be expressive of a certain stance. With Henry James, the urge to impose a framework rises almost to the level of obsession, with the narrator acting as a busy sheep dog, worrying at the flock of readers who, unattended, might wander off in a comfortable, familiar and unchallenging direction.[5] But even in these cases framework is a matter of expression; whatever is intended, the effect on the audience need not depend on their recognition of that intention.

Being both representational and expressive, narratives give us two things: a series of connected events (the story, sometimes called a *fabula*), and a framework of preferred emotional and evaluative responses to those events. The framework will usually be vague and incomplete; it rarely does more than guide our responses in a general way. But the narrative's story is vague and incomplete as well: no story manages (or seeks) to determine the world of its happenings with precision and completeness.

[5] For an analysis of the kind of expression at issue here along with illuminating literary examples see J. Robinson, 'Style and Expression in the Literary Work', *Philosophical Review* 94, 1985, 227–247.

Gregory Currie

Story and framework are distinct things, and they correspond to the answers we give to two distinct questions: 'what happens according to the story?' and 'how are we supposed to respond to those happenings?'. But we generally cannot identify the one without identifying the other. The dependence of our knowledge of framework on our knowledge of story is obvious; we can't see what the act of representing story events expresses unless we also know what that act is—what it succeeds in representing. And dependence runs the other way: the framework itself partly determines how we are to take things that are said about the story's events. Is the preferred response to the narrator a skeptical one? Knowing the answer may depend on a sense of the mood or tone of the piece. If we take her to be unreliable, we will have to radically rethink our assumptions about what happens in the story.

Working out the events of a story is often subject to indeterminacies of interpretation: there may be nothing to choose between the assumption that something happened according to the story, and that it did not. There can be similar indeterminacy with respect to what is expressed, and so there may be irresolvable disagreements about framework. There may also be indeterminacies about what is story and what is framework. We are in that region where things 'present themselves sometimes as statements but at other times as programmes of action or announcements of a stance'.[6] With so much unclarity, it is not surprising that narrative makers confuse us, and perhaps themselves, by offering what looks like narrative content, or elements of story, but which, properly understood, amount to disguised exercises in framing. Later on I'll consider two prominent works, one literary and one filmic, which have profited by this confusion.

While frameworks do have a special interest for us in cases of great literature, the motives and mechanisms that govern the workings of narrative frameworks are visible in a much broader class of phenomena. Framing is a quite general feature of communication, and one that occurs in simple, jointly constructed narratives of early childhood—probably for good developmental reasons. Showing this will be part of the project of accounting for the comparative ease with which narratives place their audiences within the frameworks they express, an ease which derives from the use of powerful mechanisms which govern human practices of

---

[6] J. Heal, *Mind, Reason and Imagination* (Cambridge: Cambridge University Press, 2003), 27. Heal is discussing cases quite different from those we are considering here.

imitation and joint attention. But there are limits, as I have indicated, to the framing capacity of narratives: an issue that has been highlighted by recent work on the problem of imaginative resistance. I will argue that this problem is, at least in one of its guises, posed by the limitations on our capacity to adopt frameworks rather than by our capacity to imagine this or that element of the story's narrative content.

2 The natural history of frameworks

Frameworks are important for understanding narrative, but so they are for understanding almost any communicative act. Sharing information is not always the only or even the primary reason for communication. Sometimes communication serves primarily to bring about a sharing of framework. Here is an example where no narrative is in play; I adapt it from an example used by Dan Sperber and Deirdre Wilson to illustrate a somewhat different point.[7]

Arriving for a holiday at Lake Como, Janet throws open the balcony doors and, in a way that is visible to John, and is clearly intended to be visible, sniffs appreciatively at the air. This is a communicative act: an action which, in Sperber and Wilson's terms, guarantees its own optimal relevance. What does Jane mean by doing this? That the air is fresh? The freshness of the air is already evident to John. Janet is arranging things so that she and John attend to the freshness of the air, in a way that is mutually manifest to both of them. But Janet is doing more: she is adjusting John's cognitive and affective take on the world: trying to get John to see the world in somewhat the way she is currently seeing it. There is a small, highly salient portion of the world visible to both of them, and Janet wants John to attend to that portion of it in the way that she is attending to it: appreciatively, gratefully, with excitement at the possibilities for the holiday that has just begun. She does not want to convey any propositions to John: she wants him to notice certain things; to engage imaginatively with certain possibilities which these things present; to see these things and possibilities as valuable in certain ways. She wants John to frame the visible world in a certain way. It would be vastly impractical—perhaps impossible—for Janet to try to *say* all this, to make explicit the way

---

[7] See D. Sperber and D. Wilson, *Relevance* (Second Edition, Oxford: Blackwell, 1994).

she wants John to frame the bit of world they are looking at. It would also be pointless: the minimal gesture does the job very well.

Frameworks have to be on or for something. Janet and John's situation provides them with a natural focus on a restricted part of the world—the view from the window—which has a significance for them they already appreciate in much the same way. Janet's gesture would convey much less—would indeed, hardly be comprehensible at all—if they did not have this part of the world as a natural and unspoken focus of attention, as well as having a shared awareness of certain salient and unusual aspects of the situation. The context enabled Janet to pick out a small part of the world and to adjust John's way of attending to it so as to bring it into line with hers. That shared background and the clarity concerning what is to be attended to—the restricted bit of the world visible in a certain direction—is what enables Janet to achieve all this with minimal activity.

Adopting a framework proffered by a narrative or by a conversational remark is an imaginative activity, often requiring us to respond in ways that call for effort, and mental flexibility, stretching ourselves conceptually and emotionally to participate in a way of seeing things which we don't spontaneously or easily enter into. In John's case as I described it, little imaginative activity is called for. He already shares the dispositions, preferences and knowledge that make Janet's response to the view a natural one; to see the scene in the way that Janet does requires very little reorientation. Still, if John were particularly unimaginative he may have trouble tuning in effectively to Janet's way of seeing. And John's task could be harder; he might be dropping Janet off at her destination, not expecting, or wanting, to share the holiday. But with imaginative flexibility, he might enter into her way of seeing things, just for the moment: sufficiently well, at least, to glimpse from the inside her sense of anticipation. If John thoroughly dislikes fresh air, lake views and Italian cooking the project will challenge his imaginative powers a good deal. Whatever the difficulties, they can't be overcome by having John simply imagining certain propositions: that fresh air and lake views are invigorating; that Italian cooking is delicious. Imagining these propositions, which he will find easy enough, won't help him to enter into Janet's way of seeing things, which is what her appreciative sniff invites him to do. What he needs to do is to enter imaginatively into a framework that includes valuing these things, even though he may not value them himself—or not so much as, or in the same way that Janet does.

I said that Janet is arranging things so that she and John attend jointly to certain things. What I am calling a framework is a pervasive feature of situations of *joint attention*. Children engage in acts of joint attention by the age of about 18 months: they draw a care-giver's attention to some object or event, not because they want the care-giver to do anything—fetch a toy, say—but in order simply to bring it about that the child and the care-giver attend together to the object or event.[8] Joint attending is enjoyed by children for its own sake, and seems to be an important milestone in the development of normal affective relations with others. Mature humans also enjoy acts of joint attention, as with shared spectatorship. One reason this is attractive is that jointly attending to certain scenes has a tendency to bring about emotional harmony between the parties, and, since it is common knowledge between us that we are jointly attending, it may also be common knowledge that we are reacting in similar or complementary ways. That is how it is with Janet and John. Where this harmony cannot be established, as with spectators supporting different teams, tension is likely to result.

My second example of framework in conversation is one where joint attention serves to aid the construction of a narrative. This is a real rather than an imagined conversation, reported by Robyn Fivush, between mother and child:

M: What happened to your finger?

C: I pinched it

M: You pinched it. Oh boy, I bet that made you feel really sad.

C: Yeah ...it hurts

M: Yeah, it did hurt. A pinched finger is no fun ... But who came and made you feel better?

C: Daddy![9]

---

[8] For an important collection of essays on joint attention, see *Joint Attention: Communication and Other Minds: Issues in Philosophy and Psychology*, N. Eilan, C. Hoerl, T. McCormack, and J. Roessler (eds) (Oxford: Oxford University Press, 2005).

[9] R. Fivush, 'Constructing narrative, emotion and gender in parent-child conversations about the past', *The Remembering Self: Construction and Accuracy of the Life Narrative*, U. Neisser and R. Fivush (eds.) (New York: Cambridge University Press, 1994), quoted in C. Hoerl and T. McCormack, 'Joint Reminiscing as Joint Attention to the Past' in Eilan *et al*. (op. cit. note 9).

Gregory Currie

In this conversation a brief, factually based narrative of past events is constructed; it tells us that the child was hurt, and felt sad as a consequence, but the intervention of daddy made things better. Christoph Hoerl and Teresa McCormack treat this exchange as an example of joint attention to the past, a means by which children come to understand the causal structure of events in time, and the role of memory in argument. They also note the extent to which, in this case, the mother guides the construction of the narrative which this conversation embodies, prompting a reminiscence of how the child felt about the past event, and correcting the child's tendency to speak of the hurt in the present tense by explicitly contrasting the past pain with the later intervention by daddy, who 'made you feel better', thus bringing the narrative to a satisfactory closure. The mother guides the construction and ordering of represented events, taking care to place events in their correct chronological order, while at the same time providing a framework within which to engage with the narrative: recalling the hurt but discouraging a strong resurgence of negative emotion by emphasizing the positive turn of events after that. As Hoerl and McCormack put it, such guided narrative constructions enable mother and child to arrive at a 'shared personal and emotional evaluation of the past'.[10] I suggest that this sense of a shared personal and emotional evaluation survives and indeed flourishes in our most mature engagements with narratives, where the sharing has come to be between audience and the authorial personality manifested in the narrative itself.

But we cannot assimilate all or even most cases of attending to narrative to cases of joint attention. As that notion is commonly understood, joint attention involves a condition of mutual openness between the parties—an essential component in the situation of the mother and child described above. It is not easy to specify exactly what is involved in this, but no condition of openness can really be satisfied when one of the two parties—in this case the author— knows nothing of the other, and may not even know whether there is such another party.[11] We might seek to avoid this problem by claiming that engagement with a narrative involves the pretence of genuine joint attending with another, just as it involves a pretence

[10]   Hoerl and McCormack, op. cit. note 9. Hoerl and McCormack acknowledge a debt to the work of Katherine Nelson.
[11]   On the openness of joint attention see C. Peacocke, 'Joint Attention: its Nature, Reflexivity, and Relation to Common Knowledge', in Eilan *et al.* (op. cit. note 9). Peacocke opposes the idea that openness need be explicated in terms of common knowledge, proposing instead that we

which gives rise to that fictional being 'the authorial personality' who, it is generally recognised, is not at all the same being as the flesh and blood author. While some encounters with narrative may be of this kind, many, I think, are not; at least, there is not much in many experiences of narrative engagement to support so complicated an hypothesis. Instead, I prefer to think of the typical situation of one engaged by a narrative as psychologically grounded in those capacities which make us apt to be seekers of joint attention, without itself constituting a case of joint attention in the strict sense. The experience of genuine situations of jointly attending to narrative is a formative and salient event in a person's development towards mature narrative engagement, and an influence on the later experience of engaging with the 'prepackaged' narratives of literature, film and the theatre. The enjoyment we get from the experience of attending with a narrative's authorial personality (however that notion is formally to be characterized) is of very much the same kind as the pleasure of genuinely joint attending, and derives, I believe, from the same set of mental dispositions that underlie that other pleasure.[12]

So let us think of joint attention as a refined form of a more general phenomenon wherein one experiences the influence of another's attention to some object on one's own attention to it; call this guided attention. The refinement consists in the fact that, with joint attention, all parties are symmetrically placed with respect to the openness of the experience. We find examples of many kinds within this broad class. In the observance of tradition, for example, we attend to something in the service of sharing a response with those who may be long dead, and it is the thought of their (possibly idealized) response to the situation that modulates our own response to it.

---

understand openness in terms of a condition of mutual perceptual availability; such a condition would not generally be satisfied in the narrative case.

[12] There are other ways in which we jointly attend to narratives, as when you and I watch a film together, and this sort of joint attending can have significant effects on one's understanding and experience of the work. But while this kind of joint attending deserves more attention than it has received, I am not going to explore it here.

Gregory Currie

The cases of guided attending I have discussed all have a distinctively emotional component.[13] They involve, and may be designed to involve, valued experiences of shared emotion, directed at a scene or object. I emphasise the role of emotion here because adopting a framework for a narrative means being *tuned* to the narrative's content; being apt to respond to it in selective and focused ways that show some stability over the length of one's engagement with its characters and events. Emotions bind together the elements of the narrative, placing some in the foreground, and making connections between what we know now and what is yet to be revealed.[14] Such a mode of engagement, because of its relatively sustained character (if only for the duration of reading) and because it involves a variety of responses to a rich pattern of events, draws on something like a whole persona, though one which may not be fully the subject's own. Adoption of a framework is, to a greater or lesser degree, a matter of the imaginative exploration of this persona.[15]

[13] For the emotional significance of joint attention see the work of Peter Hobson (e.g. 'What Puts the Jointness into Joint Attention?', Eilan, *et al.* (op. cit. note 9)). Johannes Roessler ('Joint Attention and the Problem of Other Minds', Eilan *et al.* (op. cit. note 9)) argues that the experience of having an emotional reaction to an object corrected by an adult with whom the child is jointly attending is a source of the child's sense of objectivity. Thanks here to Tom Cochrane for discussion and references.

[14] On the capacity of emotions to generate 'patterns of salience and tendencies of interpretation', see K. Jones, 'Trust as an Affective Attitude', *Ethics* 107, 1996, 4–25. See also N. Carroll, 'Art, Narrative and Moral Understanding', in his *Beyond Aesthetics* (Cambridge: Cambridge University Press, 2001). For a particularly strong thesis about the relationship between emotion and narrative see D. Velleman, 'Narrative Explanation', *Philosophical Review* 112, 2003, 1–25.

[15] Note that I draw the domain of the emotions here very widely. It is much larger than the domain we would get if we were to count emotions conservatively, including only those large-scale, recurrent, culturally salient affective states which themselves have distinctive narrative shape and a name we recognize as putting them on the list of emotions. But in addition to love, fear, jealousy, disgust and the other cases we easily recognize as emotions, there are small-scale nameless urgings that direct our attention to certain stimuli and prime us for action in ad hoc ways. When I speak hereafter about emotions I mean to include the small-scale as well as the large, the unnamed as well as the named. There are purposes for which this would not be a useful principle of grouping, but I think it meets the needs of the present case. In my very generous sense of

3 How is framework conveyed?

How does guided attending to narrative come about, and how is it kept on track through what may be a long and complex narrative with many shifts of mood and style? One kind of answer appeals to theorizing about other minds: as we read or otherwise engage with a narrative we develop a theory—perhaps not a very explicit one—about the personality expressed, and about details of this personality's take on the story, and we adjust our own take to match this personality. I don't deny a role for this in the processes by which guided attending takes place. Huge cognitive investment in self-conscious theorising about narrative can produce a few worthy souls able to adjust their affective and evaluative take on a narrative in this way. But it seems to me likely that, most of the time, framework adoption works by the activation of subpersonal mechanisms which tend to produce imitative behaviour, though we as individuals may know little about the mechanism—or indeed about the behaviour—and have limited powers to control its operations.[16] We are, it turns out, astonishingly imitative creatures, and imitation probably plays an important role in the acquisition of skills and hence in the spreading of cultural practices, as well as in achieving harmony and solidarity between group members.[17] We adopt the tone of voice of someone we are listening to, and their mood as well.[18] Certain pathologies remove the inhibition to imitation, leaving people in the grip of a drive to imitate in inappropriate circumstances.[19] Strength in imitation seems to go with high levels of empathy and with social understanding, and

---

'emotion', at least a good deal of framework adoption consists in being apt to engage emotionally with the events and characters of the narrative.

[16] On the role of what he calls 'automatic processes' in causing us to adopt imagined points of view see J. Harold, 'Infected by Evil', *Philosophical Explorations* 8, No. 2, 2005, 173–187.

[17] See e.g. M. Tomasello, *The Cultural Origins of Human Cognition* (Harvard: Harvard University Press, 2000).

[18] See R. Neumann, and F. Strack, 'Mood Contagion: The Automatic Transfer of Mood between Persons', *Journal of Personality and Social Psychology* 79, 2000, 211–223. See also my discussion of some views of N. Carroll on mood in 'A Claim on the Reader', *Imaginative Minds*, I. Roth (ed) (Oxford: Oxford University Press, 2007, forthcoming).

[19] See S. Hurley, 'Active Perception and Perceiving Action: the Shared Circuits Hypothesis', *Perceptual Experience*, T. S. Gendler and J. Hawthorne, (eds.) (New York: Oxford University Press, 2004).

children with autism—a disorder marked by rigid, unimaginative thought—tend to be poor imitators.[20] We like people better if they imitate us, and we imitate people more if we like them.[21] The best way for a waiter to increase his or her tips is simply to make sure to repeat the order back to the customer word for word.[22]

Looking back at the mother-child narrative reported earlier, it is easy to see how in that case imitation, underpinned by nothing more cognitive than the contagious expression of feeling, plays a part in bringing about the emotional adjustment in the child's way of seeing things that leads to them jointly attending to the past in an harmonious way. When mother says

> A pinched finger is no fun ... But who came and made you feel better?

We can imagine the changing tone of voice that first encourages a regretful recollection of the pain followed by an upward curve of affect leading in to the child's delighted 'Daddy!'

You might have a worry about imitation like the one I noted earlier concerning joint attention: imitation can't be the driving force behind framework adoption in the case of narrative, since the author is generally not present to be imitated, and may indeed be long dead. And imitation may account for changes in behaviour, but can hardly account for the sorts of subtle cognitive and affective changes that will be involved in adoption of a framework. I am not troubled by these objections. We have plenty of evidence for the existence of strong tendencies to deferred imitation: infants at nine months will imitate up to a week after they have seen an initial behaviour performed.[23] More significantly, we—adults included—are strongly inclined to imitate people who are not

---

[20]   See P. Hobson and A. Lee, 'Imitation and Identification in Autism', *Journal of Child Psychology and Psychiatry* 40, 1999, 649–659.

[21]   T. L. Chartrand, and J. A. Bargh, 'The Chameleon Effect: The Perception-Behavior Link and Social Interaction', *Journal of Personality and Social Psychology* 76, 1999, 893–910; E. E. Balcetis, M. Ferguson, and R. Dale 'An Exploration of Social Modulation of Syntactic Priming', draft available at http://www.people.cornell.edu/pages/eeb29/mimicry.pdf.

[22]   R. B. van Baaren, R. W. Holland, B. Steenaert, A. van Knippenberg, 'Mimicry for Money: Behavioral Consequences of Imitation', *Journal of Experimental Social Psychology* 39, 2003, 393–398.

[23]   A. Meltzoff, 'Immediate and Deferred Imitation in Fourteen and Twenty-four Month-old Infants', *Child Development* 56, 1985, 62–72; and 'Infant Imitation and Memory: Nine-month-olds in Immediate and Deferred Tests', *Child Development* 59, 1988, 217–225.

merely absent but who do not and never did exist. Ingenious experiments reveal how easily we can be brought to imitate people we have been asked to imagine, even where the imagining has been sketchy and of brief duration. Indeed, it is surprisingly easy to cause people to imitate the cognitive and affective style of a stereotypical group member when they are asked to imagine one, even in areas where we might think there was little capacity for variation of performance. Dijksterhuis and van Knippenberg asked subjects to imagine a 'typical professor' for five minutes, 'and to list the behaviors, lifestyle, and appearance attributes of this typical professor'. Subjects thus primed turned out to do better on Trivial Pursuits questions than other subjects did, whereas subjects who had been asked to imagine soccer hooligans did worse.[24] These subjects were not asked to imitate, and they were probably unaware that they were doing so.

We now have the ingredients for what I shall call the *standard mode of engagement* with narrative. Narratives, because they serve as expressive of the attitudes and feelings of their authors, create in our minds the image of a persona with those attitudes and feelings, thereby prompting us to imitate them. In taking on those attitudes and feelings, we thereby come to adopt the framework canonical for that work. This has two significant effects. First of all, adoption of that framework is likely to help us orient ourselves in rewarding ways to the represented events of the narrative. Secondly, we have the sense of sharing with the author a way of experiencing and responding to those events. We need not, I repeat, think of this canonical framework as always intended; often narrative makers express themselves unconsciously through their acts of narrative

---

[24] A. Dijksterhuis and A. van Knippenberg, 'The Relation Between Perception and Behavior or How to Win a Game of Trivial Pursuit', *Journal of Personality and Social Psychology* 74, 1998, 865–877. In these experiments imitation was consequent on the activation of a stereotypical representation (elderly person) rather than a highly individualized one, as would be the case with imitation of an authorial cognitive style. But evidence that stereotypical representations have these effects certainly suggests that individuated ones would also have them. Indeed, we are likely to draw on knowledge of stereotypes in constructing a representation of a distinctive mental economy. Tamar Szabó Gendler, who kindly drew my attention to these results, makes an important distinction between cases where the imitation results from imagining an action and cases where it results from imagining a stereotypical person. See her illuminating analyses of a complex budget of cases in 'Imaginative Contagion', *Metaphilosophy* 37 (2006, forthcoming).

Gregory Currie

making, though exponents of narrative art may consciously manipulate the expressive aspects of their work. Consciously or unconsciously, they may fashion personas which their narratives express and which are not their own real personalities.[25]

I have called this the standard mode of engagement; it is not the only one. As we shall see directly, readers sometimes resist frameworks, wholly or in part. There are readings of narrative 'against the grain', but as this description suggests, they require effort. In other cases, the framework that goes with the work seems to be intended to be resisted, though it is not always easy to distinguish these from cases of two other kinds: those where the framework is one we simply find no merit in, finding it difficult to see how this could genuinely be someone's framework; and cases where the apparent framework is undermined by subtle irony expressive of some other, less obvious framework. There are also emotional and other effects that narratives have which do not come by way of the expression-imitation nexus I have described. The ghost stories of M. R. James are chilling, but the fear we experience is not had by way of imitation of any fear expressed by the work's authorial persona; that persona seems ironically detached from the horrifying spectral creatures he describes.[26] This sense of detachment affects our own responses in various ways, but it does not generally lead to a feeling of detachment.[27] The standard model deserves its name because it works easily and naturally in so many cases, and relies very little on conscious efforts to communicate on the part of the author, or on conscious efforts to comprehend on the part of the reader.

[25] This is not a talent confined to literary geniuses; producers of formulaic romances are presumably adept at expressing the kind of personality their readers find most satisfaction in. Nor should we think of frameworks as always highly constraining. Some narratives express attitudes and feelings that embrace or at least acknowledge a range of specific responses and with which one can feel in tune while having an ambiguous, puzzled or even paradoxical response, admiring and deploring the very same traits and actions. Other narratives do seem to impose more rigidity: Dickens and Trollope as contrasted with Austen and Henry James, for example.

[26] James' technique is the opposite of that employed so often by Poe, who takes care to have his narrators express their own extreme emotional reactions to the events they recount.

[27] One hypothesis that occurs to me here is that the detachment of James' authorial persona serves to increase anxiety in the reader because it denies us exactly the comforts of a joint-attention-like experience.

4 Resisting a framework

I have presented guided attention in a positive way, emphasising the pleasures of the experience of attending with the authorial personality. But there are occasions on which the sort of sharing induced by guided attention is uncomfortable or downright objectionable; at this point we make contact with what is now called *the problem of imaginative resistance*.[28] Imaginative resistance, as perceptive commentators note, arises in different ways and for different reasons, and there's a useful distinction to be made between cases where we deny the author's right to stipulate such and such as part of the fiction, and hence deny that we have an obligation to imagine such and such, and cases where we recognise that something is part of the fiction but nonetheless resist the invitation to engage with it imaginatively.[29] The cases I'll consider are of this second kind, and I am interested in a subclass of these: those where resistance arises, not so much because we are resistant to imagining some component of the story P, but because we find it difficult, unrewarding or unattractive to occupy the framework of which the work is expressive partly in virtue of its having P as content.

Here are some examples; they illustrate the diverse ways in which this kind of resistance can be generated. Oscar Wilde said that one must have a heart of stone to read the death of Little Nell without laughing. But few of us, I suspect, do laugh, however cheap we

---

[28]   The problem was noted by Hume ('Of Tragedy') and the issue was revived by Kendall Walton ('Morals in Fiction and Fictional Morality', *Aristotelian Society* Supplement 68, 1994, 27–50) and by Richard Moran ('The Expression of Feeling in Imagination', *Philosophical Review* 103, 1994, 75–106). For a detailed clarification of the issues and a proposed solution see T. S. Gendler, 'The Puzzle of Imaginative Resistance'. *Journal of Philosophy* 97, 2000, 55–81, to which I will refer again later.

[29]   See especially B. Wetherson 'Morality, Fiction, and Possibility', *Philosophers' Imprint* 4, No. 3, available at http://www.umich.edu/%7Ephilos/Imprint/frameset.html?004003+27+images. See also Gendler on what she calls the 'That's what you think' response ('The puzzle of imaginative resistance'). Recent papers by Gendler ('Imaginative Resistance Revisited', *The Architecture of the Imagination*, S. Nichols (ed) (Oxford: Oxford University Press, 2006) and Walton ('On the (So-called) Puzzle of Imaginative Resistance', ibid) emphasise the need to distinguish different issues, and the inadequacy of the general label 'puzzle of imaginative resistance'.

think the pathos of Dickens' narrative.[30] We feel a strong pull in the direction of reacting as Dickens so obviously wants us to, though we may resent its effects on us, and our resentment may lead us to abandon the work altogether.[31] Dickens does not tell us how to react; instead he sets a tone in his writing which is strongly expressive of the reactions he seeks to wring from us. Or we may be disconserted by the author's having placed us in a position where the preferred (and tempting) reaction to tragic events is amusement, as is notoriously the case with Evelyn Waugh. Even an author whose point of view we generally admire may sometimes ask of us more than we can comfortably give, as with *Mansfield Park*, for a reader unwilling to grant so central a role to the virtue of constancy.[32] These are cases of one kind of imaginative resistance, though as I have indicated, our willingness to resist in such cases can be seriously challenged by a talented author. We may on occasions be pleased that the author's efforts to move us away from ways of responding that we find natural and convivial have succeeded. In V. S. Pritchard's novel *Mr Beluncle*, the central character is made to some degree sympathetic despite a constant emphasis on his small-minded religious zealotry, selfishness, bullying, weakness of will, self-delusion and a host of other faults. Pritchard puts the brakes on our natural tendency to enjoy roundly condemning Beluncle's character, behaviour and way of life, and by so restraining us Pritchard helps us both to understand the forces behind such an existence and to exercise our capacity for generosity.

In all these cases, engagement with the work is compromised by the difficulty we have in bringing to bear a range of affective and evaluative responses which are both mandated by the work's expressive qualities and necessary in order to make reading a worthwhile experience. We are like people asked to enjoy an exercise routine for which our muscles and joints are unprepared—

---

[30] 'Cheap pathos' is Henry James' phrase, but from a review of *Our Mutual Friend*.

[31] Carlyle—surely a good candidate for being a highly resistant reader—was reportedly overcome by grief.

[32] See A. MacIntyre, *After Virtue* (London: Duckworth, 1981), Chapter 16.

perhaps even constitutionally unsuited—and which may seem anything from interestingly challenging, through irritatingly pointless, to calculatedly cruel.[33]

But we do not find it merely difficult or unrewarding to adjust our frameworks to fit what seems to be required for certain narratives: we sometimes think that it would be wrong to try. Tamar Gendler argues that we feel this way especially when we sense a desire on the author's part to 'export' that part of the story: to suggest that what is true of the fictional world is in this respect true of the actual world. More specifically 'cases that evoke genuine imaginative resistance will be cases where the reader feels that she is being asked to export a way of looking at the actual world which she does not wish to add to her conceptual repertoire'.[34] I agree that in many cases our resistance is dependent on our sense that something suspicious is up for export, though this may not explain what is going on in the case of Little Nell: few would object to the exportation of the idea that a child's death is tragic. And anyway, why don't readers—even sensitive ones—cheerfully refuse the invitation to endorse the *truth* of the story's content, while at the same time indulging the harmless pleasure of responding *imaginatively* to the story content in the way they are encouraged to do?[35] Here are two ways we might expand on Gendler's suggestion

[33] In 'Desire in Imagination' I argued that we should recognize a category of states I called desire-like imaginings. I suggested that imaginative resistance is not resistance to imagining that such and such but rather to having certain kinds of desire-like imaginings. While I still think that we need the idea of desire-like imagining, it is not necessary to insist that they are the source of imaginative resistance. Instead I can go downstream (causally speaking) to a less controversial set of entities: emotions evoked by fictions. People who disagree with me about whether there are desire-like imaginings might yet agree with me that we do have the difficulties outlined above in responding emotionally to narrative events in the ways the narrative's framework suggests we should. We need not argue about whether these emotions—were we to have them—would be generated partly by our having states of desire-like imagining.

[34] 'The Puzzle of Imaginative Resistance', op. cit. note 29. See also Gendler's 'Imaginative Resistance Revisited', where she distinguishes between the problem of imaginative barriers and the problem of imaginative impropriety (p. 154).

[35] Gendler also puts her point in this way: 'We are *unwilling* to follow the author's lead because, in trying to make that world fictional, she is providing us with a way of looking at *this* world which we prefer not to embrace' ('Puzzle', op. cit. note 29, 79, emphasis in the original). But why

so as to answer this question.[36] I suspect they often apply together; they would apply in cases where we do not sense a desire to export, though they might appear more vivid in cases where there is export than in cases where there is not.

The first reason is this. How we feel about fictional things and events is how we *really* feel about them; fictions put us into distinctive and highly salient mental states which, even if they are not genuinely emotional states, may be phenomenologically indistinguishable from such states as warm-hearted approval, anger and loathing.[37] And I don't want to feel (that is, really feel) certain ways about imaginary situations, for that would bring me closer to those who effortlessly and naturally feel that way about them, because that is the way they feel, or would feel, about comparable situations in real life. I would be manifesting a response which I see in another as the expression of something deplorable, inauthentic or otherwise concerning. On this account, resistance to engaging as Dickens wants us to with the death of Little Nell is a matter of not wanting to share with others—and in particular with the authorial personality—an expression of sentimental and indulgent feelings.[38]

---

should we not choose to confine our use of this 'way of looking' to the fictional world? Most recently ('Imaginative resistance revisited') Gendler argues that in a range of cases, moral and non-moral, we refuse to imagine what the author would have us imagine, because we sense that the relevant proposition (or some related proposition) is one we are being asked to believe (Gendler calls these 'pop-out passages'). But in at least the three non-moral examples Gendler gives (Walton's knock-knock joke, Yablo's maple leaf and Wetherson's rational-belief-without-evidence case) I get no sense that the stories involve pop-out; they strike me instead simply as bizarre exercises in fiction-making.

[36] And Gendler's answer has the merit of moving us away from questions about why we might want, or not want, to imagine this or that proposition, and towards what seems to me the key to understanding the kind of imaginative resistance I am currently considering: that the question is not what we imagine, but how we imagine it.

[37] Kendall Walton argues that our responses to fictions are best described as 'quasi-emotional' rather than as genuine emotions ('Fearing Fictions', *Journal of Philosophy* 75, 1978, 5–27).

[38] Analogous reasoning explains why we are resistant to imitating behaviour (e.g. an insulting gesture) we find deplorable even when the imitation would not have the consequences that makes us deplore the behaviour imitated. When motivated in this way, imaginative resistance exemplifies a more general phenomenon: resistance to sharing salient, but often evaluatively neutral, properties with people who we wish to

The second reason is this: we worry that, in coming to feel that way about imaginary situations, we may put ourselves in danger of coming to feel that way about real situations. Whether or not the feelings evoked by fictions are genuine emotions, we may worry that they are capable of affecting our emotions, and our behaviour, in response to real situations. In view of the rather good evidence for the effects of fictionalised violence on aggressive behaviour and attitudes, I think we are right to worry about this.[39]

Should we say that imaginative resistance arises from our unwillingness to do something, or from our inability to do it? There is no uniform answer to this question. Whether we call any particular case in this region one of inability or of disinclination depends on our assessment of the counterfactual robustness of the conditions that lead to the resistance, together with a choice of a standard of robustness which is highly context-dependent. Given Albert's beliefs about what is morally right, his desires concerning what to do in the face of moral wrongness, together with rather basic facts about the ways he responds emotionally and viscerally to things which strike him as starkly and unmotivatedly wrong, it seems reasonable to say that he simply *can't* engage imaginatively with literature celebratory of sadism in the ways its canonical frameworks suggests he should, though he certainly and in addition thinks that it would be wrong to do so if he could, and he is unwilling to test the boundaries of his imaginative capacity by trying. If he had different beliefs, desires and emotional responses it might be a different story, but the requisite changes would have to be dramatic. It's the relative robustness of the states and dispositions which prevent him from engaging with this narrative which makes 'can't' seem the right description in this case. In other cases the change required would be less dramatic, as with *Mr Beluncle*. Here one might be more inclined to say that someone who fails to take up the challenge of the work's framework is someone who *won't* adopt it rather than someone who *can't*. If we simply say that Albert can't engage imaginatively with *Mr Beluncle* or with a narrative of sadism, that's true in something like the sense in which

---

dissociate ourselves from on broadly evaluative grounds. Compare wearing a Hitler-style moustache, or (certainly *less* troubling) a Burberry-patterned cap; while resistance might be partly aesthetic in both cases, it also exemplifies resistance to sharing.

[39] See S. Hurley, 'Imitation, Media Violence and Freedom of Speech', *Philosophical Studies* 117, 2004, 165–218.

Gregory Currie

I can't speak both Finnish and Martian. It's true that I can't currently understand a word of either, but my not speaking Martian is much more counterfactually robust than my not speaking Finnish is.[40]

Does my approach generate a new puzzle of imaginative resistance? Consider again Albert: he has no difficulty imagining *that* Nell's death is tragic; his problem is that, in imagining this, he is not able to adopt any framework of response that would make this an emotionally satisfying thing to imagine. And the new puzzle is this: why is our capacity to vary our framework of imagining so much more limited than our capacity to imagine this or that content?

Cost and benefit give us the key to this puzzle. Flexibility of response to circumstance comes at a cost, so there must be benefits that justify those costs.[41] Take first the case of imagining such-and-such. Suppose it evolved for planning purposes. In order to plan effectively I need to imagine how things might go under various counterfactual assumptions; I need to imagine this or that being the case, or doing this or that. But what I need to know about these scenarios is how they will affect me—and that means, in almost all cases, how they will affect me, constituted as I am with my own basic values, tastes and other character-defining dispositions. Not much need here for flexibility in the adoption of frameworks.

Planning may not have been the only reason why imaginative capacities were selected in our lineage: capacity to read the minds of our fellows was probably an important factor in determining the fitness of our Pleistocene ancestors. But here again there need not have been much pressure to gain flexibility in point of view for purposes of mind-reading. Social groups were, by our standards, very small, and the people one came into contact with were mostly those with very similar experiences and aspirations who faced similar problems; there were not then the differences of access to wealth and culture that so greatly exaggerate the differences between people. If our minds had evolved in an environment as mentally diverse as the *Star Wars* bar things might have been different.

[40] See D. Lewis, 'The Paradoxes of Time Travel', *American Philosophical Quarterly* 13, 1976, 145–152.

[41] On mental complexity as response to circumstance see Peter Godfrey-Smith, *Complexity and the Function of Mind in Nature* (Cambridge: Cambridge University Press, 1996).

A problem with this account is that it looks as if we have vastly *more* flexibility in imagining this-or-that than we need either for planning or for mind-reading. We take in our stride the wildly false scenarios of science fiction, though they would have had no relevance to either planning or mind-reading in the Pleistocene. The solution here is to see that, for this kind of imagining, maximum flexibility is the lowest-cost option. According to simulation theory, the capacity to imagine operates by using the same inferential system that operates for belief; that is cheaper than building two parallel systems. Such a dual purpose system has then to be insensitive to the doxastic status of the input; the system will run the same way whether the proposition is believed or not. In that case, the system will run on anything that is a potential belief. So at the very least, anything we could possibly believe becomes something we could imagine. Now there are things we can imagine but cannot believe: that I am now dead, that the world has ended, that I believe P but P is false, for example. The last of these examples is significant, since acknowledging the possibility that your own beliefs might be false is very useful; a system of imagining should therefore exceed the compass of belief. And so, very probably, it would. A rule for inputs which said 'allow just those things which might be believed' would require a gateway capable of distinguishing believable from unbelievable propositions—no easy thing to create and maintain. Once the creature concerned acquires an articulated language, the simplest rule for imaginative inputs is *allow anything that makes sense*. So imagining this or that is under quite different evolutionary constraints from those that apply to the adoption of frameworks for imagining. That sort of flexibility comes only at considerable cost, and the benefits of great flexibility with respect to frameworks were few in the relevant environment.[42]

[42] A useful model for thinking about this contrast exists in the distinction between imagining that something is the case, and imagining performing certain bodily actions. We have strong evidence that the request to imagine tapping your fingers in a certain order involves the operation of systems designed to plan and initiate actual movement. While we can easily imagine *that* we tap our fingers at arbitrarily high speeds, when it comes to imagining tapping, things are different; people generally report a maximum imagined speed at which they can carry out the tapping routine which is close to the highest speed at which they could actually tap it. And damage to certain brain areas that affects your actual performance can comparably affect the rate at which you can imagine performing. (For a review of some empirical results in this area as well as an account of the

Gregory Currie

5 Confusing framework and content

I've treated framework and story content as distinct; a more subtle analysis than I have space for here would show, at least, that they are not independent. Certainly, it is not always clear where the distinction between them lies, or even that the boundary between them is everywhere sharp. Cases arise where our wariness of the narrative is the product of a complex and perhaps confused relation between framework and story content. Here are two cases of this kind; they exemplify what we might call *resistance to metaphysics*.[43] They illustrate the ways in which a narrative may confuse us—and may be contrived to confuse us—about what is content and what is framework, promising a more balanced and harmonious relationship between these two things than they in fact deliver.

1. *Rashomon* (Kurosawa, 1950) is a film in which the same events are described by different characters, whose accounts are translated into images by means of flashbacks: we see what happens, according to each account. These accounts are different in crucial ways, particularly to do with the assignment of responsibility for the events. *Rashomon* is commonly said to illustrate the relativity of truth, and I think there is grounds for saying that this is how it is meant to be taken.[44] But I hope I am not alone in experiencing resistance to this intention; this sort of philosophy is too banal to add anything interesting to the story, and indeed it detracts from

---

contents of bodily imaginings, see G. Currie and I. Ravenscroft, *Recreative Minds* (Oxford: Oxford University Press, 2002), Chapter 4.) An evolutionary argument like the one I produced just now seems to apply here: there was little advantage to be gained for my ancestors in having a highly flexible system for the imagining of bodily movement; indeed, it would be an advantage to have your imaginings in this regard constrained by facts about your own performance in ways which don't depend on you knowing what those facts are, since mental rehearsal for action ought, by and large, to reflect the constraints of actual performance. But when it comes to imagining this or that proposition to the effect that I can tap at a certain speed, there is no advantage to be gained by making one imagining more difficult than another, and no cost in not doing so.

[43] Weatherson notes the possibility of imaginative resistance to metaphysics; but his '*Wiggins World*' case is an example of failure to make something part of the fiction's content.

[44] But note the well worked out non-relativistic reading in D. Richie, *Focus on Rashomon* (New York: Prentice-Hall, 1972).

it. So I prefer not to adopt the framework here suggested by the narrative itself: a framework which requires me to see a certain kind of significance in the events of the story. I choose not to see those events as significant in that way.

2. At various points in Proust's *A la Recherche du Temps Perdu*, Marcel experiences episodes of memory, most notably the incident of the madeleine. Along with descriptions of these events, Proust gives us, through the voice of Marcel, a very lengthy philosophical account of the nature of time, which is supposed to be illustrated by and in some way explain these experiences. This philosophy of time has many aspects; part of it seems to involve the idea that each person has an essence that stands outside time and which experiences the fusion of temporal moments from this external perspective.[45] This idea strikes me as very implausible, as making dubious sense, and certainly not as supported by the narrative's account of the experiences Marcel undergoes. The story looks better without that idea and once again I feel entitled to put it to one side.

Could my concern in these metaphysical cases be, at bottom, a moral one? Perhaps these claims about truth and about time are ones I associate with self-indulgent philosophising, and indulging one's self philosophically may be a bad thing to do; if the metaphysics in question was one I firmly rejected but for which I could see respectable arguments, I might not be so resistant.[46] But this cannot be the whole explanation. Ghost stories traffic in all sorts of entities and events I regard as epistemically unrespectable, but, given the right kind of story, I am happy to imagine them existing and happening. The ghost stories of M. R. James are fine things: not at all dubious *qua* narratives, even though ghosts and the like are epistemically very dubious indeed.[47] Appeal to the idea of indulgent metaphysical thinking won't take us far in explaining my

---

[45] For discussion see my *Arts and Minds* (Oxford: Oxford University Press, 2004), Chapter 5. For a more detailed and scholarly analysis with similar conclusions see J. Dancy, 'New Truths in Proust?', *Modern Language Review* 90, 1995, 18–28.

[46] I could be badly wrong about all this: about the works concerned, and about the merits of the philosophical ideas I've mentioned. That doesn't matter. The point is that, feeling this way makes me resist the imaginative invitations of the work. No doubt you can illustrate the same phenomenon from your own experience.

[47] *See The Collected Ghost Stories of M. R. James* (London: Edward Arnold & Co., 1942).

Gregory Currie

reactions to these works. For similar reasons, the difficulty with the indulgent metaphysics can't be that I worry that by imagining these things I will end up believing them. The same consideration would create a barrier between me and the ghost story, and no such barrier exists.

My objection to the metaphysical ideas of *Rashomon* and of Proust is not so much to their epistemic weakness or metaphysical indulgence, but to their lack of impact on the content of these narratives. M. R. James always manages to embed his ghost-metaphysics firmly in story-content. I don't mean by that that the stories always forbid a naturalistic reading; in some of them the supernatural might conceivably be explained away. But the supernatural is always a live explanatory option, and bears on particular events, their causes and their effects. And while James is a master of the genre, success in this is not so very rare; ghosts are the sorts of things that are apt to fit nicely into story-content, and one does not have to be a literary genius to make a ghost story work tolerably well. A metaphysics of the supernatural has, of course, advantages of vividness and emotional pull. But even some general and abstract metaphysical ideas occasionally make a significant impact on story content; David Lewis claims that there are time travel stories within which a consistently developed non-standard metaphysics of time governs the development of plot.[48] By contrast, the psychological and objective events of *Rashomon* and of Proust's novel seem unaffected by the metaphysical ideas in question; if it were not for Marcel's endless theorising, sober readers would never infer Proustian notions of time from the plot. *Rashomon* and Proust's novel announce (in different ways) their metaphysical themes, without going to the trouble of showing how the metaphysics is integrated into the story—something, I suggest, that would be just about impossible. Their resort is therefore to metaphysics as framework: they suggest to us ways of seeing the material as more profound than it would otherwise seem; they suggest to us certain attitudes and emotions we might have in response to this deeper message.[49] We are encouraged to see episodes of memory as portentous in vague ways, to adopt a rather knowing and superior attitude towards testimony, with hand-wringing about scepticism thrown in. This is metaphysics as anxiety—but without meeting the cost of making plausible or even

[48] See Lewis, 'The Paradoxes of Time Travel', op. cit. note 40.
[49] Barnett Newman's much-derided titles suggest a framework that the work often does not live up to.

40

visible anything to be anxious about. Oscar Wilde said that a sentimentalist is one who wants to enjoy an emotion without paying the cost of it. There is a sort of metaphysical parallel to sentimentality in such works as *Rashomon* and in Proust's novel as well: they invite us to admire certain exciting prospects, but they take care to show only a far distant and very blurred view, thus avoiding the hard work of making coherent sense of the idea they want us to be excited by. Their performance is like that of an artist who, lacking fine drawing skills, suggests we look at their work from a distance at which fine drawing will not be evident.

This does not mean the end for these narratives. Proust's novel cycle is full of literary and psychological value which survives the rejection of his metaphysics of time; Kurasawa's film has its virtues. Indeed, I have suggested that these works are experienced as more engaging, interesting and valuable without the framework designed to push emotional buttons when time, memory and truth are mentioned. This suggests an asymmetry in narrative between story-content and framework; frameworks seem to be to some extent optional, detachable things, or things about which we as readers and viewers are in some—perhaps limited—position of authority. We don't have comparable authority in story-content. Suppose I find certain speeches of Miss Bates in *Emma* to be too crudely characterised. So I fashion a new character for her, and make corresponding changes to the text. Surely I have ceased to engage with the original story, taking it instead as the basis for the construction of a new work of my own. That does not seem to be so obviously what I am doing in the cases of *Rashomon* and of Proust. With story-content, the author simply stipulates what is to be the case; while we are under no obligation to engage imaginatively with any work at all, once we do chose to engage with it, we accept the author's say-so.[50] Not accepting that say-so is then a sign of disengagement. With framework, it seems as if something is presented on which there might be a certain amount of negotiation.

Why should this be? Perhaps the answer is this. While story-content can be characterized in objective, observer independent terms, framework is essentially a matter of response. In

---

[50] Except, perhaps, in those cases where the author specifies a set of circumstances, but then goes on to claim something we might call *constitutively inconsistent* with these circumstances. Thus we would baulk at the author who, having told us that in the world of the story grass looks green to normally sighted people in normal circumstances, goes on to insist that, in that world, grass is red. On this see Wetherson, 'Morality, Fiction, and Possibility', op. cit. note 29.

Gregory Currie

presenting a framework, the author suggests a way of responding to content. In matters of response, we do not easily accept the absolute authority of another. It is reasonable to think that the author is well-placed to make suggestions about how to respond to the story, but not reasonable to think him or her in a position absolutely to dictate terms.[51]

So my worries about *Rashomon* and the Proust cycle are these. There is, first of all, a failed expectation that the proffered metaphysics will be built into narrative content; what we actually get is little more than a suggestion about how to see and respond to the events of the story by projecting onto them a general, vague emotional colouring. Yet even this exercise provides few if any opportunities for making interesting connections between events of the story and depends for its emotional force on our being persuaded that there is more depth in the metaphysical thoughts than in fact there is.

[51] Again, I have found Wetherson's 'Morality, Fiction, and Possibility' (ibid.) useful here, though I am not sure he would agree with the point made. See also S. Yablo, 'Coulda, Woulda, Shoulda', *Conceivability and Possibility*, T. S. Gendler and J. Hawthorn (eds) (New York: Oxford University Press, 2002).

The Narrative Practice Hypothesis: Origins and Applications of Folk Psychology

DANIEL D. HUTTO

1. Folk Psychological Practice

Psychologically normal adult humans make sense of intentional actions by trying to decide for which reason they were performed. This is a datum that requires our understanding. Although there have been interesting recent debates about how we should understand 'reasons', I will follow a long tradition and assume that, at a bare minimum, to act for a reason involves having appropriately interrelated beliefs and desires.

He left the party because he believed the host had insulted him. She will head for the cabin in the woods because she wants peace and quiet. These are typical examples of reason explanations, one backward looking and the other future facing. Both imply more than they say. To leave a party because of a suspected insult suggests that one desires not to be insulted, or at least it implies that the desire to avoid insult is stronger than that for some other good on offer. Similarly, to seek tranquillity in an isolated cabin implies that one believes that it can be found there, or at least more so than elsewhere. Despite the fact that the situations and characters involved in these dramas are woefully under-described, we are able to 'make sense' of these actions in a basic manner using the belief/desire schema. This involves designating a *particular pairing* of a belief and a desire, each with its own specified propositional content, in a way that rests on a quiet understanding of *the way* propositional attitudes inter-relate.

To understand which beliefs and desires were responsible for a person's action is normally only to understand why they acted in a quite skeletal way. Maximally, to understand why someone acted requires a more or less detailed description of his or her circumstances, other propositional attitudes (hopes, fears), more basic perceptions and emotions and perhaps even his or her character, current situation and history. In short, to fully grasp why someone took action on a particular occasion requires relating that

43

Daniel D. Hutto

person's 'story'. While I think this richer understanding of what it is to act for reasons is important, my primary interest is to better understand how we acquire and apply our understanding of 'folk psychology' more minimally construed.[1] I am interested in how we become skilled at the practice of predicting, explaining and explicating actions by appeal to reasons of the sort that minimally have belief/desire pairings at their core. To keep things straight, let us call this folk psychology *stricto sensu*.

It is a commonplace in Anglophone philosophy that adult humans make regular and reliable use of 'folk pyschology', so understood. Some maintain this fuels even our most basic encounters with others in daily life and that a great many of our social institutions depend upon it. In promoting these ideas, many so-called friends of folk psychology have overstated and misunderstood its role in social cognition and our lives more generally. First, they typically see it as more basic and far more pervasive than it is. We have many other—more basic, both phylogenetically and ontogenetically—means of conducting social coordinations, interactions and engagements. These yield neither predictions nor explanations *per se* but instead involve recognition-response patterns that generate 'embodied expectations'. In 'normal' contexts these are not only quicker but also far more powerful and reliable ways of relating to others and navigating social dynamics.[2] It is therefore false to say that without a capacity for folk psychology we would be bereft of *any* reliable means of interacting

[1] Some prefer to talk of 'commonsense psychology' as opposed to 'folk psychology', because the latter label was pejoratively fashioned by the enemies of this practice in order to highlight its weak scientific credentials. Calling it 'folk' psychology was meant to signal that its tenets are outmoded, limited and backward—i.e. to highlight the fact that it is indeed 'folksy'. However, since I do not think this folk practice can be usefully compared with the promises of a scientific psychology, I am happy to defend the vulgar on this (see D. D. Hutto, *The Presence of Mind* (Amsterdam: John Benjamins, 1999)).

[2] See D. D. Hutto, 'The Limits of Spectatorial Folk Psychology', *Mind and Language* 19, 2004, 548–73; D. D. Hutto, 'Unprincipled Engagements: Emotional Experience, Expression and Response', *Radical Enactivism: Focus on the Philosophy of Daniel D. Hutto*, R. Menary (ed.) (Amsterdam/Philadelphia: John Benjamins, 2006). See also H. De Jaegher, *Social Interaction Rhythm and Participatory Sense-Making: An Embodied, Interactional Approach to Social Understanding, with Some Implications for Autism* (Brighton, University of Sussex, 2006), unpublished DPhil thesis.

with others. Nor do we call on it that often.[3] Many of our routine encounters with others take place in situations in which the social roles and rules are well established, so much so that unless we behave in a deviant manner we typically have no need to understand one another by means of the belief/desire schema.[4] More often than not we neither predict nor seek to explain the actions of others in terms of their unique beliefs and desires at all.

That said, *sometimes* the actions of others cry out for explanation—sometimes they violate norms (or appear to do so) in ways that we can only make sense of by understanding them in a wider context; by acquiring the narrative that fills in or fleshes out the particular details of that person's story. Any account that has as its subject matter the reason why a person acted on a particular occasion (as restrictively defined above) I will call a folk psychological narrative.[5] The practice of supplying such narratives *just is* that of explicating and explaining action in terms of reasons—the application of the belief/desire framework. Folk psychology is thus, *in essence*, a peculiar kind of narrative practice.

Folk psychological narratives come in both third-personal and second-personal varieties. This is important since the success or otherwise of such explanations depends mainly on who is doing the telling—i.e. who produces the account. Although we often attempt to generate such accounts on behalf of others, even when this speculative activity is well supported—say, by simulative or theoretical heuristics—it is quite unlikely that such attempts will

---

[3] S. Gallagher, 'The Practice of Mind: Theory, Simulation or Primary Interaction?' *Journal of Consciousness Studies* 8, No. 5–7, 2001, 83–108.

[4] J. Bruner, *Acts of Meaning* (Cambridge, MA: Harvard University Press, 1990); J. Bermúdez, 'The Domain of Folk Psychology', *Minds and Persons*, A. O'Hear (ed.) (Cambridge: Cambridge University Press, 2003).

[5] We might also call these 'people-narratives'; for they are 'narratives in which people feature as people (and not, for example, as objects for scientific investigation), the narrative should also present what happened in a way that enables the audience or the reader to make sense of the thoughts, feelings, and actions of those people who are internal to the narrative' (P. Goldie, *On Personality* (London: Routledge, 2004), 115). For expositional variety, I use these terms interchangeably. Of course, this presupposes the uncontentious idea that there are different types of narratives and that these can be classified by their content and subject matter.

succeed in hitting on the 'right' explanation. Indeed, it seems that the likelihood of success is more or less inversely proportional to need.[6]

Although hardly foolproof, by far the best and most reliable means of obtaining a true understanding of why another has acted is to get the relevant story directly from the horse's mouth. The activity is familiar enough. Such accounts are typically delivered—indeed, fashioned—in the course of ordinary dialogue and conversation. It is because of this that they are usually sensitive to a questioner's precise explanatory needs and requirements. The nature of such engagements is complex and deserves greater attention than it has received to date, but that is not my focus here. So far, all I want to draw attention to is the banal truism that second-person deliveries of these folk psychological narratives do much of the heavy lifting in enabling us to make sense of the actions of others in daily life—i.e. when there is a need to do so.

While I suspect that we may use folk psychology far less frequently and less reliably than is generally supposed by its friends, folk psychological practice is important and our capacity to engage in it warrants explanation. The above observations, however, should immediately raise doubts about the credibility of the favoured hypotheses about its ultimate origins. Orthodoxy has it that our 'theory of mind' abilities are the consequence of the hard work of subpersonal mechanisms. And, although there is much debate about the precise character of the latter, these devices are typically thought to be a kind of native cognitive endowment, gifted to us by our evolutionary forefathers.

In light of the above and on close scrutiny, it seems quite unlikely that this ability was the ancient solution to an adaptive problem that arose for our ancestors during the Pleistocene epoch, enabling 'the rapid comprehension and prediction of another organism's behaviour'.[7] Third-personal mindreading involving the attribution of interlaced propositional attitudes would have been unnecessary for oiling our primary forms of social interaction and even for sophisticated activities such as lexicon formation and language

---

[6]   see Hutto, 2004, op. cit. note 4.
[7]   S. Baron-Cohen, *Mindblindness: An Essay on Autism and Theory of Mind* (Cambridge, MA: MIT Press, 1995), 12.

learning.[8] Moreover, if speculative uses of folk psychology to determine why someone acted are as unreliable as I have claimed, it seems quite unlikely that the folk psychological framework was originally *put in place* to provide our ancestors with a powerful predictive-explanatory tool, as it is so often claimed. In this light, we would do well to rethink the role and function of folk psychological 'explanations' in our lives, since their main job is not to generate third-party speculations about what others are likely to think or do or why they acted as they did. This is no way diminishes—indeed it may well enhance—our understanding of the importance of folk psychology and its place in our lives and other practices.

In what follows, I promote the view that our childhood engagement with narratives of certain kinds is the basis of these sophisticated abilities—i.e. it is through such socially scaffolded means that folk psychological skills are normally acquired and fostered. Undeniably, we often use our folk psychological apparatus in speculating about why another *may* have acted on a particular occasion, but this is at best a peripheral and parasitic use. Our primary understanding and skill in folk psychology *derives from* and has its *primary application* in special kinds of second-personal engagements.

It is possible to explain how budding folk psychologists come by a practical grasp of the core folk psychological concepts, as well as the ability to structurally represent how these propositional attitudes normally relate, schematically without postulating any inherited hard-wired 'theory of mind' mechanisms.[9] A distinct kind of narrative practice, one involving particular kinds of story, engenders folk psychology abilities in the normal populace (of certain cultures, at least). Encounters with narratives about those who act for reasons best explain the origins of folk psychological

---

[8] See D. D. Hutto, 'First Communions: Mimetic Sharing without Theory of Mind', *The Shared Mind: Perspectives on Intersubjectivity*, J. Zlatev, T. Racine, C. Sinha and E. Itkonen (eds.) (Amsterdam/Philadelphia: John Benjamins, 2007).

[9] In what follows, I will be presupposing that the children in question already have a basic practical grasp of the core concepts of belief and desire. I provide a more detailed account of how they come by these in other writings. I also argue that no existing version of theory-theory or simulation theory can better explain the origin of the core metarepresentational concept of belief in particular. See D. D. Hutto, *Folk Psychological Narratives: The Sociocultural Basis of Understanding Reasons* (Cambridge, MA: MIT Press, forthcoming).

abilities, both phylogenetically and ontogenetically. Such stories familiarise us with the *forms* and *norms* of folk psychology. This is the core claim of the Narrative Practice Hypothesis (or NPH). The aim of this paper is to introduce this proposal and to make a *prima facie* case for its acceptance.

2. What does it take to be a Folk Psychologist?

Not everyone has what it takes to be a folk psychologist. The birds and the bees don't do it; chimps don't do it. Even little kids don't do it! This should not surprise us. Folk psychology isn't easy—it is a quite sophisticated skill. Mastery of it rests on having met a number of pre-requisites. At the very least, one has to have:

  (i) a practical understanding of the propositional attitudes;
 (ii) a capacity to represent the objects that these take— propositional contents as specified by that-clauses;
(iii) an understanding of the 'principles' governing the interaction of the attitudes, both with one another and with other key psychological players (such as perception and emotion);
(iv) an ability to apply all of the above sensitively (i.e. adjusting for relevant differences in particular cases by making allowances for a range of variables such as the person's character, circumstances, etc.).

Any interesting explication of folk psychology should not only say what having this rich set of abilities entails, it should also say how it is acquired. On the assumption that these abilities do not come as a 'package deal', I will focus on providing an acquisitional account of (iii) and (iv) in terms of children's engagement in a special kind of narrative practice. This is of interest since, contrary to their advertisements, the rival offerings—theory theory and simulation theory—do not provide any deep understanding of (iii). All the existing theories presuppose some kind of commerce with folk psychological principles, whether this is imagined to take the form of a tacit or explicit theoretical understanding or a practical capacity to manipulate one's own mental states in accord with them (thus, quite literally, embodying them). But presupposing the existence of such abilities is not the same as adequately explaining how they first came to be in place. Ultimately, I think it can be demonstrated that the existing theories do not meet this explanatory demand.[10] Yet, worse than this, as far as I can see, they do not trouble themselves with giving an account of (iv) at all.

Before getting started, it is worth saying a few words about what distinguishes what it is to have an understanding of desires, beliefs (and even desires *and* beliefs) from what it is to have an understanding of reasons. Doing so will help us to properly characterise our true quarry. It is empirically well established that children make some propositional attitude ascriptions before they learn to explicate, explain or predict actions in terms of reasons. For example, at around two years of age, children are in secure possession of 'an early intentional understanding of persons having internal goals and wants that differ from person to person'.[11] The two-year-old's understanding of desires can be rather sophisticated: children understand, for example, how desires relate to emotions and perceptions and what would relevantly and consistently satisfy specific desires—thus they exhibit some fluency with counterfactual thinking of a limited sort.

As impressive as this is, it goes without saying that these abilities do not equate to an understanding of beliefs. Nor would an understanding of desires *and* beliefs conjunctively equate to an understanding of reasons. These are all logically distinct abilities. We can see the main point at issue if we consider that for a great many coordinating purposes it is often enough to know simply what it is that McX likes or wants. Young children are certainly capable of noting this sort of thing and making good use of it—it is what enables them to make certain low-level, inductively driven predictions about what others are likely to do. But this capacity in itself is quite different from understanding why McX might have acted for a reason. More is needed for that—in particular, the child would have to be able to understand that McX's action issued from a complex 'state of mind', one having a particular kind of implicit structure. Said structure is what one alludes to when one says McX not only likes yoghurt but is eating it for breakfast *because* he believes it will make him healthy—implying, of course, that good health is also something he seeks.

[10] Ibid.
[11] H. Wellman, A. Phillips, 'Developing Intentional Understandings', *Intentions and Intentionality*, B. Malle, L. J. Moses and D. A. Baldwin (eds.) (Cambridge, M.A.: MIT Press, 2001), 130; K. Bartsch and H. Wellman, *Children Talk About the Mind* (New York: Oxford University Press, 1995), chapter 4.

Daniel D. Hutto

I mention this because while it is quite unlikely that anyone would confuse the ability to understand and attribute desires with that of being able to understand and attribute beliefs, there is a fairly widespread tendency to conflate the latter sort of ability with a capacity to understand and attribute reasons. This mistake stems from assuming, as is commonly done, that children are *already* in the possession of the bulk of their theory of mind at the point at which they begin to pass false belief tests. Hence, success on these tests is taken to be the mark of their having acquired the final piece of the 'theory of mind' puzzle. Having mastered the core concept of belief, it is supposed that they have mastered the full set of folk psychological principles.

But if we give due consideration to what false belief tests actually test there is reason to doubt this. In the original version of the false belief test, of which there are now many well-known variants, children were introduced to a puppet, Maxi.[12] The test was conducted in a room in which a pile of biscuits was the main attraction. In the course of events, Maxi, like the children, observes as the biscuits are put in one of two cupboards. The puppet subsequently leaves the room and during his absence the children watch as an experimenter moves the biscuits into the other cupboard. The question they are asked is: where will Maxi think the biscuits are on his return? For anyone with a sound grasp of the concept of belief, and how perception fixes belief, answering this ought to be straightforward. But, famously, for some—children below a certain age and those with specific impairments—it is not.

Such children have difficulty in ascribing the Maxi-puppet a belief which differs from their own belief about the location of the biscuits. They are unable to ascribe the puppet a false belief, or so it seems. The reason for this is, it has been plausibly suggested, that they are unable to understand that the puppet (or anyone) has a cognitive take on the facts that diverges from their own. Younger children and those with infantile autism cannot simultaneously represent how they take things to stand with the world (from their point of view) and also how things stand from another cognitive vantage point. Thus, in lacking an ability to ascribe false beliefs they demonstrate a lack of an understanding of belief, if we suppose, as we ought, that grasping that concept requires having a metarepresentational ability.

[12]   H. Wimmer and J. Perner, 'Beliefs about Beliefs: Representation and Constraining Function of Wrong Beliefs in Young Children's Understanding of Deception', *Cognition* 12, 1983, 103–128.

If we stick to the evidence and put aside any prior attachment to theory theory for a moment, it is quite clear that merely having demonstrable metarepresentational abilities—i.e. showing command of the concept of belief—is not equivalent to understanding reasons *per se*. It is easy to be misled on this score due to the great emphasis that developmental psychologists place on the moment when children begin to pass false belief tasks. As noted above, these are often called 'Theory of Mind' tests but in fact, just as their name suggests, they only test for an explicit understanding of false belief and nothing more. To call them 'Theory of Mind' tests therefore gives a quite erroneous impression, which trades on the assumption that folk psychological abilities simply fall into place automatically once children master the application of the concept of belief. This is simply untrue. Knowing that children manage to pass false-belief tests, reliably enough, at a certain age under very particular experimental conditions, gives no insight into the extent of their understanding of that concept in *other* contexts. This being the case, such tests certainly do not tell us about the general abilities of children to ascribe or understand reasons, *per se*.

The myopia associated with conducting and analysing 'false belief tests' has tended to blind researchers to the fact that children's nuanced folk psychological skills only develop securely after ages 4 and 5. Thus, 'Proponents of the dominant theories have been notably quiet about what happens in development after the child's fifth birthday. However research that explores whether 5-year-olds can use simple false belief knowledge to make inferences about their own and other's perspectives finds that they singularly fail to do so'.[13] Apparently, it takes some time for them to incorporate their newfound understanding of belief within wider explanatory strategies.

The simple truth, as I said, is that having an understanding of belief is logically distinct from having an understanding of what it is to act for a reason. One can ascribe beliefs using a simple inference rule of the following sort: if McX says (or sincerely asserts) that P then McX believes that P (*ceteris paribus*). Knowing that McX believes that P is useful for at least some social coordination purposes—for example, it enables one to predict what else McX might believe. This might be achieved by focusing on

---

[13]   J. I. M. Carpendale and C. Lewis, 'Constructing an Understanding of the Mind: The Development of Children's Social Understanding within Social Interaction', *Behavioural and Brain Sciences* 27, No. 1, 2004, 79–151, 91.

what McX ought to conclude from thinking that P (on the assumption that X observes standard norms of rationality). Very well, but this does not equate to ascribing X a reason: that would require ascribing to X a complex state of mind, minimally consisting of a belief/desire pair with interlocking contents. Reasons are not to be confused with isolated thoughts or desires. To think of an action as performed for a reason it is not enough to imagine it as being sponsored by a singular kind of propositional attitude; one must also ascribe other kinds of attitudes which act as relevant and necessary partners in motivational crime.

This is not always evident given the way reason explanations are often presented. As noted before, they are generally truncated. But what I have sought to emphasize is that having a discrete understanding of the core propositional attitudes—belief and desire—is only a necessary but not a sufficient condition for being a practising folk psychologist. Having issued that reminder, we can now turn to the main event.

3. Acquiring Folk Psychology in ontogeny

How, during childhood, do we come by our everyday folk psychological skills and understanding? This familiar achievement rests on a complex series of foundations—i.e. children must already have a number of more basic imaginative abilities and interpersonal skills in order to learn how to make sense of actions in terms of reasons successfully. Long before they are able to do this, they are at home in navigating their social worlds in embodied and imaginative ways: they get by in the earliest stages of their interpersonal careers without ever attributing desires, beliefs, or reasons to anyone. In time, they get a practical grasp on the different kinds of propositional attitudes—learning about each in discrete stages, as their command of language and its syntactic constructions grows. I have elsewhere argued at length that there is good reason to think that children come into the possession of all the pieces needed for playing the understanding-action-in-terms-of-reasons game before they can actually play it.[14] What they are missing in their early years, if I am right, is not the components needed to play this game: they lack knowledge of the basic rules for doing so.

For, as noted in the previous section, proficiency in making isolated propositional attitude ascriptions—attributing certain

[14]   Hutto, ibid.

goals, desires, thoughts and beliefs—is not the same as *knowing how* these combine to become reasons. This stronger condition must be satisfied if one is to be a folk psychologist. This requires mastery of the norms governing the interplay between these attitudes. What children are missing, even upon acquiring a practical grasp of the concept of belief, is not therefore another ingredient needed for baking the folk psychological cake—rather it is the instructions for mixing all the ingredients properly to make many such cakes. But if the instructions for this are not built into their minds, how exactly might they be acquired?

The Narrative Practice Hypothesis (NPH) claims that children normally achieve this understanding by engaging in story-tellling practices, with the support of others. The stories about those who act for reasons—i.e. folk psychological narratives—are the foci of this practice. Stories of this special kind provide the crucial training set needed for understanding reasons. They do this by serving as exemplars, having precisely the right features to foster an understanding of the *forms* and *norms* of folk psychology. By participating in this kind of narrative practice children become familiar with the way the core propositional attitudes, minimally belief and desire, behave with respect to each other and their familiar partners: emotions, perceptions, etc. More than this, in such stories a person's reasons are shown *in situ*; against appropriate backdrops and settings. For example, children learn how a person's reasons can be influenced by such things as their character, history, current circumstances and larger projects.

It is because they have just these features that folk psychological narratives as well as the fact that they are complex objects of mutual attention can play this crucial role. Most children are not only repeatedly exposed to such stories, but normally this occurs in a very rich setting, with engaged participants on both sides. It is helpful to remind ourselves of this, lest we are swayed by misguided poverty of the stimulus arguments into believing that the postulation of inherited 'theory of mind' devices is unavoidable.[15]

---

[15] Several philosophers have suggested that a Poverty of the Stimulus Argument concerning the acquisition of folk psychology could be developed that would parallel the version Chomsky developed in support of his claims about the existence of innate linguistic knowledge, see P. Carruthers, 'Moderately Massive Modularity', *Minds and Persons*, A. O'Hear (ed.) (Cambridge: Cambridge University Press, 2003), 71; G. Botterill and P. Carruthers, *The Philosophy of Psychology* (Cambridge:

Daniel D. Hutto

The assumption behind that line of thought is that the acquisition of folk psychology 'poses the same degree of a learnability problem as does the rapid acquisition of linguistic skills, which appears to be similarly rapid, universal and without sufficient stimulus from the environment'.[16] Yet, with respect to folk psychology, the argument has not been spelt out in any detail. Any *prima facie* plausibility it has derives simply from the idea that children could not possibly fashion the rich product that is folk psychology by applying their general reasoning abilities in response to impoverished stimuli. But this idea is only remotely credible if we have in a mind a quite implausible picture of how children *might* become aquainted with the rules of folk psychology in the first place; to be sure they do not encounter these as set of serial announcements issued by their parents. And, of course, acquiring an understanding of folk psychology by means of participating in narrative practices, with the support of others, is nothing like being read off a set of explicit principles or rules to be committed to memory. It is only if one has this second model in mind that it is tempting to agree with Goldman that few children 'have mothers who utter [folk psychological] platitudes'.[17]

Engaging with narratives, and those of the folk psychological variety in particular, is anything but a passive affair: a wide range of emotive and imaginative abilities are typically brought into play. For example, even to appreciate such stories children must be initially capable, at least to some degree, of imaginative identification with the characters of the story. And not only will they be exercising their recreative imaginations in this way, they will also be responding emotively, just as they do in basic social engagements, such as joint attention. In this respect, 'conversations about written and oral stories are natural extensions of children's earlier

---

Cambridge University Press, 1999), 52–3; J. A. Fodor, *Psychosemantics* (Cambridge, MA: MIT Press, 1987), 133; see also K. Sterelny, *Thought in a Hostile World* (Oxford: Blackwell, 2003), 214).

[16] S. Mithen, 'Mind, Brain and Material Culture: An Archaeological Perspective', *Evolution and the Modern Mind: Modularity, Language and Meta-Cognition*, P. Carruthers and A. Chamberlain (eds.) (Cambridge: Cambridge University Press, 2000), 490.

[17] A. I. Goldman, 'In Defense of the Simulation Theory', *Mind and Language* 7, 1992, 104–119, 107.

experiences with the sharing of event structures'.[18] It is therefore of no surprise that young children's first narrative encounters are with picture books that only depict objects, emotions and actions—but not *reasons* for actions. They slowly graduate to stories that concentrate on the kinds of complex psychological attitudes of characters; those who find themselves embedded in increasingly complex social dramas.

But it is not just the content of such stories that matters. Sophisticated demands are also placed on children in the course of hearing, discussing and learning from them. Thus it is normal for children to be directed by caregivers to attend to the thoughts, desires, and feelings of story characters and these are often explained to and contextualised for them. Throughout these interactions children will be calling on a prior bit limited mastery of mentalistic terms and concepts. Crucially, however, these are not simply mentioned in story-telling practices, rather children are prompted at crucial points to offer their own explanations; they are invited to apply, demonstrate and extend their prior understanding. For example, while reading stories it is typical for adults to press for answers to questions such as: 'Why do you think X did that?'. Moreover, those who tell stories to young children generally go beyond the strict text—using voices, enacting character responses, and providing details that reveal or hint at the motivations and rationales of characters. Such exchanges are a mix of dramatic re-enactment, contextualisation, and exposure to further examples, all of which prompt further requests from listeners and opportunities for correction from the story-tellers.[19]

In these guided encounters with such stories children come to see the relations that hold between the various psychological attitudes—crucially, but not exclusively, the focus is on beliefs and desires. This is important because, as stressed above, not only must children have an understanding of the core propositional attitudes, they must also learn how these inter-relate. Thus the way beliefs and desires conspire to motivate actions—which, *in abstracto*, we

[18]   N. R. Guajardo, A. Watson, 'Narrative Discourse and Theory of Mind Development', *The Journal of Genetic Psychology* 163, 2002, 305–325, 307.

[19]   Also, this kind of interpersonal activity occurs at the right point in the developmental schedule of most children, making it plausible that it might form the basis of their folk psychological training. People-focused conversations happen early on and story-telling activities of the relevant sort are usually well under way by the time children reach the ages of three and four.

might think of as the folk psychological schema—is a constant feature of these narratives. But this requires knowing not only how they inter-relate with one another, but also how they do so with other standard players in psychological dramas. In sum, these comprise what we might think of as the 'core principles' of intentional psychology.

According to the NPH these 'princples' are revealed to children not as a series of rules but by showing them in action, through narratives, in their normal contexts of operation. In this way, narratives not only show which features are constant to folk psychological explanation but also, importantly, what can vary in such accounts—such as the particulars of what a person believes and desires, how these attitudes can change over time and why, and also how character, history, and other commitments might impinge on why a person acts as they do. All of this is put on show. In this way children learn which kinds of factors must be taken into account and adjusted for when it comes to making sense of the stories that others tell about the reasons why they acted, as well as learning what needs mentioning when providing their own. It is in this way and in this sense that children acquire an understanding of the core structure of folk psychology, its governing norms, and guidance on its practical application. This is not a process through which children distil a set of general rules.

To understand the NPH aright, two senses of 'narrative' must be distinguished—i.e. the narratives which are the third-personal objects of focus, and the narratives through which these are presented and shared—i.e. the acts of narration that constitute the second-personal story-tellings. As an object, a narrative—the story itself—might be spontaneous production, an autobiographical account, a bit of gossip, or an established cultural artefact. Many of the latter are texts of which there may be multiple versions—such as Perrault's 'Little Red Riding Hood' or its Grimm Brothers variant 'Little Red Cap'. Indeed, this is one of the best known folk psychological narratives:

> Little Red Riding Hood *learns* from the woodcutter that her grandmother is sick. She *wants* to make her grandmother feel better [she is a nice, caring child], and she *thinks* that a basket of treats will help, so she brings such a basket through the woods to her grandmother's house [beliefs and desires lead to actions]. When she arrives there, she *sees* the wolf in her grandmother's bed, but she *falsely believes* that the wolf is her grandmother [appearances can be deceiving]. When she *realizes* it is a wolf, she

is *frightened* and runs away, because she *knows* wolves can hurt people. The wolf, who indeed *wants* to eat her, leaps out of the bed and runs after her trying to catch her.[20]

Tales of this sort are legion. This is not, I take it, in doubt, although as yet I have no precise data on how many of these children encounter in the normal course of their development; I leave it to the reader to speculate about this. What matters is that they are the best means of revealing how propositional attitudes work together in motivating actions and indicating which other factors might make a difference. Given their content, they have precisely the right properties for this work.

Well crafted cultural artefacts, like the familiar fairy tale cited above, are a secure medium of achieving this. They are amongst the earliest forms of published fiction, typically deriving from orally preserved folk tales. Yet any story that describes reasons for action, even those related through casual conversations, has the potential to do so, even if they are not as well-structured as the canonical texts used in much pre-school story-telling. With this in mind it is diffcult to imagine how to motivate a poverty of the stimulus argument in this domain, since these narratives are regularly traded in run-of-the-mill conversations. Indeed, it is through listening to and participating in conversations about people and why they act that children first hear propositional attitudes being discussed and described, and it is likely that it is through this route that they learn about the kind of objects these take—complex linguistic constructions embedded in that-clauses. It is stories featuring people and their reasons for acting—*however these are conveyed*—that familiarise children with the folk psychological framework and practical knowledge of how to apply it.

Children are not simply learning generalisations—i.e. mere soft laws—about what people typically do; they are learning how to apply the folk psychological framework.

Although I previously emphasised the imaginative identification and emotional responding that characterises engagement in narrative practice, it is also worth highlighting how straightforward it would be for children to pick up the *structural template* of means-end reasoning through such encounters. It is into this framework that particular propositional attitudes, beliefs and desires, are inserted, like arguments in place of variables—based on

[20] A. Lillard, 'Other Folk's Theories of Mind and Behaviour', *Psychological Science* 8, 1997, 268–274, 268, emphases mine.

what we learn (or are told) about why someone acted (or why we speculate they may have acted). Similarity-based connectionist—non-sentential—accounts of cognitive processing that trade in stereotypes, prototypes and exemplars are well placed to explain the working of the underlying mechanisms which might make this possible. Picking all this up from narrative encounters would be easy work for our pattern-completing, form-finding brains.

A major virtue of the NPH is that it does not need to characterise this aspect of the learning process as one of 'scaling up' or 'bootstrapping'; to do so is rightly to be accused of hand waving.[21] For in this case the training 'input' is *identical* to learned 'output': the structures to be acquired are clearly detectable in the exemplars—the folk psychological narratives—themselves (this can be seen by replacing the italicised mentalistic verbs in the 'Red Riding Hood' excerpt with a series of neutral symbols). And it is well known that connectionist networks can 'learn' both lexical categories (e.g. nouns, verbs) and grammatical structures (e.g. agreement and dependence of embedded clauses) using their humble resources. In summarising the evidence on this score, Prinz remarks that 'Elman shows that a dumb pattern detector can pick up on structural relations'.[22] Note too that the folk psychological template is a much simpler kind of structure than even the most basic of syntactic patterns. All that is required in order to make the NPH credible on this score is the assumption that the child's world is adequately populated with folk psychological narratives and that they have enough opportunities to engage with them. This seems to be the case, in most cultures.

It should also be recognised that although this framework is derived from ambient stories, and is not part of a built-in theory, this in no way detracts from the power and depth it affords in making sense of others in particular cases. Its source does not affect its capacity to 'go beyond the evidence' when explaining and predicting what actors are likely to do in 'novel' cases (although, as stressed, such third-personal uses are not a reliable method of

[21] A. Gopnik, The Theory Theory as an Alternative to the Innateness Hypothesis, *Chomsky and His Critics*, L. M. Antony and N. Hornstein (eds.), 2003, 238–254, 243.

[22] J. Prinz, *Furnishing the Mind: Concepts and Their Perceptual Basis* (Cambridge, MA: MIT Press, 2002), 206.

discovering another's reasons for acting).[23] Folk psychology exhibits precisely the sorts of features that led philsosophers, such as Lewis, to mark it out as being theory-like—i.e. it has characteristics that makes the 'theory theory' a compelling hypothesis.[24] Nevertheless, despite having a coherent framework at its core, folk psychology is not, in fact, theoretical in its origins or principal applications.

It is worth saying a bit more about this. Many philosophers who are attracted to theory theory are of the view that the content of theoretical concepts is determined by the role they play in a network of principles—principles which, when working in unison, enable the prediction and explanation of action. It is also commonly held that the 'meanings' of mental predicates, those which form the basis of such principles, are fixed in the same way; i.e. terms such as belief, desire and hope are defined by the way they systematically interrelate with one another and with other terms.

However, the claim that the meaning of mental predicates depends wholly on their lawful relations is apparently undermined by the fact that children develop a practical understanding of the different propositional attitudes at distinct stages in their early careers. Thus they have a grasp of the concept of desire, quite independently of and prior to having an understanding of belief. And an understanding of both of these attitudes appears to precede an understanding of the roles they play in making sense of a person's reasons for action. At best, then, it seems that children significantly extend their understanding of the core propositional attitudes when they learn how these cooperate with one another (and others of their ilk) in the context of reason explanations. It is not that the later ability constitutes their understanding of mental predicates. Nevertheless, it is getting to grips with the roles played by the attitudes in this context that is, minimally, what is required to be capable of understanding what it is to act for a reason.

[23] The capacity to go beyond the evidence has been singled out as 'the most important evolutionary benefit of developing theorising abilities' (A. Gopnik and A. N. Meltzoff, *Words, Thoughts, and Theories* (Cambridge, M.A.: MIT Press, 1996), 37). Good theories run deep: their power to anticipate, explain and control stems from their tapping into the world of the unseen and the abstract.

[24] See D. Lewis, 'How to Define Theoretical Terms', *Journal of Philosophy* 67, 1970, 427–446; D. Lewis 'Psychophysical and Theoretical Identifications', *Australasian Journal of Philosophy* 50, 1978, 249–258.

Daniel D. Hutto

To be a practising folk psychlogist rests on having an understanding of the roles that mentalistic concepts play in a framework of this sort. Some have concluded, because of this, that the framework in question is a theoretical one and mental predicates thus have a theoretical status. But that is a mistake. It may be an essential feature of all theories that they have complex network structures—and it may even be that the meanings of theoretical terms are determined entirely by the roles they play within such networks (well, maybe). All of this could be true without it being the case that folk psychology is a theory. Clearly, the mere fact that something has a framework structure does not entail that it is a theory or that the meaning of its concepts is holistically constituted. Ordinary games, such as cricket or chess, have rules, but these activities are not theoretically but conventionally grounded; they are well-established, regulated social practices. Folk psychology, too, has a framework structure, but it is neither a game nor a theory.

So, it looks like we should agree with holistically minded theory-theorists only up to a point: in order to understand what it is to act for a reason we must understand the roles played by the mental predicates. But this gives us absolutely no reason to think of such concepts as theoretical constructs—similar to 'electrons', 'atoms', or 'gravity'. To be sure, to understand the distinct roles that such concepts play in folk psychology requires having an understanding of their place in a network of possibilities. But, at most, this means that, *in this context*, mentalistic terms may be similar *in this one respect* to certain theoretical terms (on the disputable assumption that this is the best way to make sense of the meaning of theoretical constructs). Folk psychology need be like a theory in no other interesting aspect, neither in its origins nor its primary applications.

For all these reasons, using the label 'theory of mind' as a byword for folk psychological practice is highly misleading. The practice should be shunned in light of the bad effects it has had (and continues to have) on the imaginations of many philosophers, psychologists and others working in this topic.

4. Norms of practical applicability

Successful application of folk psychology involves more than merely getting to grips with its core structure, it requires development of refined skill. One must be able to use it, sensitively, occasion by occasion. Encounters with folk psychological narratives help foster this practical ability as well. For, although the structure of intentional psychology is a constant in all folk psychological narratives, they vary in other aspects. Through them children also learn that many non-mentalistic factors are pertinent to why someone has acted or might act. For example, they learn that what a person believes or desires matters to the actions they take but also how their character, unique history and circumstances might affect their motivational set. These are the sorts of features, inter alia, that differ from story to story, within a single story over time, and often from protagonist to protagonist within the same story. They are prominent in nearly all interesting stories even if only in the background. Knowing how to make relevant adjustments to accommodate just such factors is necessary for the skilled application of folk psychology. The simplest person-narratives engender this kind of practical knowledge by introducing children to distinct characters and their specific background beliefs and desires, particular agendas, unique histories, personality traits and so on. Although the stories in which they figure are at first quite simple, they become more sophisticated over time.

The main point, yet again, is that these stories have precisely the right properties for familiarising children, not only with the core mentalistic framework, but also with the rudimentary norms governing its practical application. By putting examples of people acting for reasons on display, they show both how the items in the mentalistic toolkit can be used together to understand reasons in general, as it were, but also how and when these tools might be used—i.e. what to adjust for—in specific cases. They not only teach children this but they also give some hints about how to make the relevant adjustments (e.g. a character with suspicious tendencies is likely to form certain beliefs in such and such a situation, etc.). Encounters with such stories look ideally suited to provide children with the requisite specialised know-how—i.e. to teach them how to apply folk psychology, with sensitivity, in everyday contexts.

The NPH therefore has the potential to explain something its rivals do not; insight into how we might acquire our workaday skills in wielding folk psychology. This matters, for if an effective use of folk psychology requires getting to grips with the sorts of factors mentioned above, there is little to recommend the thought that such 'practical worries' can be shunted to one side and dismissed when it comes to understanding FP abilities. Surprisingly, this is the standard strategy. Thus, it is widely supposed that questions about day-to-day 'application' can be relegated to the sideline and dealt

Daniel D. Hutto

with by a liberal invocation of *ceteris paribus* clauses. Consequently, although everyone acknowledges that there are many factors—psychological and non-psychological—that are relevant to any particular attempt to make sense of an action in terms of reasons, our ability to cope with these in practice is treated as if it is outside the scope of folk psychology *per se*. The mainstream offerings, theory theory and simulation theory, are conspicuously silent on the question of what grounds this aspect of folk psychological practice. To my eye, this is a serious lacuna.

Most theorists do not accept that there is a need to give an account of such practical knowledge because they imagine, quite wrongly in my opinion, that 'folk psychology' just is the name of a theory or procedure; one which can be understood quite independently from its practical application. I take the opposite view: although folk psychology has a core framework—which can be abstractly described as a set of principles—it is first and foremost a practical enterprise. Its business just is the application of a special narrative framework in specific cases of making sense of actions. Any theory of folk psychology that fails to recognise and to account for this will ultimately fail to satisfy. And this, I fear, is true of all existing accounts.

Take theory theory as an example. Here the sole focus is on explaining the nature of the basic rules of folk psychology—understood *in vacuo*—those which define its core mentalistic framework. Little attention is given to the question of how children learn to apply these rules in practice. Rather it is often supposed that we somehow rely on a tacit understanding of 'idealised rational agents' when making mentalistic predictions and explanations.[25] This is, so it is claimed, a necessary condition for getting any mentalistic attribution off the ground. Thus, if I know that McX is thirsty for a glass of water, and I know that he believes he could get one by going downstairs to the refrigerator I will probably predict that he will do just this (all else being equal and assuming he has the right sort of background beliefs and desires, etc.). But I will only expect this of McX if I think he will behave as any 'rational agent' would. For if McX is irrational, interpreting or predicting his behaviour in terms of his reasons is a non-starter.

---

[25] Cf. D. C. Dennett, *Brainstorms* (Cambridge, MA: MIT Press, 1985), 16–22; D. C. Dennett, *The Intentional Stance* (Cambridge, MA: MIT Press, 1987), chapter 4; S. Stich, *The Fragmentation of Reason* (Cambridge, MA: MIT Press, 1990), chapter 2, chapter 3.

In one sense this is surely right. But knowing this is hardly sufficient for being a practising folk psychologist; our everyday skill involves much, much more than knowing in some thin, attenuated sense that a person has acted or might act thus and so because they have a certain belief/desire pairing and that they are not irrational. Alone, knowing all of this would not be much help in making a person's actions intelligible. In those interesting cases in which we might need to make sense of McX's action we would need a much thicker description not just of his psychological set, but of his character, his history and his circumstances. In effect, we need to know his particular story.

Sustained experience with folk psychological narratives primes us for this richer practical understanding by giving us an initial sense of: which kinds of background factors can matter, why they do so, and how they do so in particular cases. Stories can do this because they are not bare descriptions of current beliefs and desires of idealised rational agents—they are snapshots of the adventures of situated persons, presented in the kinds of settings in which all of the important factors needed for understanding reasons are described; those that are relevant to making sense of what is done and why.

The various *personae dramatis* in such tales, even the not very interesting ones, each have their own unique psychological profile consisting not only of occurrent psychological attitudes but also habitual tendencies or other personality traits (which may conflict in various ways). They depict reasoners to be sure, but not ideal ones. The principal players in narratives have substantial attributes; these may make them admirable, pitiful or deeply or tragically flawed. It is the knowledge that people too have such attributes— learning what to watch out for and how to recognise these—that, in large part, fuels the activity of making sense of their actions (and indeed our own). This is at a far remove from making generalisations about what we can expect that any rational 'someone' might do or might have done in specified circumstances.

Once again, this works because story characters, like their real-life counterparts, do not pursue their projects in a vacuum. Often their reasons for taking a particular course of action are influenced by their character, larger projects, past choices, existing commitments, ruling passions or unique circumstances and history. My claim is that our ability to make sense of intentional action in practice—and our proficiency at doing so—rests on our knowing in general which details might be relevant and knowing how and when to make the appropriate adjustments in particular cases. Folk psychological narratives are uniquely well-suited to foster this kind of understanding because they provide examples of people acting for reasons in appropriately rich settings.

Admittedly, a full and properly nuanced awareness of what is involved in acting for a reason requires acquaintance with narratives of a much more sophisticated kind than those that feature in pre-school dialogues and simple fairy tales. There is much more on offer in adult conversations and grander literary offerings. The characters that populate children's stories would struggle even to pass muster as, what E.M. Foster called, 'flat characters'; those who 'can be summed up in a single sentence'.[26] Typically, storybook characters and the situations in which they find themselves are not very complex. Little Red Riding Hood is no Madame Bovary, to be sure. But this does not change the fact that such early narrative encounters supply the basics needed for acquiring a first understanding of reasons. This is folk psychology 101, after all, not grad school.

I opened this paper by saying that it is a test of adequacy for any good theory of folk psychology that it should be capable of explaining (at least potentially) not just how we acquire an understanding of the core mentalistic framework but also how we acquire our normal capacity to apply it sensitively in practice. This is integral to what we most want to understand about the distinctive but everyday phenomenon of making sense of intentional actions; it is not an optional extra. The importance of this can be best seen if one considers that it is possible to learn about the core folk psychological principles without knowing how or when to apply them (or at least not with the same fluency that ordinary practitioners of intentional psychology exhibit). One could learn how the core mentalistic predicates relate to one another in conceptual space without knowing, for example, how they function in a richer setting i.e. without having any idea of how or when they should be ascribed, as might happen if one learned such principles by means other than by engaging with folk psychological narratives in early childhood. Pretty clearly, on its own such an understanding would be of limited value.

Let me be clear about one other aspect of the central claim of the NPH. Although exposure to person-narratives is the normal route for learning the forms and norms of folk psychology, it is possible to achieve this (or something approximating to it) by other means. Apparently, it is possible to learn the basic rules of folk psychology

---

[26] Goldie, ibid, p. 3.

off by heart, as some individuals, initially diagnosed with infantile autism, have seemingly managed to do. The process is described as a purely 'logical one', using observation to fashion a set of useable generalizations that are then committed to memory, as are the principles for their application. On this basis, autistic individuals have been described as being able to 'compute' and 'calculate' what others are thinking and feeling based on available evidence, as if they were using a set of algorithms.[27] This is achieved in later life, perhaps thanks to their strong general intelligence and powerful rote memories, in order to compensate for their lack of insight into the reasons why others act. This is the most likely explanation of how such individuals eventually become capable of passing false belief tasks.

Picking up the relevant folk psychology principles and rules for their application as sets of explicit regulations is quite unlike the training I suggest is imparted through storytelling practice. And the effects of this alternative kind of training regime are transparent. Those who acquire their folk psychology skills in this way remain quite awkward in their dealings with others; they never fully develop a capacity to make sense of actions in the easy and familiar way that most of us do.[28] The phenomenological differences are also salient.[29] For example, Temple Grandin, an autistic individual who has, by her own account, succeeded in fashioning rules for understanding others in this way still 'describes herself as like an anthropologist on Mars'.[30]

Of course such feelings of estrangement have deeper roots, but the point is that these persist even after autistic individuals learn to master false belief tasks. This suggests that they never quite achieve the kind of understanding of others that is the norm for most

[27] See D. Bowler, "Theory of Mind' in Asperger's Syndrome', *Journal of Child Psychology and Psychiatry*, 33, 1992, 877–893; S. Gallagher, 'Understanding Interpersonal Problems in Autism: Interaction Theory as an Alternative to Theory of Mind', *Philosophy, Psychiatry, Psychology* 11, 2004, 199–217.

[28] See R. Eisenmajer and M. Prior, 'Cognitive Linguistics Correlates of 'Theory of Mind' Ability in Autistic Children', *British Journal of Developmental Psychology* 9, 1991, 351–364; F. Happé, 'The Role of Age and Verbal Ability in the Theory of Mind Task Performance of Subjects with Autism', *Child Development*, 66, 1995, 843–855.

[29] D. Zahavi and J. Parnas, 'Conceptual Problems in Infantile Autism Research', *Journal of Consciousness Studies* 10, 2003, 53–71.

[30] J. Kennett, 'Autism, Empathy and Moral Agency', *The Philosophical Quarterly* 52, 2002, 340–357.

people. If nothing else, consideration of such cases should discourage the tendency to think that folk psychology is nothing more than the name for a theory or set of rules, as opposed to a special sort of rule-based know how. This is a salient reminder that our true explanandum, our real quarry, is a highly nuanced and skilled practice—albeit one that makes use of the core mentalistic framework.

Extracting this schema and becoming familiar with the norms for its application through experience with a certain class of discursive narratives is the culminating, non-negotiable requirement for a basic mastery of our everyday folk psychology abilities. Engaging in the relevant kind of story-telling practice is the normal route through which this practical knowledge and understanding is procured.

5. The myth of Jones (remixed)

But if this is right, what should we say about the ultimate origins of our folk psychological abilities? Here I take a leaf out of Sellars' book; both in making clear the limit of my ambitions while also adapting the central feature of his basic proposal. Sellars concocted a famous myth—which he explicitly identifies as a piece of anthropological science fiction—in order to show the conditions under which our Rylean ancestors—who would have been wedded to a kind of methodological behaviorism—might have graduated to a more non-observationally based understanding of 'inner episodes of thought'. This is accomplished, Sellars imagines, by a genius, whom he calls Jones, who came amongst them. The great Jonesean insight was to model the inner thoughts of his compatriots on their overt speech acts and by doing so he developed a new means of explaining their intelligent acts, even when these were unaccompanied by any outward verbal behaviour.[31]

In the very same way, we can imagine that reasons—minimally, logically interlaced belief/desire pairings—might have been originally modelled on overt narrations. These would have been temporally extended, public speech acts that detailed, at bare minimum, the episodes of practical reasoning that detailed one's rationale for acting. They would have provided accounts, for example, of plans constructed and acted upon on the basis of

[31] See W. Sellars, *Empiricism and the Philosophy of Mind* (Cambridge, Mass.: Harvard University Press, 1956/1997), 102–107.

manipulating propositional beliefs and desires in appropriate ways. We can suppose then that just like the overt speech acts that served as Jones' original inspiration, these more complex narratives would have been supplied by the authors of these activities, in the first instance. Of course, this assumes that these narrators had command of a logically complex natural language; since they would have had to be at home with the practice of making plans based on bouts of practical reasoning involving propositional attitudes, expressing themselves in this way, and so on.

What matters is that in such story-tellings one's reasons for acting would have been put on exhibit for all to see. Presumably, such narratives would have been public spectacles, taking the form of complex third-personal representations for the benefit of a shared audience—i.e. they would have been issued in second-personal contexts. In short, we can imagine that such public narrations would have provided the model for what it is to act for a 'reason' in just the same way that less complex utterances served Jones in developing his understanding of inner episodes of thought.[32]

The importance of this Sellarsian myth is that it serves to remind us of the primacy of second-person, public practices in establishing our understanding of ourselves and others as persons who act for reasons. Given this ambition it may seem odd that I have borrowed from Sellars. After all, he is frequently presented as an arch theory-theorist, indeed possibly even the progenitor of the kind. Surely, his myth is better suited to support the idea that, at its root, folk psychology is a model used for third-personal explanation. Indeed, it is common to hear that 'Early formulations of the notion of folk psychology stressed the idea that folk psychology is *an explanatory theory*. This is much to the fore, for example, in Sellars'

---

[32] Like Sellars, I do not want to elevate this suggestion beyond the status of a myth in the sense that I make no claims about exactly how this might have come about. But if we assume that the basic logic of this story is right, it would seem that the practice of folk psychology is likely to have emerged relatively late in the pre-history of our species. Even though we do not know exactly when sophisticated linguistic abilities and the relevant discursive practices might have emerged, it is a good bet that, 'symbolic language, with the central function of narrative making, emerged only with *Homo sapiens* about thirty-five thousand years ago and was accompanied by a rapid acceleration of cultural growth'. See K. Nelson, 'Narrative and the Emergence of a Consciousness of Self', *Narrative and Consciousness*, G. D. Fireman, T. E. J. McVay and O. Flanagan (eds.) (Oxford: Oxford University Press, 2003), 24.

Daniel D. Hutto

influential mythical account of how folk psychology might have emerged'.[33] However, one really should not read *too much* into Sellars' talk of a Jones having created a 'theory', especially given the source of his model. Certainly, the way the story plays out, Jones *uses* his model in order to effect third-personal speculations. And this is surely a possible use of folk psychology; though it is—to be sure—not a very reliable one. Even so, this gives us no reason to suppose that supporting such third-personal speculation is or was the primary use of the folk psychological framework.

Even so, it might be objected, Sellars emphasizes the fact that the way in which Jones constructs his model of non-observational 'inner episodes of thought' parallels the way in which theoretical posits are, in general, constructed. But consider that he only ever claimed that his 'story helps us to understand that concepts pertaining to such inner episodes are *primarily and essentially intersubjective*, as intersubjective as the concept of a positron, and that the reporting role of these concepts—the fact that each of us has a privileged access to his thoughts—constitutes a dimension of the use of these concepts which is built on and presupposes this intersubjective status'.[34] I too have been at pains to stress this intersubjective, indeed socio-cultural, basis of our understanding of reasons, but this hardly commits me—or anyone who follows suit—to the idea that that understanding is theory-based, theory-like or formed as a product of explicit theorizing.

To see this it may help if one observes that in my new version of the Sellarsian myth, my Jones, like the orginal one, is not really a creative mastermind; he is more an attentive listener. He pays close attention to the stories of his fellow practical reasoners. For it is by hearing these often enough (or, more plausibly, by actively participating in conversations about these) that he becomes acquainted with a basic understanding of what it is to act for a reason. This would have supplied him with a framework that he can apply again and again when making sense of actions performed for reasons. My proposal is that the story is much the same with us.

---

[33] Bermúdez, ibid., 47, emphasis added.
[34] Sellars., ibid., 107, emphasis added.

Dramatic Irony, Narrative, and the External Perspective

PETER GOLDIE

Introduction

There is a frequently asked philosophical question about our ability to grasp and to predict the thoughts and feelings of other people, an ability that is these days sometimes given the unfortunate name of 'mentalising' or 'mind-reading'—I say 'unfortunate' because it makes appear mysterious what is not mysterious.[1] Some philosophers and psychologists argue that this ability is grounded in possession of some kind of theory or body of knowledge about how minds work. Others argue that it is grounded in our capacity to take on in imagination the perspective of others; sometimes called simulating or centrally imagining another person, we entertain in our minds what the other person is thinking about and feeling: if he is thinking 'p' and 'if p then q', then we think 'p' and 'if p then q', and if he is feeling angry with someone, then we imagine feeling angry with that person. We thus recreate as well as we can in our imagination his mental life as it is 'from the inside'. We can do this in two different ways: I can put myself in the other's shoes, simply imagining what I would do were I in his situation, or I can empathise with him, imagining *being* him, taking on in imagination his relevant traits and other mental dispositions; I will from now on use the term *perspective-shifting* to cover both of these imaginative activities.[2]

---

[1]   The term is sometimes chosen for the very reason that it does make this ability seem mysterious; see for example S. Nichols and S. Stich, *Mindreading: An Integrated Account of Pretence, Self-Awareness, and Understanding Other Minds* (Oxford: Clarendon Press, 2003).

[2]   I am skating over innumerable complexities here, which are not important for what follows. For some recent discussion of some of these complexities, see Nichols and Stich, op. cit., and the collection of papers in the following work by Heal, where she is careful to distinguish her notion of co-cognition from a more scientific notion of simulation: J. Heal, *Mind, Reason and Imagination* (Cambridge: Cambridge University Press, 2003).

I do not want to engage directly with this frequently asked question, interesting and important as it is. I want rather to bracket it off and consider another interesting and important question, which is not given so much prominence. The question is this: In order to manage our interactions with other people, *given* that we already have a reasonable grasp of their thoughts and feelings and can make reasonably accurate predictions of what they will think, feel and do, how are we best to use the psychological resources at our disposal, including our imagination, to *engage* with these thoughts and feelings? There *is* a question here, I think: it is a mistake to assume that all we need for managing our social and ethical relations with others is a grasp of what is in their minds sufficient for making predictions. We need also to think *about* their thoughts and feelings. For example, if you already know that your sensitive friend is upset because you have taken a disliking to her fiancé—and you know this because she has told you as much—there remains a further question as to how best to engage with her thoughts and feelings in order to find the best way of managing things between you and of negotiating your way around a shared social world.[3]

Perspective-shifting is often supposed to have its rightful place here too, as well as, supposedly, in relation to the first question. Against this, I will try to argue that perspective-shifting is (at least generally) not the best way to engage with the thoughts and feelings of other people. We should rather adopt what I will call an external perspective on them. In thinking about another person, if I think 'he thinks that p' and 'he thinks that if p then q', then I am thinking of him from an external perspective. And in visually imagining someone from an external perspective, I imagine him as another person so that he is part of the content of what I visually imagine. I thus do not in any way adopt his perspective in imagination, or in any way try to think the same thoughts as him or feel the same feelings.[4]

I should make one point clear from the outset. The notion of perspective-shifting that I am arguing against is not the same notion as empathy when this notion is taken in a wider sense. When

---

[3] My way of addressing this question has been much influenced by the excellent notion of 'micro-ethics' introduced by A. Morton, *The Importance of Being Understood: Folk Psychology as Ethics* (London: Routledge, 2003).

[4] For discussion, see R. Wollheim, *The Thread of Life* (Cambridge, Mass.: Harvard University Press, 1984).

our feelings resonate to those of another (like sympathetic strings), such as when we are nervous for the person as we watch her taking her viva, there is an obvious sense in which our emotion is generated by, and matches, that of the other person. In one sense of the term 'empathy', this is empathy, but not in the sense I am concerned with, which specifically involves the notion of perspective-shifting—of imaginatively shifting one's perspective to that of another person. Martin Hoffman uses the term 'empathy' in the wider sense. 'The key requirement of an empathetic response according to my definition', he says, 'is *the involvement of psychological processes that make a person have feelings that are more congruent with another's situation than with his own situation*'.[5] Now empathy in this sense, as Hoffman points out, is 'multi-determined'. Perspective-taking is just one of five possible psychological processes that he discusses, and it is quite distinct in that it requires none of the other processes, and none of the other processes require it.[6] Of the other four processes, three are 'pre-verbal, automatic and essentially involuntary'; these are motor mimicry and afferent feedback, classical conditioning, and 'direct association of cues from the victim or his situation with one's painful past experience'. The fourth is, like perspective-shifting, a 'higher-order cognitive mode', which involves 'association of expressive clues ... mediated by semantic processing ...' So an empathetic response in Hoffman's sense might be arrived at through perspective-shifting, but it certainly need not be. And I have no brief against the other four processes that Hoffman discusses under the general rubric of empathy.[7]

So it is precisely in contrast to perspective-shifting that I will argue for adopting an external perspective on another person. In taking such a perspective, one's stance is resolutely thinking of the other, although a human being just like one is oneself, as another person, with a possibly significantly different perspective to one's

[5]   M. Hoffman, *Empathy and Moral Development: Implications for Caring and Justice* (Cambridge: Cambridge University Press, 2000), 30.

[6]   Ibid., 8.

[7]   Many of these processes will involve what Shaun Gallagher calls implicit simulation, 'involving sub-personal activation of mirror neurons, shared representations, or, more generally, resonance systems'. He questions, rightly in my view, whether it is right to characterise such processes as simulations. S. Gallagher, 'Logical and Phenomenological Arguments Against Simulation Theory', *Folk Psychology Reassessed*, D. Hutto and M. J. Ratcliffe (eds.) (Dordrecht: Kluwer Academic Press, forthcoming).

Peter Goldie

own—diverging both in occurrent thoughts and feelings, and in traits of character and personality as well as in other mental dispositions. It is necessary to adopt an external perspective if we are to appreciate these diverging perspectives and to evaluate them in comparison to our own. This is exemplified in what I will call dramatic irony.

What do I mean by dramatic irony? In drama, we the audience sometimes know something that one of the characters in the drama does not know. In Sophocles' *Oedipus Rex*, we know that Oedipus killed his father at the crossroads, but Oedipus believes that he killed a stranger. In the *Odyssey*, we know that Odysseus has returned home to Ithaca, but Penelope, at least initially, does not know this. In *King Lear*, we know that blinded Gloucester, who wants to die, is wrong when he thinks that he is on the edge of the cliffs of Dover, and that with one step he will be able to cast himself over the edge to his certain death. This is dramatic irony—a strange term one might think, because, at least on the face it, it does not have much to do with irony.[8] I want now to extend the idea of dramatic irony beyond drama into the real world, to include the divergences that can open up between one's own beliefs and those of other people—divergences that here too can only be appreciated from an external perspective.

I will begin with a few remarks about the beginnings of a child's appreciation of dramatic irony. Then I will discuss how this kind of appreciation continues to develop, or ought to continue to develop, in a mature person, and how appreciating the complexities and diverging perspectives in good novels helps in this development, and thus helps us in negotiating our way around the real social world. And finally, in what must here be a rather brief discussion, I will turn to an ethical objection to my complaints against perspective-shifting. I will argue that seeing the other person as another, from an external perspective, far from alienating one from other people, brings one closer to them, and puts one in a better position to treat them in an ethically appropriate way, with sympathy or otherwise. Perspective-shifting, by putting oneself in the other's shoes or by empathising, is not the ideal route to ethics.

---

[8]   However, there is this in common between dramatic irony and irony: in irony, what is literally said and what the speaker means have to be grasped both independently and in contrast one to the other; and in dramatic irony there is a similar structure, requiring the audience to grasp independently how things in fact are and how another thinks they are, and also to grasp the contrast between the two.

Dramatic Irony, Narrative, and the External Perspective

The child's developing understanding of dramatic irony

Let me begin, then, with development in children, and what is generally known as the false belief task. For those who are not familiar with it, I will give a very quick summary of what is involved in the original experiment, from which there have been innumerable variations since.[9] The child is asked to watch a puppet show, in which Maxi the puppet puts a chocolate in a box. Maxi then goes out to play. Then, whilst Maxi is out, the child watches Maxi's puppet mother move the chocolate to a cupboard. The child is then asked where Maxi will look for the chocolate when he returns. The four-year-old child, unless he is autistic, reliably answers as an adult would: Maxi will look in the box because that is where Maxi, falsely, thinks it is—understandably enough, because Maxi was out of the room when it was moved. But the three-year-old reliably gets the answer wrong, saying that Maxi will look in the cupboard; after all, that is where it is.

The generally accepted conclusion drawn from this experiment is that a significant developmental change takes place in a child's grasp of the concept of belief at around the age of three-and-a-half, although the debate continues to this day as to what experiments like these suggest about how and why this change comes about. Does the child have some kind of tacit *ur*-theory of the mind, possibly innate, which emerges at about this time, or does the child learn how to grasp and predict the thoughts of other people through some kind of simulation of the other? However, as I said at the outset, this is the debate that I want to put to one side. I want to focus on something else that the false belief task shows.

The three-and-a-half-year-old child who first passes the false belief task has shown the beginnings of a grasp of dramatic irony: he realises that Maxi believes something that is not the case, just as we realise that Gloucester falsely believes that he is on the edge of the cliffs of Dover. This is, precisely, dramatic irony.[10]

Now, dramatic irony can only be appreciated from an external perspective, in which Maxi's thoughts are grasped by the child as

[9]   The *locus classicus* is H. Wimmer and J. Perner, 'Beliefs about Beliefs: Representation and Constraining Functions of Wrong Beliefs in Young Children's Understanding of Deception', *Cognition* 13, 1983, 103–128.

[10]   Whilst there is nothing ironic about dramatic irony, there are structural commonalities between the two (see note 8 above), and I take it that it is no coincidence that autistic children not only have difficulties appreciating dramatic irony, but also have difficulties appreciating irony.

those of another ('Maxi thinks that the chocolate is in the box'), rather than being grasped from a perspective which emulates or simulates Maxi's own perspective ('the chocolate is in the box'). Even if the child shifted his perspective to that of Maxi as a methodology to enable him to ascribe to Maxi the belief that the chocolate is in the box (the issue about which I am remaining neutral), the child still has, so to speak, to return to the way he (the child) sees things, to his own perspective, in order to appreciate its divergence from Maxi's perspective. Things are precisely the same with our appreciation of *King Lear*: if we put ourselves in the shoes of Gloucester, the dramatic irony of his position will be lost from view. Simulating or centrally imagining the other's mental life from the inside, whilst it might well sometimes deliver up a correct ascription of belief to the other, is not sufficient for appreciating dramatic irony.

So by about the age of three and a half, a child is able to grasp the diverging perspectives in dramatic irony. But even if the false belief task reveals a significant change in this respect in children of about this age, all the evidence points towards a progressive developmental story in the grasping of diverging perspectives, rather than something that comes about, all at once, at this age. For example, children seem able to grasp diverging desires before they are able to grasp diverging beliefs. And after they are able to pass the false belief task, and thus demonstrate a grasp of diverging beliefs, there remains a delay before they are able to grasp what the implications are of having false beliefs for emotion, even though they might be able to grasp what the implications are of false beliefs for action. This is interesting and somewhat puzzling. Consider the story of *Little Red Riding Hood*—a wonderful example of dramatic irony. Little Red Riding Hood has the false belief that it is Grandma whose teeth she is admiring, and the four-year-old child is able to appreciate this. Surprisingly, though, it is not until around five to six years old that the child is able to appreciate the emotional implications for Little Red Riding Hood of her false beliefs—that it is understandable that she should be unafraid as she knocks on Grandma's door, and as she discusses the size of 'Grandma's' teeth. The four-year-old child projects his own fear onto Little Red Riding Hood, whilst not projecting his own belief. Moreover, children manifest the same failure to appreciate emotional implications of false beliefs in their own case: for example if the child is, like Maxi, the unwitting victim of a chocolate switch, looking back on their past feelings, they would 'claim to have felt the emotion they now feel, having discovered the actual situation'.[11]

Thus it would seem that as children grow up, they find their way slowly into a world of diverging perspectives, becoming increasingly able to appreciate the implications of these diverging perspectives for their relations with others. This appreciation, I would maintain, is a necessary condition for anything like a fully-fledged appreciation of narrative. Perhaps it is very early on that the young child is able to give a breathless, babbled narrative to her mother of what happened to her on the bus on the way back from playschool, and this is done from a perspective, but this in no way suggests that she is able to appreciate the possibility of dramatic irony and of diverging perspectives.[12]

As we grow up: diverging perspectives in literature and in real life

Our ability to appreciate diverging perspectives ought to be a skill that we continue to foster and develop into maturity. Novels are the most wonderful source of the phenomenon: in novels there can be diverging perspectives between character and character, between internal narrator and other characters, between character and reader, between narrator and implied author, between implied author and author, between implied author and reader, between reader and reader, between actual reader and ideal reader, and many more besides. To understand these possible divergences is part of what it is to understand and appreciate a novel.

Usually we take all this for granted, as it comes to us so easily. But at times it is something of a struggle to achieve and the effort makes evident to us what is also involved in the effortless case. Let me illustrate this with Willa Cather's *My Ántonia*. It makes use of an interesting device: an introduction which, so to speak, sets the scene for the first-personal narrative that is to follow, at the same

[11]   Many thanks to Paul Harris for discussion here; the citations are from personal correspondence. See also his *Children and Emotion* (Oxford: Blackwell, 1989).

[12]   For discussion and reference to the literature, see Nichols and Stich, op. cit., 74. See also Katherine Nelson's discussion in her 'Narrative and the Emergence of a Consciousness of Self', *Narrative and Consciousness*, G. Fireman, T. McVay and O. Flanagan (eds.) (Oxford: Oxford University Press, 2003), 17–36.

time giving the rest of the novel a false and superficially misleading air of factuality or reality. The same device is found in Nabokov's *Lolita*, and versions of it are very common in the novels of Conrad.

In Willa Cather's wonderful novel, we have Jim Burden's first-personal story, set in frontier Nebraska, of the incredible hardships in the life of his friend, Ántonia Shimerda, an immigrant from Bohemia, with whom he grew up from childhood. But Willa Cather sets the scene of the novel with an Introduction, in which an unnamed character, writing in the first person, tells of meeting Jim Burden, a childhood friend, on a train. Burden, now old, a railroad lawyer, unhappily married, and full of disappointments, reflects on that Bohemian girl whom they had both known all those years ago, and tells this person, the narrator of the Introduction, that he had been writing down what he remembered of Ántonia. The Introduction ends as follows:

> When I told him [Jim] that I would like to read his account of her, he said I should certainly see it—if it were ever finished.
>
> Months afterwards, Jim called at my apartment one stormy winter afternoon, carrying a legal portfolio. He brought it into the sitting-room with him, and said, as he stood warming his hands, 'Here is the thing about Ántonia. Do you still want to read it? I finished it last night. I didn't take time to arrange it; I simply wrote down pretty much all that her name recalls to me. I suppose it hasn't any form. It hasn't any title either.' He went into the next room, sat down at my desk and wrote across the face of the portfolio the word 'Ántonia'. He frowned at this a moment, then prefixed another word, making it 'My Ántonia'. That seemed to satisfy him.[13]

And then we have Jim Burden's story, narrated by Jim. What this introduction does, in a rather moving way, is to open up and make starker the diverging perspectives: we have Willa Cather; we have the first-personal narrator of the introduction (and what is this character's relationship to Willa Cather?); we have Jim the young lad; we have Jim Burden as a disappointed railroad lawyer with a failed marriage looking back on his life, making dismissive remarks about the lack of form in the writing; and so on. As readers of the novel, we have to make a real effort to keep track of these diverging perspectives and the dramatic ironies involved. The difficulty is not

[13] W. Cather, *My Ántonia* (London: Virago Press, 1980, first published 1918).

like that in grasping multiply-embedded propositional attitudes, where beyond a certain level of iteration it becomes impossible. Rather, the difficulty, as we read the novel, is of keeping in mind, and evaluating, this variety of perspectives that can diverge from each other and from our own. And we need to maintain an external perspective in order to do this. If we empathise with, or put ourselves in the shoes of, one of these characters or people—Jim the narrator, say—we will lose sight of the divergence between Jim's perspective and our own.[14]

But here you might object. Surely the ideal reader of a novel is expected precisely not to maintain this external perspective but to shift his or her perspective to that of one or other of the characters in the novel. Am I not flying in the face of millennia of great narrative works of fiction? I am not so sure about this. Could it not be that what a good author or playwright wants of us, as good readers or audiences, is not in imagination to shift our perspective to one of the characters, but to do all sorts of other things: to know in full and fine detail what that character thinks and feels; to focus our attention on one character and not on some other character; to think what it must be like for that character (terrifying perhaps); to draw on our own experiences; to understand him; to resonate with his feelings; perhaps to sympathise or feel for him; and yet at the same time to evaluate him, and to respond emotionally to our evaluation. This kind of engagement, or cluster of engagements, involves plenty of imagining, including in particular imagining from an external perspective; and moreover, it involves plenty of emotional engagement. We should not be under the illusion that the only way of being a good reader or audience, of being someone who responds emotionally to the fiction in the right way, has to

[14] Sometimes in literary theory the term 'external perspective' is used when we are speaking or thinking of the characters in novels as characters, and so in that sense 'externally'; see, for example P. Lamarque and S. Olsen, *Truth, Fiction, and Literature* (Oxford: Clarendon Press, 1994). For example, in this sense we might say that Pierre in *War and Peace* is a better drawn character than Levin is in *Anna Karenin*, whereas if we were to say that Pierre was a man of great sensitivity yet capable of terrifying and blind rage we would be taking an internal perspective on Pierre. Although useful in many ways, this is a quite different distinction from the one that I wish to draw. I discuss the external perspective in literature and contrast it with the simulationist account of Greg Currie in P. Goldie, 'Narrative, Emotion and Perspective', *Imagination and the Arts*, M. Kieran and D. Lopes (eds.) (London: Routledge, 2003).

involve perspective-shifting, by putting ourselves in the shoes of one of the characters or by empathising with him or her.[15]

Reading great literature, then, can remind us of the complexities of diverging perspectives in narratives—perspectives that sometimes only come into view with careful attention. The point applies not only to fictional narratives, but to works of history, to autobiographies, to diaries and contemporary historical documents, and to confessions. But we must not let the tail wag the dog here, for we find the same divergences, and possibilities of divergences, in our engagement with other people in a shared social world. Dramatic irony is found not only in narratives but in real life too. If I may put it like this, our negotiating our way around narratives—novels, drama and other narratives besides—is just an aspect of our wider social involvement; and it is for this reason that good novels can be a kind of training ground for appreciating and dealing with dramatic irony and other kinds of diverging perspective in the so-called 'real world', and for evaluating and responding to those perspectives that diverge from our own: the therapist's perspective diverges from our own qua patient, the bank manager's from our own qua customer, the house-buyer's from our own qua house-seller, the child's from our own qua parent, the colleague's from our own qua colleague, the politician's from our own qua voter, and so on. It was surely with this in mind that Harold Macmillan, himself a great reader of Trollope, once impatiently told an ambitious young politician to go away and read a novel.

This is not to suggest that all our dealings with others are adversarial or competitive, and the fact of diverging perspectives does not imply it. Indeed, there are often diverging interests when two people or more are cooperating in a joint task, such as moving a piano. I do not want to get my clothes dirty and she does not want to strain her back which has been giving her trouble recently; things will go better for our joint task if these concerns are reflected in how we divide things up between us. And even if there are no divergences in a particular case—you are, as the saying goes, *ad idem* on some matter—there still should remain in one's mind the *possibility* of divergence, which might perhaps begin to become actual as things develop. It is highly dangerous to work on a default presupposition of identity of perspectives and of shared interests;

---

[15] I discuss these issues in P. Goldie, 'Wollheim on Emotion and Imagination', *Philosophical Studies* 127, 2006, 1–17.

better surely to assume that there might well be divergences, and be gratified when it turns out that our interests are shared in this particular case.[16]

An objection to my line of argument might go as follows. Of course it is not always best to shift our perspective onto the other, by empathising or putting ourselves in the other's shoes, and of course it is important not to lose sight of our own perspective, and of how perspectives can diverge. But still, so this objection continues, why should we not shift our perspective where we are relevantly like the other in psychological makeup and where the situation is a familiar one, and then return to our own external perspective once we have done this? Why can we not oscillate between the two, or even keep both perspectives in mind at the same time? I have three comments.

First, I have nothing against this approach as such, although I believe it is not effective nearly as frequently as is generally supposed, even in the most simple situation. Even shared rationality is in question when it comes to being relevantly similar to the other person in psychological makeup; rationality is such a thin notion, with plenty of scope for variation. Indeed, I think it is too much emphasis on the familiar and simple type of situation that has in part led to too much emphasis on perspective-shifting.[17]

Secondly, I think that the first comment points towards deeper epistemological difficulties, because the effectiveness of the process of perspective-shifting depends crucially on determining that, either there are no relevant differences, or that the differences that there are can be identified as relevant and then suitably adjusted for. This requires not only profound knowledge of the traits of character and personality, emotions, and other mental dispositions of both ourselves and of the other person. It also requires profound knowledge of the ways in which these traits and other mental dispositions interact with our conscious thought processes (let alone our unconscious thought processes). This seems to me to be wildly optimistic.

---

[16]   I discuss these issues in relation to diverging mental dispositions, and in particular diverging emotional dispositions, in Goldie (2006), ibid.

[17]   Jane Heal discusses this in her 'What are psychological concepts for?', in her (2003), op. cit. note 2, and I discuss the thin notion of rationality in P. Goldie, 'There are reasons and reasons', *Folk Psychology Reassessed*, D. Hutto and M. J. Ratcliffe (eds.) (Dordrecht Netherlands: Kluwer Academic Press, forthcoming). Morton has some excellent examples of the importance of simulation in game theory, op. cit. note 3.

Peter Goldie

My third comment is that the process of perspective-shifting can easily take a wrong turn, ending up in something of a blind alley. To show what I mean, consider this example. Your colleague tells you about her experience of being delayed because of the lateness of her train. You shift your perspective in imagination and, as is natural, you do so by bringing to mind a similar situation that you experienced some time in the past. 'I know just how you feel', you say, 'something just like that happened to me the other day.' And then, your mind being on *your* experience, you start to tell her about what happened to you, so that what began as an attempt to empathise ends up as something rather self-indulgent. It is a familiar enough phenomenon. Hoffman nicely calls it 'egoistic drift', and specifically associates it with perspective-shifting.[18] Hospitals ought to have notices to patients about it: 'You are advised not to tell other patients about your suffering, for they will reply by telling you about theirs'.[19]

Ethics and the external perspective

The final objection to my argument might at first glance seem to be the most forceful. The objection is that, whatever the role might be of perspective-shifting in our engagement with literature, any reasonable ethics of real life requires us to shift our perspective to that of another. This is supposed to be what properly sensitive and imaginative people do, and it seems to be what is implied by the Golden Rule, which is found in so many religions and secular ethics across the world in one formulation or another: 'Do unto others as you would they should do unto you'. And to find out what you would they should do unto you, you need to imagine how you would feel with the roles reversed. It is a not unfamiliar refrain:

[18] Op. cit., note 5.
[19] In contrast to real life, when we come to reading literary works, my own experience is that egoistic drift can sometimes be both harmless and enjoyable: for a moment one stops reading about the torrid holiday romance to reflect on one's own past experiences of torrid holiday romances, and to think about how similar one's own experiences were to those of the character in the novel.

'Before you do that, put yourself in my shoes. How would you like it if I did the same thing to you?'[20]

Of course it *could* be a useful heuristic to put ourselves in the other person's shoes when we are relevantly similar to that other person. For example, you might be considering the possibility of keeping someone waiting for an hour at a railway station whilst you dawdle in the bookshop, and then be brought up short on imagining how you would feel in such circumstances. But I have four comments.[21]

In the first place, surely we should all just *know* not to do things like that; the very fact that someone should need to engage in a role-reversing imaginative exercise indicates that their moral thinking is somewhat lacking in sensitivity. Moreover (and by now this should be a familiar refrain), simple role-reversal will only come up with the right answer if you have the same relevant preferences as the other person. Let us assume that they are not the same. If no adjustment is made, then, as Don Locke has pointed out,[22] the Golden Rule becomes open to the telling remark of George Bernard Shaw: 'Do not do unto others as you would have them do unto you—their tastes may be different'. If adjustment *is* made, so that you take on in imagination their preferences whilst abandoning yours, then one may, in certain circumstances, be blocked from action altogether where these preferences include ones which are directly opposed to your own. For example, you like holding hands with your partner in public; your partner does not. Should you hold hands in public? If you shift perspective in the appropriate way, you will determine that you should not. If she also shifts her perspective, she will determine that you should. You are no further forwards in determining what the right thing is to do.[23]

---

[20]   I leave to one side the affinities of the Golden Rule to the Categorical Imperative. Kant himself denied any affinity; see his *Groundwork of the Metaphysics of Morals* (1785), H. J. Paton (trans.) (New York: Harper and Row, 1964).

[21]   One thing I will not discuss is how to judge someone who refuses to imagine what the Golden Rule prescribes us to imagine, what the censure is on them, and whether their failing is one of rationality or one of morality. R. M. Hare's work is the source of much discussion of these issues; see, for example, his *Freedom and Reason* (Oxford: Clarendon Press, 1963).

[22]   D. Locke, 'The Principle of Equal Interests', *The Philosophical Review* 90, 1981, 531–559, 536.

[23]   Again, this is delightfully demonstrated in Locke (1981), ibid.

Peter Goldie

My second comment is that making perspective-shifting central to moral thinking fails to pay sufficient credit to the importance of the sympathetic stance towards others. The sympathetic stance is from an external perspective. In thinking of the other person as another, our sympathy does not mirror his suffering: it is an ethical response *to* his suffering; we feel *for* him. In sympathising with him, in contrast with perspective-shifting, we are free to think of him in all his particularities, appreciating his perspective on the world as ineliminably his, and perhaps as radically unlike our own. Our focus is, precisely, on *him*, on *his* thoughts and feelings, on what kind of person *he* is, and so on. For example, our friend tells us that his wife has left him, and he has no idea what to do. In sympathising, we feel terrible for him. We might ourselves know what it is like to be betrayed in a relationship. But we do not dwell on our own past experiences, partly because of the risk of egoistic drift. Nor do we imagine it happening to us, with our sensitivities in play rather than his. Rather, from an external perspective, we dwell on *his* experience. This allows us not only to draw on the advantage of dramatic irony. It also allows us to bring to bear in our thinking our evaluation of him from our own perspective (for perhaps to some extent what has happened is of his own doing), and this evaluation would be closed off from us if we shifted our perspective to his.

Thirdly, from the external perspective we are not only better able to appreciate the situation the other person is in and to evaluate his perspective. We are also better able to give advice. For example, returning to our friend whose wife has left him, if we advise him to do what we would do if we were in his shoes, we would not be in a position to take account of the divergences between our two evaluative perspectives; and if we fully empathise with him, then the advice that we give would be no different from what he would decide on without our involvement. The right model for our giving advice to others, I suggest, is one based on the right way to buy a present for someone. What does *she* want? What sort of tastes has *she* got? How does *she* respond to surprises? Here too we should not forget Bernard Shaw's dictum.

And fourthly, seeing the other as another, from an external perspective, where the other person is both substantially different from us and has done something terrible, can also yield up a depth of understanding that perspective-shifting closes out. For the outcome of perspective-shifting is limited by our powers of imagination, and these powers are in turn limited by our knowledge. Someone does something wrong in strained circumstances that are unfamiliar to us, and, putting ourselves into his shoes, we exclaim 'I couldn't *imagine* doing such a thing', or perhaps 'How could *anyone* do such a thing?' At this point it is often so easy to rest on this sheer incomprehension, as when we describe some forms of violence perpetrated by people on other people as 'mindless'. Violence is never mindless.

So in a way I have turned certain views of ethical thought on their heads. Where these views suggest the right ethical outlook is to think of others as being very much like ourselves, and to treat them as we would ourselves be treated (the Golden Rule again), my view involves resolutely thinking of them as others, with perspectives, at least potentially, significantly different from ours. We can then treat them not necessarily as we would be treated, and not necessarily even as they would themselves be treated; but we can treat them as they ought to be treated, which is at least with understanding and proper consideration—and, of course, as people.

With this last remark in mind, let me return, finally, to the debate that I put to one side at the outset—the debate about the respective merits of theory theory and perspective-shifting. It is sometimes complained that the trouble with the theory approach is that it treats people very much like other material things in the world, so understanding and prediction of what someone will do becomes similar to understanding and predicting what an atom or a volcano will do; and yet people are not to be understood in this way.[24] This may well be a justified complaint, but agreement with it should not force one into the arms of perspective-shifting. One might think this if the complaint against the theory approach were expressed as if what is wrong with its stance towards other people is that it is 'third-personal'. The complaint, rather, ought to be that the theory approach involves a stance which is *impersonal*—in other words, it is the stance of the sciences. If the third-personal and the impersonal are conflated, we run the risk of deeming the external perspective, being third-personal, also therefore to be impersonal, and thus perhaps unfavourably contrasted in this respect with perspective-shifting. Yet this is precisely what I have been at pains to say is not the case: there is no difficulty in thinking of another person in the

[24] See, for example, Jane Heal's excellent remarks in her Introduction to her (2003), op. cit. note 2.

Peter Goldie

third person, and yet at the same time thinking of him as a person; in this respect, it is no different from thinking of him or her in the second-person.[25]

That, then, concludes my plea for adopting an external perspective in our engagement with characters in literature and in other narratives, and in our engagement with other people in the real world. I do not claim hegemony for it, but I do believe that it is often neglected, as if the theory approach and perspective-shifting were the only two possibilities here. Indeed, I think that the external perspective is so pervasive in our engagement with others that it almost goes unnoticed, so that we are, in this respect, rather like Monsieur Jourdain in Molière's *Le Bourgeois Gentilhomme*, who was surprised to be told that he spoke prose.

---

[25] I discuss these matters in *The Emotions: A Philosophical Exploration* (Oxford: Clarendon Press, 2000).

Episodic Ethics

GALEN STRAWSON

I guess I wont send that note now, for the mind is such a new place, last night feels obsolete (Emily Dickinson, 1830–1886).[1]

She said: 'Rejoice, for God has brought you to your fiftieth year in the world!' But she had no inkling that, for my part, there is no difference at all between my own days which have gone by and the distant days of Noah about which I have heard. I have nothing in the world but the hour in which I am: it pauses for a moment, and then, like a cloud, moves on. (Samuel Hanagid, 996–1056, Vizier to the King of Granada)

1 Four temporal temperaments

The first thing I want to put in place is a distinction between one's experience of oneself when one is considering oneself principally as a human being taken as a whole, and one's experience of oneself when one is considering oneself principally as an inner mental entity or 'self' of some sort—I'll call this one's self-experience. When Henry James says, of one of his early books

> I think of … the masterpiece in question … as the work of quite another person than myself … a rich … relation, say, who … suffers me still to claim a shy fourth cousinship'[2]

he has no doubt that he is the same human being as the author of that book, but he doesn't feel he is the same self or person as the author of that book. It's this phenomenon of experiencing oneself as a self that concerns me here. One of the most important ways in which people tend to think of themselves (quite independently of

---

[1] Letter to Mrs. J. G. Holland, early October 1870. When I cite a work I give the first publication date or estimated date of composition, while the page reference is to the text referred to here. E. Dickinson, *Emily Dickinson: Selected Letters*, T. H. Johnson (ed.) (Cambridge, MA: Belknap Press, 1830/1971).

[2] 1915: 562-3.

Galen Strawson

religious belief) is as things whose persistence conditions are not obviously or automatically the same as the persistence conditions of a human being considered as a whole.

I'm going to use the terms 'Diachronic', 'Episodic', 'Narrative' and 'non-Narrative' with capital letters to denote four psychological tendencies, four natural ways of experiencing life in time. To be *Narrative* is

[N] to see or live or experience one's life as a narrative or story of some sort, or at least as a collection of stories.

To be *non-Narrative* is not to live one's life in this way; one may simply lack any Narrative tendency, or one may have a positively anti-Narrative tendency.

Everyone, I think, agrees that there is such a thing as Narrativity, although there's a large debate about what it is, exactly, and about whether or not it's a good thing. I'm not going to say much about it here, though, because I'm more concerned with the less familiar distinction between Episodics and Diachronics.[3]

If one is *Diachronic*

[D] one naturally figures oneself, the self or person one now experiences oneself to be, as something that was there in the (further) past and will be there in the (further) future.

Diachronics needn't be Narratives, even if (as may be doubted) Narratives are bound to be Diachronics, for the basic Diachronic experience of self and life can exist as just defined in the absence of any specifically Narrative—story-discerning, unity-seeking—attitude to one's own life. Many human beings, it seems, are Diachronic. Others are Episodic, where the defining feature of being *Episodic* is that

[E] one does not figure oneself, the self or person one now experiences oneself to be, as something that was there in the (further) past and will be there in the (further) future

although one is of course fully aware that one has long-term—lifelong—continuity considered as a human being. Episodic experience is the direct opposite of Diachronic experience.

Many think that a good human life must be both Narrative and Diachronic. They think that an Episodic person cannot live a fully

---

[3] I discuss Narrativity in 'Against Narrativity', *Ratio* 16, 2004, 428–452.

moral life. An Episodic, they say, cannot properly inhabit the realms of responsibility, duty and obligation—not to mention those of friendship, loyalty, and so on.[4]

Is this true? In discussing the question I will use 'I*' ('me*', 'mine*', etc.) as I have done before to represent that which I experience myself to be when I'm apprehending myself specifically as a self or inner subject considered as something different from GS, i.e. the human being that I am considered as a whole. (The asterisk attaches equally well to other personal pronouns and adjectives—'you*', 'their*', etc.—to denote others' sense of themselves as selves or inner subjects as opposed to their sense of themselves as human beings considered as a whole.)

According to Kathy Wilkes

> morality is a matter of planning future actions, calculating consequences, experiencing remorse and contrition, accepting responsibility, accepting praise and blame; such mental phenomena are both forward—and backward—looking. Essentially ... Emotions such as love or hate, envy or resentment, would not deserve the name—except in some occasional rare cases—if they lasted for but three seconds, and were thereafter claimed, not by any me*, but by some former self ... *The Episodic life could not be richly moral and emotional*; we must have a life, or self, with duration. We are, and must consider ourselves as, relatively stable intentional systems. Essentially.[5]

This is forcefully put, and I agree with quite a lot of it. It does, however, misrepresent what it is to be Episodic, and I think that its central claim is false. The Episodic life is certainly not the same as the Diachronic life, any more than the non-Narrative life is the same as the Narrative life, but it is certainly not less moral, or less feeling. Nor is it less human or humane, less vivid, less understanding, or less responsible. A happy-go-lucky person can be the best among us.

[4]   The notion of Diachronicity is close to the special notion of consciousness of past events that Locke employs in his discussion of personal identity. Consciousness in his sense is essentially accompanied by 'concernment', a sense of ownership and involvement. See M. Schechtman, *The Constitution of Selves* (Ithaca: Cornell University Press, 1996), 105–109; G. Strawson, *Locke on personal identity* (in preparation).

[5]   K. Wilkes, 'ΓΝΩΘΙ ΣΕΑΥΤΟΝ (Know Thyself)', *Journal of Consciousness Studies* 5, 1998, 153–165, 155, criticizing G. Strawson, ' "The Self" ', *Journal of Consciousness Studies* 4, 1997, 405–428 (my emphasis).

Galen Strawson

To some this is obvious, others find it hard to see. Human beings have radically different moral styles or personalities, and some types have a rather dim view of others.[6] Diachronics may think that an Episodic's attitude to others must be thin or cold or incomplete in some way. There is, however, no systematic quantative difference in the warmth, completeness and depth of Episodics' and Diachronics' relations with others. Human beings can flourish in very different ways, and Plutarch shows great ignorance when he writes in *On Tranquillity* as follows:

> the present good, which permits us to touch it only for the briefest period of time and then eludes perception, seems to fools to have no further reference to us nor to belong to us at all. As in that painting of a man twisting rope in Hades, who allows a donkey grazing near by to eat it up as he plaits it, insensible and thankless forgetfulness steals upon most people and takes possession of them, consuming every past action and success, every pleasant moment of leisure, companionship and enjoyment. Forgetfulness does not allow life to become unified, as when past is interwoven with present. Instead, separating yesterday from today as though it were different, and also tomorrow, it immediately makes every event to have never happened because it is never recalled.

> Those in the Schools who deny growth and increase, on the ground that Being is in continual flux, turn one into ... a series of persons different from oneself. So too, those who do not preserve or recall former events in memory, but allow them to flow away, make themselves deficient and empty each day and dependent on tomorrow—as though what had happened last year and yesterday and the day before had no relation to them, and had never happened at all.[7]

Diachronics may see a lack of interest in what one has made of one's life as chilling or alien—even slightly frightening—when it is

---

[6]   Cf. e.g. O. Flanagan, *Varieties of Moral Personality* (Cambridge, MA: Harvard University Press, 1991). One of the most profound differences is between those for whom the moral-emotional categories of resentment and humiliation are central, and those for whom they hardly figure.

[7]   Plutarch, 'On Tranquillity of Mind', *Moralia* VI, Plutarch, W. C. Helmbold (trans.) (Cambridge, MA: Harvard University Press, c 100 CE/1939), 214–217 (473B-474B); my thanks to Richard Sorabji for showing this to me. Forgetfulness is not in fact a necessary part of Episodicity, but Plutarch's overall opposition to the Episodic life is clear.

set down on paper. They should not, however, conclude that they will find people who experience things in this way chilling or frightening; some of their best friends may be like this. It is not hard to develop a sense of where people fall on the Diachronic-Episodic spectrum, although one needs to bear in mind that things like increasing age may bring about significant change, and that the strength and emotional loading of one's awareness of oneself* as something that has a past or a future can vary considerably according to what one is thinking about.

Adequate studies of the ethical differences between Diachronics and Episodics would fill a bookshelf—they already fill many, if one looks to literature—and I'm not going to attempt a systematic exposition. After forestalling one possible misapprehension I'm simply going to offer, in no particular order, a number of points in defence of the flourishing Episodic life. (It is a further question whether the non-Narrative life can be a fully moral or human life; the answer is 'Of course'.)

The misapprehension is this. In the passage quoted above Wilkes is replying to a paper in which I propose that the best thing to say about human selves, given the assumption that such metaphysical entities exist at all, is that they exist for at most two or three seconds. Now this is a strictly metaphysical proposal, motivated partly by considerations from experimental psychology, and it is meant to apply equally to all of us, Diachronics and Episodics alike, however we experience ourselves in time. It does not carry any sort of suggestion that anyone's subjective experience of their* duration will tend to be of the order of two or three seconds, and the grounds for making it would remain the same even if we were all profoundly Diachronic. As things are, it seems that some Episodics experience their* duration as the same as that of the specious present, around a second; for others, perhaps, it is experienced as considerably longer, extending, perhaps, for a few minutes, or half an hour, or a day, or for some much longer indeterminate period of time, in the Proustian or Jamesian manner.

Many will look no further than their friends and acquaintances, real and fictional, in realizing that Episodics are not as a group somehow morally worse off than Diachronics—although strong Diachronics may have to make more effort than others, in as much as they assume that the Diachronic form of moral experience is required.[8] The fact that Episodics are not morally inferior as a type should also be immediately clear to many moral philosophers—all those, for example, who hold that moral principles are either consequentialist, or deontological, or rights-based, or some mixture of these. For respect for these principles need not depend in any way on whether one is Episodic or Diachronic.[9] The same is true in the case of 'virtue ethics', but some virtue ethicists, i.e. those who take the concepts of virtue and moral character to be central to ethics, may think it obvious that Episodics must fall short of Diachronics.

To make their case, these virtue ethicists will have to show that there are some dispositions of character that are not only essential to a fully moral life (whether or not they are rightly called 'virtues') but are also unavailable, or significantly less available, to Episodics. I don't think this can be shown. I am, however, going to accept Wilkes's terms of debate, and take it that we are concerned with the conditions of a 'richly moral and emotional' life in her sense, not just with moral life more narrowly construed. Moral goodness is fundamentally a matter of feeling and desire, of right feeling and right desire, and there is a clear sense in which machinelike consequentialists or crabby 'Kantians' fail to live a richly moral and emotional life even if they are morally impeccable by their own standards.[10]

[8] Almost all of us assume that other people are more like ourselves, psychologically, than they are. In this domain we automatically employ something like the 'argument from analogy' and are seriously restricted in our capacity to imagine radical difference. We fail, as Murdoch (following Simone Weil) observes, to think of others with sufficient realism, imagination, and attention—where these three virtues are indissolubly connected (I. Murdoch, *The Sovereignty of Good* (London: Routledge and Kegan Paul, 1970)).

[9] Still less should it. Consider people who subscribe to a morality of divine command and who all have an equal degree of religious belief. Suppose we find out that the Diachronics among them are somewhat more likely than Episodics to observe the dictates of that morality. That will hardly show that they are, intrinsically, morally better people. It may be that they are more self-concerned, or simply that the practical effects of self-concern are different in Episodics and Diachronics.

[10] For a striking discussion of how adherence to Kantian principles can go wrong, see J. Annas, 'Personal Love and Kantian Ethics in *Effi Briest*', *Philosophy and Literature* 8, No. 1, 1984, 15–31.

2 Remorse, contrition, regret, guilt

It's important, to begin, that the Episodic sense of self is not absolute in the way Wilkes imagines. Episodics vary greatly among themselves, from extreme to moderate, and one's general sense of one's temporal being may also vary considerably depending on what one is doing or thinking about, or one's chemistry or mood.[11] There are things in what is for most people the remoter future—e.g. their death—and the remoter past—e.g. moments of great embarrassment—that even strong Episodics may tend to figure as involving themselves*. They may for example apprehend a past triumph as involving themselves* and feel satisfaction. They may apprehend dubious actions in the remoter past as involving themselves* and duly feel remorse or contrition.

Remorse and contrition seem particularly important, when one asks whether an Episodic can be a fully moral being. They seem to be emotions to which one ought to be susceptible in certain circumstances. Neither of them, however, depends on any sort of Diachronic connection with one's remoter past, for both are often felt intensely immediately after action, and are for that reason alone as available to a strong Episodic as anyone else. Nor is either of them essential to the moral life. One can rightly regret things one has done without any special experience of remorse or contrition (in many cases neither is appropriate), and a morally good agent may never have occasion to feel either.

> – Isn't the *capacity* to feel remorse or contrition, at least, essential to the moral life?

The first reply is that an Episodic may have this capacity as robustly as anyone else, as just remarked. The second reply is No. There is, for one thing, a distinctively moral species of sinking feeling that lacks the special phenomenology of remorse and contrition although it possesses in equal measure anything that is good about them. There is a certain distinctive negative thud of realization of what one has done that has the same ethical value, whatever exactly that value is. There is a kind of dismay of which the same is true, and one's own actions can occasion sorrow or sadness in one in an ethically influential way, and in a way in which others' actions (or indeed news of disaster) would not, without being self-concerned in the manner of remorse or contrition or mortification. There is, again, a kind of matter-of-fact moral

[11] See e.g. Strawson, op. cit. note 4, 419–21.

Galen Strawson

self-criticism that is not a morally inferior way of experiencing
one's own wrongdoing even though it may have very little of moral
emotion in it (in so far as it is accompanied by emotion this is not a
matter of remorse and contrition, but rather a kind of condemna-
tory exasperation or crossness with oneself, a feeling of severity).[12]

When this sort of moral self-criticism occurs in an Episodic like
myself it is directed at me* experienced as something existing in
the present, even if it is thought about the past that brings it on.
But it doesn't follow from the fact that it is thought about the past
that brings it on that I do really and in spite of my assertion of my
Episodicity think of myself* as there in the past. For one thing,
thought about the past can bring it on because I am as I know a
person of a certain kind and my GS-past can be a very good
indicator of what kind of person $I^{(*)}$ am (it is an understatement to
say that my GS-past has special relevance to me as I am now). The
content of the experience is plain: the object of my attention is
simply me* now, and I have no sense that I* was there in the past.
My concern in this moral self-criticism is with my* moral nature or
being, and this no more includes my past than my present physical
being includes all the particles of matter that have previously made
me up. I* was not there in the past. But this is not to say that $I^{(*)}$
cannot feel bad about past harm I have done to others; $I^{(*)}$ can.

– Shouldn't this feeling become indistinguishable, in an
Episodic, from feeling bad about past harm that others
(strangers) have done?

It might in some Episodics, but it need not—to any extent that it
should not. Feelings are not bound by consistency or rationality
considerations, although they can certainly respond to such
considerations, and it is, as just remarked, an understatement to say
that my GS past has special relevance to me as I am now. If, then,
some difference remains between my feelings about my own past
wrongdoing and my feelings about others' past wrongdoing, we
need not be surprised.

We should also bear in mind that contrition, appropriate and
attractive as it can be, is the more attractive the more fully it
involves grasp of and sorrow about the harm done, and the less it
involves focus on the fact that it was oneself who did it. This last
element cannot disappear altogether if the feeling is to count as
contrition, but the focus on self grows suspect if the emotion

[12] It may also be accompanied, dangerously for some, by self-disdain,
self-contempt.

persists too long, and even contrition can easily become entangled with elements of self-indulgence. The same is (all too) true of remorse and feeling mortified, which are emotionally thicker than contrition along a certain dimension, but a good thing for the same reasons.[13] These moral emotions may be instrumentally useful both personally and socially, in as much as they dispose people to future good behaviour; they are, so far, good things in their place. And we feel warmly about contrition and remorse even when we consider them non-instrumentally, especially in so far as they are fuelled more by an awareness of harm to others than by an essentially negative attitude to oneself. Susceptibility to such feelings is not, however, a necessary ground of future good behaviour, nor a very good one, even when it is practically effective.

Certainly *guilt* adds nothing—nothing good—to moral being. It is a common feeling, but it is rightly not mentioned by Wilkes. Cyril Connolly has guilt-trouble —

> When I contemplate the accumulation of guilt and remorse which, like a garbage-can, I carry through life, and which is fed not only by the lightest action but by the most harmless pleasure, I feel Man to be of all living things the most biologically incompetent and ill-organized. Why has he acquired a seventy years life-span only to poison it incurably by the mere being of himself? Why has he thrown Conscience, like a dead rat, to putrefy in the well?[14]

— but the fact that experiencing guilt is disagreeable does not alter the fact that there is in the end nothing in it that is not essentially superficial, essentially self-indulgent (especially when associated with religious belief) and above all petty, as Connolly would be quick to grant. It is, to be sure, a chimpanzee thing, and wholly so, an ancient adaptive emotional reflex in social animals, encrusted, now, with all the fabulous complications and dreadful superstitions

---

[13] Nietzsche attacks remorse, predictably, but fails to distinguish it sufficiently from guilt. See his 'Against Remorse' (1887), *Writings from the Late Notebooks*, K. Sturge (trans.), R. Bittner (ed.) (Cambridge: Cambridge University Press, 1885–8/2003).

[14] C. Connolly, *The Unquiet Grave* (New York, NY: Persea Books, 1944–51/2005).

of human consciousness, but otherwise unchanged, an internal prod that evolved among our remote but already highly social ancestors.[15]

Some think that it's impossible for anyone who takes such a negative view of guilt to be fully moral. They think that such a view shows a basic failure of moral understanding. This, though, is an unfortunate charge, because it proves in its proponents what it charges in others. The negative view of guilt isn't a strategy of self-exculpation. It isn't a view held by moral flippertygibbets or strident self-styled 'Nietzscheans', or by those who don't themselves feel guilt. It's at least as likely—perhaps more likely—to be held by those who are susceptible to guilt. It isn't a comfortable self-protective truth. It's an uncomfortable self-exposing truth (at least at first). It is much less comfortable than guilt for the millions who make their comfortably uncomfortable home in guilt, and grasping it is, perhaps, the beginning of genuine personal morality.

> – I agree that there's a great ocean of unwarranted guilt, bad guilt, narcissistic, masochistic guilt. But what about feelings of guilt that occur in people because of genuine wrongdoing on their part? Aren't these feelings of guilt, at least, intrinsically morally good, rather than (at most) instrumentally valuable?

Surely not. There can be sorrow and remorse without guilt, as already remarked. There can be regret and contrition and just self-reproach. None of these things is self-indulgent or self-important in the way that guilt is, and the same is true of shame, although shame is delicately balanced. It has forms that are not in any way self-indulgent (their availability is as likely to be a matter of cultural differences as of individual psychological differences), but it can, like self-hatred (fatally easy for some, unimaginable for others), degenerate fast into a particularly insidious form of self-indulgence.[16]

[15] My father and eldest son once startled me by maintaining that there is nothing more to feeling guilty than fear of being found out. Reflecting on this view is a good exercise for those given to guilt, but it cannot be wholly right because one can feel guilty about actions performed in full view of others, and feelings of guilt can persist even when one's misdemeanour is discovered. We need to add fear of being ill thought of and punished, at least, to the fear of being found out.

[16] Guilt in the Christian manner seems irredeemably obnoxious, but there is a Jewish cultural tradition that treats it as an object of rueful humour in a way that makes it seem positively charming.

It is a striking fact that a capacity for negative self-concerned moral emotions (remorse, guilt, and so on) is widely thought to be essential to fully fledged moral being—especially, I have found, when the issue of Episodic ethics is raised—while there is much less tendency to hold similar views about the indispensability (or even importance or desirability) of positive self-concerned moral emotions.[17] We don't really seem to have words for attractive, positive, distinctively moral self-concerned emotions, although we have a rich way of talking about unattractive ones—as when we say that people are self-satisfied, smug, self-righteous, complacent and holier-than-thou.[18] We tend to be overcome by the idea that if positive self-concerned moral emotions were in any way agreeable to those who felt them then they would diminish or destroy the value of the very thing that would otherwise justify them, as when a child's charm is spoilt by the fact that she is aware of it. We are too aware of how such emotions might constitute a suspect motive for being moral, or become infected with self-deception. Our model of morally good people seems to require that they be somehow ignorant of the fact that they are morally good, on pain of corruption; or at least that they be utterly unmoved by it. If positive moral emotions are to be a matter of occurrent feeling at all, then they must somehow be ghostly to the point of invisibility. If we posit as attractive an emotion of quiet happiness in doing justice, say, it must not know or examine itself, it must somehow ignore itself.

It is not as if there is no room at all, in our ordinary moral scheme, for positive feeling to flow from, and in that sense be concerned with, one's moral behaviour. Everyone—even Kant—can agree that good deeds may give one a sense of being in harmony with things, and with oneself, and that this is a good and desirable thing, that virtue in this sense can be its own reward.[19] Few would find anything wrong in a person's being filled with happiness by being kind and thoughtful. Once again, though, it seems that these feelings cannot themselves be moral feelings in the sense that they

[17] It is an ancient idea that you have to like yourself—well enough—to live a good life, and similar ideas are common in present-day psychotherapy; but they do not usually extend to positive self-concerned emotions that are specifically moral in character.

[18] 'Pride' names something good as well as something bad, but it is hard for us to think that 'moral pride' might be a good thing.

[19] I'm interpreting the dictum narrowly and psychologically as a statement about the positive effects of virtuous action on one's subjective state. A wider reading finds rewards beyond any subjective effects.

involve a moral opinion about oneself. It is all right to feel oneself to be morally bad, but it is simply too dangerous, according to our ordinary scheme, to feel oneself to be morally good.[20] Even when theorists allow that a sense of harmony deriving from good conduct may have considerable intrinsic and instrumental value—against the standard background of the view that negative self-concerned moral emotions are important or essential to fully moral being—one hears little or nothing of the correlative idea that susceptibility to such positive emotions might be important or even essential to being a genuinely moral agent.

Well, I'm not at all sure it is essential, but why is there this sour bias? Why isn't the disposition to feel the negative emotions also judged to have instrumental value at most, and to be otherwise regrettable and in any case inessential to full-fledged moral flourishing? The answer lies in part in the difficult domain of evolutionary psychology. Here it is enough to note that the question bears immediately on the question of Episodic ethics, for if I am right that ethical wellbeing and responsibility don't require susceptibility to the negative emotions then it does not follow, from the claim that these emotions require a Diachronic outlook, which is in any case dubious, that only Diachronics can be fully moral.

Suppose we think that susceptibility to the positive emotions is a good thing, but not a morally good thing. Should we continue to maintain that susceptibility to the negative feelings is specifically a morally good thing, even after having abandoned the idea that it is essential to fully moral being—continuing to insist that an individual's possession of a disposition to have the negative feelings is not merely instrumentally valuable but also makes that individual an intrinsically better person, morally speaking? This seems utterly dubious. It may at first be thought to connect with and derive support from the venerable idea that morality is at bottom to be negatively defined,[21] as a device to counteract egoism, say, but that doctrine typically incorporates a strongly instrumental attitude to morality, and is vulnerable to Nietzschean polemic and Aristotelian puzzlement.

It may be added that an instrumentally valuable negative attitude to one's own wrongdoing need not involve any particular moral

[20] Perhaps there are cultural differences at work here—American/ European differences, for example.

[21] See e.g. T. Hobbes, *Leviathan*, Richard Tuck (ed.) (Cambridge: Cambridge University Press, 1651/1996); G. Warnock, *The Object of Morality* (London: Methuen, 1971).

emotion. As for the supposed instrumental value of guilt—the belief that one has done something wrong can motivate one to act without any trace of the feeling of guilt, and I would back clear belief over guilt any day, if there is any hope of the wrongdoer making things better. And consider dear Lucy, who has, regrettably, performed some action A. Suppose that she is thinking that A-ing is wrong, and suppose she has acquired a particularly vivid sense that A-ing is wrong specifically because she herself has A-d in the past. This can be so without her being in any way disposed to fix on or give special weight or attention to the fact that *she herself* has A-d.[22] Even if it is the experience of actually performing the action that has provoked her sense of its wrongness she needn't be specially fixed on the fact that it was she herself who A-d, and it is better if she isn't.

She may be Diachronic or Episodic, Narrative or non-Narrative; it makes no difference. Newly acquired moral understanding, like many other kinds of understanding, can be integrated into how one is without being explicitly tagged as deriving from something one did in the past, even if it is the fact that one did it in the past that has made its wrongness especially plain to one. There is a powerful, phylogenetically ancient psychological mechanism by which many of us learn vividly about morality from our own actions, and the attendant sanctions of others, but the learning of the lesson does not depend on any marked or sustained self-concern, or any persisting sense of oneself* as having been the agent of those actions. The operation of the mechanism may be accompanied by such forms of self-concern in Diachronics and may seem to depend on them, but it does not.

3 The Emotional Priority Thesis

When we consider the complexities of conscience and moral emotion specifically as they relate to a person's past, I think we are in danger, as theorists, of getting things the wrong way round. It may seem to us that these feelings depend essentially on possession of a Diachronic sense of self (although not necessarily on Narrativity). But the true dependence, I suggest, runs the other way. The grounds of the mechanisms—the feeling-mechanisms—of conscience and responsibility are ancient. They predate the·

[22] She may be equally likely to acquire a vivid sense that A-ing is wrong from being the victim of someone else's A-ing.

Diachronic sense of self, both phylogenetically and ontogenetically, and they are in that straightforward sense independent of it and can operate without it. Rather than being essentially dependent on the Diachronic sense of self, which is after all something that can exist only in creatures like ourselves that have evolved into fully fledged concept-exercising self-consciousness, they are among its deep foundations.

One might call this the 'Emotional Priority Thesis'. It states that the past-concerned moral emotions, and in particular the feeling of responsibility, do not in their basic forms presuppose a Diachronic outlook, although we tend to conceptualize them in ways that make it seem analytic that they do. It is because the independently and phylogenetically grounded feeling of responsibility is so salient and vivid among the many things that nourish and structure the Diachronic outlook, in those who have it, that the former comes to seem to depend on and presuppose the latter.

There is a clear parallel between the Emotional Priority Thesis and P. F. Strawson's argument in his famous paper 'Freedom and Resentment'.[23] We all ordinarily believe that people are free agents in some strong, straightforward and unequivocal sense given which they are truly and wholly and ultimately responsible for what they do in some equally strong, straightforward and unequivocal sense, and this belief is vividly manifested in what Strawson calls our 'moral-reactive' and 'personal-reactive' attitudes to other people—our feelings and attitudes of gratitude, resentment and so on. It seems plain that such reactive attitudes are unwarranted, inappropriate, out of place, fundamentally mistaken, if people do not really have 'strong' free will of the sort just outlined: it seems plain that the reactive attitudes depend logically on the belief in strong free will for their full appropriateness.

There is, however, an extremely powerful argument, which I will not give here, that shows that strong free will of this sort is incoherent, logically impossible.[24] Does this mean that we should give up the reactive attitudes? The question does not really arise for us, as Strawson points out, for it raises the question whether we can give them up, and the answer to that question is, for all practical purposes, No. And although the reactive attitudes do clearly

[23] P. F. Strawson, 'Freedom and Resentment', *Freedom and Resentment* (London: Methuen, 1962/1974).
[24] See e.g. G. Strawson, 'The Impossibility of Moral Responsibility', *Philosophical Studies* 75 (1994), 5–24, where I offer a further characterization of strong free will.

depend logically on the belief in strong free will for their full appropriateness, in spite of the fact that feelings are not bound by logic, it does not follow that they depend *causally* on this belief in such a way that it must in some sense precede them and give rise to them and sustain them. It seems, on the contrary, and as Strawson says, that it is the other way round. The reactive attitudes are the primary and prior phenomenon. They are the true foundation of the typically wholly unexamined and utterly-taken-for-granted belief in strong free will, rather than being founded on it. Logically, the reactive attitudes depend on belief in strong free will for their full appropriateness. Causally, the dependency is the other way round.[25]

It is not just that the reactive attitudes clearly precede any clear and explicit formation of a belief in free will, both phylogenetically and ontogenetically, and standardly persist untouched in the face of extremely powerful theoretical arguments directed against the possibility of free will (arguments that lead many to say, quite sincerely, that they do not believe in free will). The further claim is that the belief in free will actually arises from the reactive attitudes (it is perhaps best seen as a kind of conceptualized *post hoc* expression of the reactive attitudes, rather than as an independent element in a person's mental economy). The corresponding claim about Diachronicity is that feelings that apparently presuppose Diachronicity—embarrassment, guilt, resentment, remorse and so on—actually precede it. They are not essentially posterior to Diachronicity and dependent on it. They are part of what drive and vivify Diachronicity in those who are Diachronically inclined.[26] Most strongly put, the claim is that the Diachronic outlook is not the necessary ground of the feelings it seems to be the ground of. It is, rather, grounded in them—in those who have it at all.

The parallel between the Emotional Priority Thesis and Strawson's argument is partial, for in the free will case it is not only the reactive attitudes but also the belief in free will itself that seem to survive acceptance of the force of the argument that free will is

---

[25] I differ from my father in suspecting that the most fundamental source of the continuing conviction of strong free will is one's experience of one's own agency rather than from one's experience of one's reactive attitudes to others (see G. Strawson, *Freedom and Belief* (Oxford: Clarendon Press, 1986), ch. 5). I will drop the word 'strong' from now on.

[26] By the same token, people who are naturally low in the feelings that most powerfully underwrite the Diachronic outlook may be less Diachronic for that reason alone.

impossible; the reactive attitudes and the belief in free will are very tightly locked together. In the present case, by contrast, the starting assumption is that the person is Episodic and simply does not have the belief that constitutes the Diachronic outlook, and the question is to what extent moral feelings and attitudes that seem to presuppose the Diachronicity belief can survive or even exist in such a person.

4 Responsibility and conscience

I do not need to show that this is possible in the case of feelings that are not essential to fully moral being, for my aim is only to show that Episodics can be fully moral. But even when we have put aside guilt, and even remorse and contrition, there are some feelings—feelings of responsibility, feelings of obligation, feelings involved in having a conscience—that may seem to be essential to fully moral being and, equally, to depend essentially on the Diachronicity belief; especially, perhaps, in so far as they depend for their full expression on a sophisticated conceptually articulated outlook.

I will begin with responsibility, where the central point is quickly made, because the heart of moral *responsibility*, considered as a psychological phenomenon, is just a sort of instinctive *responsiveness* to things, a responsiveness in the present whose strength or weakness in particular individuals has nothing to do with how Episodic or Diachronic or Narrative or non-Narrative they are. Moral responsibility in this fundamental sense is non-historical. Fully moral being, fully felt awareness of moral right and wrong, no more depends on a sense of one's past, or on a sense that one* was there in the past, than mathematical knowledge.

– I disagree. Episodics will inevitably lack a proper sense of responsibility if they don't feel that it was they themselves* who performed their past actions.

Not true. Full moral responsibility is in no sort of conflict with an Episodic outlook. If my past acts have given me obligations, including obligations of reparation, these are obligations I* now fully feel myself to have without any sense that I* performed those actions. This is an experiential fact for many Episodics, make of it what you will.[27] A proper sense of responsibility for my (GS's) past

[27] It is worth noting that fulfilling legitimate expectations is for many people a pleasure and is not experienced as a burden.

actions is lodged in me* as I am in the present, even though I do not feel that it was I* who performed those actions, just as memories of my (GS's) past experiences are lodged in me* as I am in the present, although I have no sense that it was I* who had those experiences. This is hardly surprising, if only because I know as well as any Diachronic that other people have legitimate GS-related expectations in the present—and what more could one need for a proper sense of responsibility? *Nothing* depends on my sense of myself in the past. I am and now experience myself as myself*, who was not there in the past, but I am also GS, and I know this, and I know that others know this, and I know that I am for others fundamentally GS, the continuing person and human being, and there is for this reason alone a straightforward respect in which that is how I primarily figure myself when I am engaged with others. Although there is a sense in which my primordial referential intention always cleaves first and foremost to I*, my overall referential intention can equally well embrace both I* and GS, and when I am thinking about and mentioning myself in public I certainly and solidly mean GS, whatever else I mean. One might say that the GS reference is automatically secured for me by the pragmatics of the context, independently of the way I figure myself in my referential intention; but there is more to it than this, because I am of course aware of the context and this awareness is active in my referential intention.[28]

Consider the sense one has that one ought to do what one has said one will do because one has said one will do it. If Lucy tells Louis she will do A, and dear Louis is expecting or relying on this, then, other things being equal (A is not, for example, something bad), she ought to do A. Anyone who agrees with this should agree that the fact that she ought to do A does not depend on her having a Diachronic sense of herself. But nor does Lucy's sense or feeling that she ought to do A depend on her having a Diachronic sense of herself. All she needs is an awareness of the fact of obligation, given the fact of expectation. If it is true that she has an obligation, it is a truth that is independent of the particularities of the way she

[28] The intended reference of 'I' in everyday thought and talk is sometimes oneself*, sometimes the whole human being that one is, sometimes both these things, and sometimes indeterminate. It is a common mistake in analytic philosophy to think that it can only be to the whole human being (see e.g. G. Strawson, 'Postscript to 'The Self'', in *Personal Identity*, R. Martin and J. Barresi (eds.) (New York: Blackwell, 2002), 363–70).

Galen Strawson

experiences herself in time. And just as there is no difference between Diachronics and Episodics, in such cases, in respect of the fact that they have an obligation to do what they have said they will do, so too there is no systematic or significant difference between Diachronics and Episodics in respect of the strength of their feeling that they ought to do what they have said they will do.

If the brakes fail in my car through no fault of mine, and it damages another car, I feel full responsibility for the damage, even if I also think I have had bad luck. This is worth noting because it shows the facility of the feeling of responsibility, but it should not be misinterpreted. In having a normal—strong—sense of responsibility for one of GS's past failures I do not as an Episodic have any sense in the present that it is my* bad luck that GS did whatever regrettable thing he did; nor do I lack awareness of the fact that I have some sort of special connection with the action that I do not have with my car or its brakes.

There are other relevant facts of this sort, such as the way in which people feel responsible for (ashamed of, proud of) the actions of members of their family or community, country or species, even though they did not perform the actions themselves. We can, though, put all such things aside, for the basic fact is simply that there is a phenomenon of natural transmission of a sense of responsibility that does not depend in any way on Diachronic self-experience.

Turning to the notion of conscience, one might put the point by saying that conscience is not essentially retrospective. The thing for which it is best known—the stab from the past, the essentially retrospective 'agenbite of inwit'[29]—is not its essence, or what constitutes it. It is simply one of its consequences. Conscience casts its lines into the future as readily as the past and is in its most general, original sense simply a matter of inner mental self-awareness in the present.[30] Taken in a slightly narrower sense it is a faculty of self-awareness specifically concerned with thought or action, by means of which one is aware of what one is up to when

[29] The re-bite of conscience, 're-bite' deriving from Latin *remordere*, from which we get 'remorse', a word which has since (like 'poignant') acquired a softer meaning. James Joyce famously uses this phrase eight times in *Ulysses* (J. Joyce, *Ulysses* (Harmondsworth: Penguin, 1922/1986)).

[30] In French 'conscience' still means 'consciousness' as well as 'conscience' in the English sense. The 'con-' prefix introduces the reflexive element. See e.g. J. Locke, *An Essay Concerning Human Understanding*, P. Nidditch (ed.) (Oxford: Clarendon Press, 1689–1700/1975), 2.27.9.

one is up to it, and a small further narrowing brings us to the standard meaning: conscience is a matter of being aware of what one is up to *within a specifically moral frame of thought*, a matter of moral self-awareness. But here too it is in the basic case wholly directed on the present moment. It is nothing other than the self-aware play of moral sense or understanding on the situation in which one finds oneself. It need not involve any memory of one's past actions at all (you are not deprived of your conscience in suffering amnesia), let alone any Diachronic or Narrative sense of involvement with them. It is neither an essentially backward looking faculty nor an intrinsically recriminatory one.

This isn't a hopeful piety or a revision of ordinary understanding. It records a fundamental part of our most ordinary understanding of what conscience is. The affective snap of the agenbite of inwit is, as remarked, merely one of the consequences that having a conscience has in certain circumstances. One's past can be preserved, active, in conscience, just in so far as one has a negative (or positive) attitude to certain sorts of actions partly because one has oneself performed them in the past. One need not have any sense that one* performed such an action, nor, of course, any sense of guilt (pride). Human beings can grow and deepen in ethical efficacy by a kind of unstudied osmosis that draws particularly on their own past performances without any explicit book-keeping or any Narrative or Diachronic sense of themselves and their deeds. Certainly Episodicity and non-Narrativity are compatible with profound constancy of character, personality and general outlook, and with a deep, steady and unwavering sense of who one is (which need not, of course, be something that one reflects upon, or could easily express in words). This is my own experience, although I am not I think an extreme Episodic. There may even be a connection between the two things, in as much as felt steadiness of personal identity removes any need for one of the things that Diachronicity and Narrativity may exist to provide.

– You claim that one can have a proper sense of responsibility for one's past actions although one does not feel or believe that one* performed them. But it seems to me that to have a proper sense of responsibility with regard to one's past actions just is—*eo ipso*—to have a Diachronic outlook. Diachronicity is not a merely theoretical attitude to oneself, it is expressed in action; essentially. If this is not so given your definition of 'Diachronic', then your definition is wrong. I agree with your criticism of views that tie a proper sense of responsibility to a capacity to feel guilty, chronically remorseful, and so on. The fact remains that any viable definition of Diachronicity must register the fact that it is a necessary precondition of a proper sense of responsibility, that if you have a proper sense of responsibility you must have a Diachronic outlook. What is your definition? You say that to be Diachronic is simply to 'have a sense that one* was there in the past and will be there in the future'. So be it. I say that having a proper sense of responsibility just shows that one does have a sense that one* was there in the past and will be there in the future—*even if it can somehow seem to one that one does not* (I'm not doubting the sincerity of your claim to be Episodic, or to have a proper sense of responsibility so far as your past actions are concerned).

Our disagreement is clear.

– But you can't just leave it at that! There's a great deal at stake. One loses a vital moral constraint on action if one cares little about one's past.

Many have made this objection, but it is a mistake. One doesn't have to care about one's past in any essentially self-concerned way, still less feel or conceive it as one*'s own, in order to act well or be disposed to act well. What matters morally in any situation one is in is the moral structure of that situation. In some cases facts about one's past actions are part of the moral structure of the present situation, in which case one's own past is part of what matters, but, again, one will not need to care about it in an essentially self-concerned way, or now conceive it as one*'s own. There is no more difficulty in this idea than there is in the idea that Louis can be and feel legally and morally related to Lucy in such a way that he can inherit her debts and obligations. The legal and moral relation can hardly be stronger than it is in the present case, for one is of course the same person in 2000 as one is in 2020, legally and morally and bodily speaking, just in so far as one is the same human being, and one is also (barring certain sorts of brain lesions and major changes in brain chemistry) fundamentally the same in respect of character and personality, however spectacular the phenomena of personal revolution; however Episodic one is.

One does not, then, lose any vital constraint on one's action if one does not care about one's past in any self-concerned way or feel or conceive it as one*'s own. Nor does one have to be governed by concern about one's *future past* (the past one will have, and have to live with, in the future) in order to be a fully moral being, or to act well. I encountered this objection the first time I defended Episodic ethics in a lecture in 1997, but it seems particularly unfortunate and is positively at odds with most moral outlooks (it has affinities with the idea that it is a good thing if people are worried about their fate in the 'afterlife' because it helps them to stay morally in line). Being a moral agent makes one responsible in the future for what one has done in the past, but it does not follow, and is not true, that one's sense of oneself as an agent confronted in the present with a moral issue need include any sense of oneself$^{(*)}$ as something having a future. Many people, I believe, find concern about their future past *completely* absent from the phenomenology of moral engagement. Many also find concern about their actual past as irrelevant as concern about their future past. Most, in so far as they are moved by moral considerations, find that their concern is simply to do what should be done because it is what should be done, or—omitting the Kantian layer—simply to do what should be done. Judgements about what to do obviously require one to take account of the consequences of one's actions and so to look to the future, but, equally obviously, Episodics can do this as well as Diachronics. One can take account of the future without having any clear sense that one* will be there in the future.

One can even adopt Nietzsche's doctrine of the eternal return considered specifically as a technique of moral seriousness (the idea is that when you are facing a choice about which action to perform you should have it vividly in mind that whatever action you choose to perform will be repeated by you for ever in the eternal return) without any trace of a Diachronic or Narrative outlook. One can care passionately about the moral quality of the action, and about the fact that performing it will not only make it part of the history of the universe for ever but will in addition cause similar such actions to occur over and over again, for ever, without thinking about oneself or one's moral standing at all.[31] To factor in the eternal return when trying to decide what to do is certainly to look to the future, and to give weight to the thought of the future, but, once again, one need not conceive it as one*'s own future in Diachronic fashion in order to be strongly motivated to avoid bad actions.

[31]   This use of the doctrine of the eternal return as a technique of moral guidance is of course strictly speaking incompatible with its status as a deterministic metaphysical doctrine to which the appropriate ethical response is *amor fati*, for one is already just repeating one's forever unalterable pattern. (There are obvious connections, here, with the psychology of strict Calvinism.)

Episodics are less likely to suffer in Yeats's way:

> Things said or done long years ago,
> Or things I did not do or say
> But thought that I might say or do,
> Weigh me down, and not a day
> But something is recalled,
> My conscience or my vanity appalled[32]

but if Diachronics propose that the inability of Episodics to be weighed down in Yeats's way is a moral failing, Episodics may be provoked to reply that when it comes to the past, most of what is thought to be conscience, and so good, is merely egoism and vanity—not good at all. It does not make one a better person if one is, or capable of being, weighed down like Yeats. It certainly does not make one a better person in some internal spiritual sense, in respect of 'beauty of soul'. As for the idea that Narratives or Diachronics may behave better overall, morally speaking, than non-Narratives or Episodics, that is an empirical claim, and evidently false.

5 Loyalty, vengefulness, resentment, hatred, friendship, gratitude

I have argued that a Diachronic outlook is neither necessary nor sufficient for a proper sense of responsibility. Diachronic personalities are certainly not more punctilious than Episodic personalities. Diachronics can fail to feel properly responsible for their past actions even though they feel that it was they* who performed them; Episodics can feel properly responsible for their past actions even though they do not feel that it was they* who performed them. Diachronics can fail to take responsibility for their past actions even if they do feel that it was they* who performed them; Episodics can behave highly responsibly, given their past actions, even though, once again, they do not feel that it was they* who performed them. There is no significant positive or negative correlation between either Diachronicity or Episodicity and responsible behaviour.

I am now going to downplay the real and important differences between 'Episodic' and 'non-Narrative', on the one hand, and

---

[32] W. B. Yeats, 'Vacillation', from *The Winding Stair and Other Poems* in *Selected Poems* (London: Macmillan, 1933/1950), 284.

'Diachronic' and 'Narrative', on the other. I will use 'EN' to join the former pair and their lexical cognates and 'DN' to join up the latter pair and their lexical cognates. 'EN' and 'DN' may be read to mean 'Episodic or non-Narrative' and 'Diachronic or Narrative' where 'or', as in classical logic, does not exclude 'and'.[33] The question, then, is whether there are any essentially DN moral traits. Guilt is not an example, and nor is shame, if only because both can be rapid reactions as available to ENs as to DNs, as powerful in acute (short-lived) form as in any chronic form. The same goes for almost all moral-psychological traits: they can be rapidly manifested in their fullest form, and they are not less themselves for being immediate.

Isn't loyalty, at least, an essentially DN virtue? Not. Loyalty may be deep and intense in those who are Episodic and picaresque and it has a non-Narrative form as strong as any Narrative form. Loyalty is a matter of one's attitude and relation to a person in the present, and the EN/DN difference is no more than the difference between those whose loyalty happens to be psychologically linked in some way to an ability or tendency to think about the past they share with those to whom they are loyal and those whose loyalty is not so linked. The phenomenon of loyalty may be grounded in the past in the EN case as much as it is in the DN case, but it need not be bound up with any tendency to think of the past, still less with any tendency to think of one's own past specifically as one*'s own.[34]

It is worth adding that loyalty, like other virtues, has intensely powerful false forms. A great deal that passes for loyalty is a blend of self-love, narcissism and fear. Those who genuinely possess the virtue are slow to attribute disloyalty to others and tend to react to evidence of disloyalty with doubt, and to proof of disloyalty with grief and regret. Those who possess the mixed vices masquerading as the virtue are quick to suspect disloyalty where there is none and have a strong tendency to react to disloyalty to themselves (real or imagined) with sulkiness, anger, accusation and a desire for revenge.

What about resentment, vengefulness, susceptibility to humiliation or insult? Are these essentially DN emotions, in the sense that

[33] One might say that the [A or B] form is best understood to abbreviate the following more complex form: [[A or at least B] or [B or at least A]].

[34] It is a striking fact (neutral for the purposes of the present case) that intensely powerful feelings akin to feelings of loyalty can spring up almost immediately in human beings who have been divided into different teams for a game.

a DN outlook is a necessary condition of their instantiation? Not: they all have EN versions in their acute form, although not their chronic form. If it is taken to be definitive of resentment that it requires a present sense that one* has been insulted, humiliated, cheated or otherwise done down, then ENs are not able to sustain it very well, and there is a way of brooding over past wrongs that is not available to them. To the extent that resentment is wrongly thought of as an essentially chronic condition, ENs are not very good at it.[35] ENs may mistrust, or dislike, or have a sinking feeling about, individuals who have wronged them in the past if they think of them, or come up against them in the present, but one can mistrust or dislike someone—this being a standing condition—, and dislike them specifically because of past wrongs, without any persisting feelings of resentment or vengefulness, insult or humiliation, just as one can be put off a food for life after it has made one ill (the mechanism is essentially the same).

So much the better, for every second spent on vengeful feelings—after the heat of the moment—is a further defeat by the person who inspires them in one. Some exult in chronic resentment and thoughts of revenge; it gives form to their lives. Others see perseveration in such feelings as what it is—a form of subjugation to the one resented. 'Pleasure in revenge is proof of a weak and narrow mind', as Juvenal says; 'revenge is sweeter than life itself—so think fools.'[36] Whole cultures can be weak, fools, narrow in this way. Retaliation may sometimes be necessary, as the Dalai Lama in his wisdom has observed about the school playground, but retaliation is not a feeling.[37]

---

[35] For some people, resentment is balefully cumulative, but this is no part of its essence. In others resentments are intense but short lived, vanishing on the air as if they had never been.

[36] 'Semper et infirmi est animi exiguique voluptas Ultio', *Satires* XIII: 189–190; 'vindicta bonum vita jucundius ipsa nempe hoc indocti', *Satires* XIII: 180. See L. Blumenfeld, *Revenge: a Story of Hope* (New York: Washington Square Press, 2003) for some remarkable stories of vengefulness.

[37] Alas for cultures that say 'revenge is a dish best eaten cold', or that a person who has waited thirty years to take revenge has been 'hasty'. The fundamental ground of chronic vengefulness is boredom: as a specifically cultural phenomenon it dates back to a time when there was far less to entertain people outside their work. This is vividly observed by Gorky in his *Autobiography*, I. Schneider (trans.) (Amsterdam, the Netherlands: Fredonia Books, 2001).

Plainly all this could be true—ENs could have special immunity to chronic forms of these disagreeable emotions—while the individuals who were in fact least touched by them, on this earth, at this time, were predominantly Diachronic and Narrative.

– But if ENs are not much good at chronic resentment, because they do not feel that they* were there in the past, presumably they are not much good at lasting gratitude either, and for the same reason. Surely they must fall down badly here?

Gratitude is the greatest *prima facie* problem for Episodic ethics. I will approach it by way of fidelity, love, and forgiveness.

Fidelity, like loyalty, is equally available to both sides. ENs are far less likely to experience fidelity as a kind of answerability to or honouring of the past, but this offers no support to the idea that they experience the emotion of fidelity with any less strength than DNs. Fidelity of heart, including true sexual fidelity, is a matter of present commitment, a matter of present feeling, and is found equally on both sides with equal strength.

The same is true of love. Enduring love of a person is, at any moment, a matter of present disposition. Its manners and customs may be shaped by the past, but it does not require any tendency to engage in explicit recollection of the past, nor any trace of any Diachronic sense that one*—or the one* one loves—was there in the past. (The deep reason why Jill matters to Narrative Jack, unfortunately, is that Jill is part of *Jack's* life and past; his feeling is fundamentally about himself. He feels safe—validated and at home—in his sense or story of his past and clings to things, including people, that it contains principally for reasons of self-love and self-support, or out of fear of the unknown.)

The same goes for friendship. Michel de Montaigne, a great Episodic, renowned for his friendship with Etienne de la Boétie, famously gave the best possible answer, when asked why their friendship had been what it was: 'because it was him, because it was I'. A gift for friendship doesn't require any ability to recall past shared experiences, nor any tendency to value them. It is shown in how one is in the present. Montaigne judges that he is 'better at friendship than at anything else' although there is nobody less suited than I am to start talking about memory. I can find hardly a trace of it in myself; I doubt if there is any other memory in the world as grotesquely faulty as mine is![38]

He finds that he is often misjudged and misunderstood, for when he admits he has a very poor memory people assume that he must suffer from ingratitude: 'they judge my affection by my memory', he comments, and are of course quite wrong to do so. 'A second advantage' of poor memory, he goes on to note, 'is that ...I remember less any insults received.'[39]

> – Narrative or Diachronic lovers and friends can be present in the present in every way in which their Episodic counterparts are, but they also have something more—their sense of themselves[(*)] as together in the past. Their history can be alive in their thought as their[(*)] history, and this is a great good unavailable to Episodics.

Episodics may reply that this may be so, but that the dangers of sentimental falsification and confabulation are awesome, and that they also and equally have something more—a way of being present in the present in which the past is present without being present as the past—that is unavailable if one's shared history is or tends to be alive in one's thought as one*'s shared history. Each side may concede that there is something they cannot know, and all will be well on all sides as long as no one proposes that Narrative or Diachronic love is somehow essentially deeper or more powerful than Episodic and non-Narrative love, or forgets that many couples are happily made up of a DN and an EN. (Explicit recognition of this fact can be helpful.)

Forgiveness? Once again, neither side is intrinsically more disposed to be forgiving than the other. One can't, perhaps, forgive if one has forgotten, but one may have forgotten because one has already forgiven. It may be said that one must not only remember what was done to one, in order to be able to forgive, but must also feel that it was oneself* who was there in the past—so that ENs may lose opportunities for forgiveness even when they have excellent memories. But I can see no reason to believe this. There do not seem to be any deep differences, specifically so far as the phenomenon of forgiveness is concerned, between the case in

---

[38] M. de Montaigne, *The Complete Essays*, M. A. Screech (trans.) (London: Penguin, 1563–92/1991), 32.

[39] Ibid, p. 33.

which one forgives a wrong done to oneself(*) and the case in which one forgives a wrong done to another (unlike someone who says 'I cannot forgive him for what he did to her'). And if this is so, then even if one does not think that it was one* who was there in the past, one's capacity for forgiving a wrong is not touched; only the emotional accompaniments are different. And if there is after all some sense in which ENs do lose opportunities for forgiveness, in spite of having excellent memories, these will be opportunities of which they have no need. 'Mirabeau had no memory for insults and vile actions done him and was unable to forgive simply because he—forgot ... Such a man shakes off with a single shrug many vermin that eat deep into others.'[40]

What about the wrongdoers, in such cases? They may feel a need for forgiveness, and feel that it is denied them by ENs. But they already have it in sufficient measure, for the ENs no longer feel wronged, although they remember what happened, and that is forgiveness. If a DN wrongdoer wants something more, and feels that a wronged EN individual is not really giving it to her, her desire is merely selfish—and perverse.

Can one fail to forgive a past wrong done to one even though one genuinely doesn't feel that it was oneself* who suffered it in the past? Perhaps one's present actions could make this seem the best thing to say. Others, though, may interpret these actions differently. What such a behaviourally manifested failure to forgive shows, they may say, is that really one does still have a sense that it was oneself* who was there in the past, and deludes oneself when one denies it.

This is an objection in a by now familiar pattern. It assumes that an adequate explanation of the unforgiving feelings that have been attributed to one (perhaps wrongly) on the basis of one's behaviour

---

[40]   Nietzsche, quoted in T. Sommers, 'The Objective Attitude', *Philosophical Quarterly* 57, 2007, 1–21. Some are less able to forgive a wrong done to someone else—whether or not it is someone they know well—than a wrong done to themselves, but it is not as if something good lies behind this. It is rather something extremely dangerous, very ugly, and very human, the most dangerous force in all human public affairs: righteous indignation in the pejorative sense, righteous indignation felt on behalf of others or on behalf of the group of which one is part. Righteous indignation of this sort often incorporates a sense of absolute justification precisely because its object is not oneself—a sense of purity of justification that seems to those who feel it to license absolute violence. Its deep root, no doubt, is anger felt about one's own life or situation, anger that, once disguised in this way, is able to express itself without any inhibition.

must cite a belief that it was oneself* who was there in the past; so that one can after all infer a fundamentally DN outlook from indirect behavioural evidence of the presence of unforgiving feelings. I think, on the contrary, and in line with the Emotional Priority Thesis, that the existence and naturalness of such feelings may be a crucial part of what gives rise to or sustains the DN outlook, and that such feelings can persist, though perhaps only in a relatively attenuated form, even in the absence of the DN outlook. As P. F. Strawson observes, moral emotions like resentment and gratitude *effortlessly* survive acceptance of the force of the argument that the (strong) free will that they presuppose is impossible. So too, moral emotions like gratitude and resentment may exist in an Episodic who genuinely does not feel that it was he* to whom good or ill was done in the past, even if such moral emotions seem logically to require that he does think that it was he* to whom good or ill was done in the past.

It is, however, far less clear that these emotions can remain untouched in the case of Episodicity, as compared with the case of belief in (strong) free will. In the latter case it seems that not only the moral emotions but also the very belief in free will survive acceptance of the force of the argument that free will is impossible. In the former case, by contrast, and as remarked, the starting assumption is that the person genuinely lacks a Diachronic outlook (this is the parallel to genuinely lacking the belief in free will) and the question is to what extent the moral emotions that seem to presuppose the Diachronic outlook can survive in such a person.

My own experience, self-deluded or not, is that the feeling of gratitude survives while the feeling of resentment does not.[41] Resentment of a person can quickly decay into negative affect that entirely lacks the peculiar phenomenology of resentment and on into neutrality (it may yet leave one specially tuned to resent that person for new reasons). Gratitude, by contrast, standardly survives in a form of liking whose special tone distinguishes it quite clearly from liking that has no foundation in gratitude.[42]

[41] The word 'gratitude' is not only used to denote a feeling—one can say truly that one is grateful to someone without any feeling of gratitude—but I will put aside this other use. (It is a question whether one can really feel gratitude to someone one doesn't like. It seems so—at least at first.)

[42] It is perhaps diagnostic of the emotion of gratitude that it can persist, in the face of disagreeable behaviour on the part of its inspirer, in cases where mere liking does not persist.

Montaigne, evidently, felt the same, and I have seen it in many others. But how is this asymmetry possible? Well, it can't be any more surprising than the asymmetry found in people in whom resentment persists even while gratitude decays, and this second asymmetry may be said to restore a basic symmetry between gratitude and resentment, in as much as either can decay while the other does not. I like to think that empirical tests would show that gratitude is more robust than resentment in the population as a whole, given reasonable conditions of life (including sufficient means of entertainment—see note 36), and other things being equal; but there are, certainly, those in whom resentments and grudges accumulate year on year, whether or not gratitude decays.[43] This last fact, though, has no special bearing on the Episodic predicament, where my sense, to repeat, is that gratitude is more likely to persist than resentment, in a form of liking that has a special tone.

It may be said that resentment can persist in a similar fashion, in a form of dislike whose special tint distinguishes it quite clearly from dislike that has no foundation in resentment. This doesn't seem accurate to me, but it is plain that this could happen to some Episodics, given other features of their personality and circumstances. The question whether it is the glow of gratitude or the stain of resentment that is more robust in Episodics is open to empirical test. Some people are immune to bitterness, others are made of it, but what happens in an individual case may be more a function of external circumstances than fundamental character.

Could it be that resentment decays because it is a psychological burden (and a waste of time), while genuine gratitude is not? It is plain that a person's psychology can have this happy disposition, but it is no less plain that it can lack it. So too, some retain memories of other people's kindness and lose memories of their ill-doing, while others are the other way round. There is nevertheless something in this idea. In the long run, I think, many people have a lot of good sense. They have, in particular, a fundamental capacity for *acceptance*, where this does not involve any sort of capitulation or admission of defeat or retreat from humanity, but is rather a matter of wider perspective, an increase of humanity, of realism, an understanding, however late, that some

---

[43] There are also those in whom reasons for gratitude become causes of resentment. Some fear that this process is inevitable and universal; see e.g. Joseph Conrad as described in F. M. Ford, *Joseph Conrad, A Personal Remembrance* (New York: Ecco Press, 1924/1989), 131ff.

things are indeed a waste of time. Acceptance of this sort
undermines resentment by its very nature, while having no adverse
effect on gratitude. One reason why we may underestimate its
presence and force in human life, I think, is that it receives far less
attention in novels, films and songs than most other important
features of human psychology.

So I continue to believe that there is a positive asymmetry. And
this belief finds further support, perhaps, in an apparent
asymmetry between gratitude and resentment that has nothing to
do with their rates of decay. We often feel grateful—the quality of
the emotion is unmistakable—for a cool breeze or an outbreak of
sun, but we are certainly not resentful, rather than disappointed,
when the breeze drops or the day turns muggy.[44] Gratitude, it
seems, has a greater natural reach than resentment. The case cannot
be cordoned off by saying that there are two kinds of gratitude,
personal and meteorological (impersonal), and that the first is
independent of the second, and that the second impersonal kind
cannot really ('logically') be the real thing. We use the same word
for the cool breeze and the kind act because it is the same basic
feeling, whatever other differences of feeling are found in the two
cases.

I don't think we have to personify nature to have this feeling of
gratitude, animistic and anthropomorphizing though we are as a
species. (If meteorological gratitude depended on surreptitious
personification, we would, *ceteris paribus*, expect meteorological
resentment in equal measure.) To this extent it seems that gratitude
has, in some way, an impersonal or at least larger field, while
resentment remains essentially personal. This does not mean that
one can't resent one's washing machine; only that one has to adopt a
psychologically anthropomorphic attitude to it. But perhaps the
weather is a special case; for I do not think one could feel gratitude
towards one's washing machine without some sort of animistic
attitude to it.

There are no strong generalizations to be made in this area. Our
moral-emotional personalities are too complex and too varied.
Obviously it seems very neat for an Episodic like myself to claim
that he can't manage to sustain significant resentment for more
than a few days (although it can be reanimated in conversation) but
has no such trouble with gratitude. I am nevertheless going to leave
you with that claim.

[44] See T. Sommers, *Beyond Freedom and Resentment: An Error Theory
of Free Will and Moral Responsibility*, PhD Thesis, Duke University
(2005).

6 Conclusion

My larger claim is that Wilkes is wrong to think that the EN life could not be richly moral and emotional. There is I suggest no interesting correlation between moral worth and being Episodic or Diachronic, Narrative or non-Narrative, although ENs and DNs may experience morality in significantly different ways. There is no special connection, let alone a necessary connection, between [a] a lack of felt connection with one's past of the sort characteristic of Episodics and [b] a propensity to behave badly or, more particularly, [c] a propensity to behave worse than those who have a characteristically Diachronic sense of connection with their past. All moral traits have both EN and DN forms of expression, even if some achieve their fullest or most familiar expression only in ENs or DNs.[45]

---

[45] Some have suggested an association between Episodicity and depression and dissociation (J. Lampinen, T. Odegard and J. Leding, 'Diachronic disunity' *The Self and Memory*, D. Beike J. Lampinen and D. Behrend (eds.) (New York: Psychology Press, 2004)). It may be, though, that while this is characteristic of depressed and dissociated Diachronics, the reverse is true in the case of Episodics—in whom greater Diachronicity could be a form of dissocation.

I would like to thank members of the audiences at Union College, Schenectady, NY, St Olaf's College, Northfield, MN, and the 2005 Royal Institute of Philosophy conference on 'Narrative and Understanding Persons' for their comments.

On the Distance between Literary Narratives and Real-Life Narratives

PETER LAMARQUE

It is a truth universally acknowledged that great works of literature have an impact on people's lives. Well known literary characters—Oedipus, Hamlet, Faustus, Don Quixote—acquire iconic or mythic status and their stories, in more or less detail, are revered and recalled often in contexts far beyond the strictly literary. At the level of national literatures, familiar characters and plots are assimilated into a wider cultural consciousness and help define national stereotypes and norms of behaviour. In the English speaking world, Shakespeare's plays or the novels of Jane Austen, the Bronte sisters, Dickens, and Trollope, provide imaginative material that reverberates in people's lives every bit as much as do the great historical figures, like Julius Caesar, Elizabeth I, Horatio Nelson, or Winston Churchill. What is striking is how often fictional characters from the literary tradition—like the well-loved Elizabeth Bennett, Jane Eyre, Oliver Twist, Pip, Tess of the d'Ubervilles—enter readers' lives at a highly personal level. They become, as Martha Nussbaum puts it, our 'friends'[1], and for many readers the lives of these characters become closely entwined with their own. Happy and unhappy incidents in the fictional worlds are held up against similar incidents in the real lives of readers and such readers take inspiration from the courage, ingenuity, or good fortune of their fictional heroines and heroes. Nowhere is it more true that life imitates art.

Works in the canonical literary tradition—more so than merely popular fiction, whose influence is lost over time—are thought to be especially valuable for holding up a mirror to life. Their characters appear richer, more rounded and more finely developed than in lesser productions, their plots better structured and their writing more elevated and elevating. Such works also exemplify the fundamental genres of narrative that are supposed to help structure ordinary lives: from the broad genres of the tragic, comic, epic, or romantic, to narrower genres of the anti-hero, the picaresque, the

---

[1]   M. Nussbaum, *Love's Knowledge: Essays on Philosophy and Literature* (Oxford: Oxford UP, 1990), 44.

noir, or the coming of age. It seems natural for people who are telling stories about themselves to take as a model the very works that define the literary tradition, that is, define what stories at their best are like. All this might seem both obvious and innocuous.

But the underlying picture, I maintain, is a serious distortion of what makes literary narratives distinctive and valuable. Closer inspection reveals that the role of fictional characters in literature does not closely mirror the role of real people living real lives. Nor do real-life narratives bear a close relation to literary narratives. It is not just that ordinary lives tend to be more humdrum, less dramatic, or less structured. To see literary characters as our friends, as ordinary people like ourselves, their lives as essentially like our lives, is to set aside nearly everything that makes great literature what it is. In effect it is to ignore all essentially literary qualities and reduce literature to character and plot at the same level of banality as found in the stories we tell of ourselves.

The first inkling that this is the case can be found in the poverty of general knowledge of the great iconic characters. Most people who have heard of Oedipus, Hamlet, Faust, or Don Quixote, as in my earlier list, know little more about them than the most rudimentary facts: Oedipus unknowingly killed his father, Hamlet hesitated in avenging his father's murder, Faust made a pact with the devil, Don Quixote tilted at windmills. Such impoverished knowledge should not be mocked; it provides a core means of identifying iconic characters and serves to locate them in cultural mythology. But it is plain that characters of this kind as they enter the cultural mainstream are bare abstractions. Their literary origins are irrelevant and often not known. It makes no difference, for example, which version, if any, of the Faust story underlies this usage. It is the same with the lesser characters mentioned, like Elisabeth Bennett and Oliver Twist; to the extent that they are loved and emulated they are again mere abstractions far removed from literary detail. A summary of their lives would do just as well as the original novels in capturing what is appealing about them. (The popularity of film versions confirms the point.)

To reduce literary works to abstracted characters and summarised plots is precisely to lose everything that makes them literary in the first place. When literary characters become our friends and offer models for our behaviour they lose their literary bearings; they cease to be literary. If this is right—and I will offer further arguments for it—then it seems that real-life narratives are far removed from literature per se. The thought that there is something special about the narratives of the canonical works in guiding our lives comes to seem less plausible. The more we try to restore the distinctively literary features of such narratives the more remote they become from real life. Indeed a stronger point can be made. To the extent that literary features are brought to bear on real-life narratives they have a distorting and pernicious effect on the self-understanding that such narratives are supposed to yield.

II

The case that literary works are remote from the narratives of real life rests on the peculiar features of such works. It might be thought that the case cannot get going without a preliminary definition of literature. And that, it might seem, is where the argument gets bogged down right from the start. In fact I will not attempt to define literature but will rest my argument as far as possible on fairly uncontroversial observations drawn from literary criticism and the ontology and epistemology of fiction.

The first point to make is that 'literature' and 'fiction' name separate concepts, with different meanings and different extensions.[2] Fiction is a species of language use (applied to names, sentences, and discourses) and is neutral as to value. Literature, even in the narrowest sense applied to imaginative and creative writing, is a kind of discourse, essentially valued, which affords and invites a distinctive kind of appreciation. Not all literary works are fiction, nor all fictional works literature. It would be wrong to suppose that literary works are merely a subset of fictional works marking off those, for example, that are especially well written or especially admired for other reasons. A work of fiction could reach the highest standards as fiction—say, within a popular genre— without even aspiring to the aims of literature. One condition on literature, which does not apply to fiction *per se*, is the aspiration to a kind of moral seriousness; a literary work in some way or other must have more to say, of general interest, beyond the particularities of its plot. Literary works are not just examples of good story–telling or fine writing.

Examining the role of character in literary works, we see a principal example of the richer connections between content and mode of presentation. There are two ways in which fictional characters enter the consciousness of readers. One is through the imagination. In what

[2] See P. Lamarque & S. H. Olsen, *Truth, Fiction, and Literature: A Philosophical Perspective* (Oxford: Clarendon Press, 1994), ch. 11.

Peter Lamarque

I have called the internal perspective[3]—that is, a perspective internal to a fictional world—characters are imagined to be real humans, speaking, acting and interacting just as ordinary people do. Of course one must be careful about generalising across genres for realism is not always a literary aim. But even works that transport us into non-realistic or extra-human realms invite imaginings. The second way is through linguistic modes of presentation; this is a perspective external to fictional worlds, rooted in the real world of artifice, style, and narrative technique. As well as imagining characters, readers can become aware of the descriptive means by which the characters are presented. Broadly speaking it is a characteristic of literary works that they invite attention to their own literary artifice, while genre fiction of a non-literary kind encourages more transparent access to its imagined content.

There is an ontological point about characters near at hand. Their identity conditions are bound up with their modes of presentation. Let us call this the Character Identity Principle:

In literary works character identity is indissolubly linked to character description.

Part of what this means—the familiar part—is that characters come into being only through being described. They have their origins in narratives. This is a necessary truth, though the scope of the necessity is debatable. It is a matter of contention whether, for example, Emma Bovary might have been created by some author other than Flaubert and even in some other novel than *Madame Bovary*.[4] Note that an Emma Bovary that cuts loose, as it were, from Flaubert, can be given only coarse-grained identity conditions of the kind that allows the character of Faustus a trans-work identity across its exemplifications in Christopher Marlowe, Johann Wolfgang von Goethe and Thomas Mann. But fictional characters cannot come into being independent of narrative altogether.

Another part of what the Character Identity Principle means is that the manner of character description determines the very nature of the character described. This applies to fine-grained identity conditions according to which we might say that the Marlowe, Goethe and Mann versions of Faustus depict different

[3] P. Lamarque, *Fictional Points of View* (Ithaca, NY: Cornell UP, 1996), 12 ff; Ch. 8.

[4] See P. Lamarque, 'How To Create a Fictional Character', *The Creation of Art*, B. Gaut and P. Livingston (eds.) (Cambridge: Cambridge UP, 2003).

characters. Characters under these fine-grained conditions are in a special sense perspectival entities.[5] This implies not just that the precise nature of the characters rests on the precision of their identifying descriptions but, for example, that the descriptions embody points of view on them both physical and evaluative. Take an example from Dickens' *Our Mutual Friend*. When Dickens first introduces the despicable Veneerings, he does so with a well-known flourish both comic and contemptuous:

> Mr and Mrs Veneering were bran-new [sic] people in a bran-new house in a bran-new quarter of London. Everything about the Veneerings was spick-and-span new. All their furniture was new, all their friends were new, all their servants were new, their plate was new, their carriage was new, their harness was new, their horses were new, their pictures were new, they themselves were new ... [A]ll things were in a state of high varnish and polish. And what was observable in the furniture, was observable in the Veneerings—the surface smelt a little too much of the workshop and was a trifle sticky.[6]

The superficiality, the worship of possessions and ostentatious wealth, the shallowness connoted in the very name 'Veneering', are all intrinsic qualities of the characters themselves. Dickens' judgment of the Veneerings, which he invites us to share, indeed which we must share if we are to grasp the role of the characters in the novel, is part of the very identity of the characters. It is not as if there is some other perspective on the Veneerings under which they subsist as decent, honest, kindly, altruistic folk who have somehow been falsely captured by the mocking tone of the narrator. The mocking tone, as it were, makes them the characters they are.

If characters are perspectival in this way, then the Character Identity Principle reveals a further important fact about characters which points to something fundamental about literary appreciation. The character descriptions, indissolubly tied to character identity, are seen to have a dual function: a characterising function and a connective or thematic function. The characterising function is simply to provide us with information about the characters: we take it to be true of the Veneerings that everything they own is new. This guides our internal imaginative perspective on them so that when we picture the Veneerings we picture them as surrounded by brand-new objects shiningly clean. But the mocking tone that

---

[5] See Lamarque & Olsen, op. cit. note 2, Ch. 6.
[6] C. Dickens, *Our Mutual Friend* (New York: Signet, 1964), 20.

informs the description has a wider function in the novel as a whole. It serves to locate the Veneerings in the social scheme of things, to situate them among a cluster of characters, like the Lammles and the Podsnaps, who see no value beyond monetary value. It also sets up a thematic contrast with characters like John Harmon, Eugene Wrayburn and Lizzie Hexam who reject these false values and the social attitudes they engender. The Veneerings are not just people in a world but elements in an artistic design.

In addition to the Character Identity Principle we should take note of another, related, principle which I will call Opacity. According to the Opacity Principle:

> *In literary works not only are characters and incidents presented to us but attention is conventionally drawn to the modes of presentation themselves.*

This principle is well known to literary critics and informs critical practice. It acknowledges the fact that linguistic resources are not merely contingent elements in literary artifice—the thought that somehow the very same content might have been presented in other ways—but also what Roman Jakobson called the 'palpability of signs' and other structuralists called 'foregrounding'.[7]

It is a peculiarity of literature, in contrast to fiction *per se*, that attention is drawn to the connective and thematic functions of character descriptions. Rather than being merely transparent vehicles for prompting imaginings the descriptions provide a more opaque kind of perspective for observing and making sense of a fictional world. Although of course imaginings are prompted by literary works and we are able to picture the goings-on as if they were real events, we find in the literary case that there is a nice interplay between what we imagine and what we notice of the literary artifice that prompts the imagining. At the same time as we picture the Veneerings we notice the modes in which they are presented to us, in particular the attitudes we are invited to take, and the significance of those attitudes in the wider canvas of the novel.

Another familiar principle of literary criticism also encourages the thought that there is more to literary description, be it of character or incident, than the conveying of fictional facts. This concerns the curious role of descriptive detail. We have already seen in the Character Identity and Opacity principles how detail

---

[7] See V. Erlich, *Russian Formalism: History-Doctrine* (The Hague, rev. edn., 1965), 183.

determines identity. But detail also is assigned significance. What operates is a Principle of Functionality, as follows:

It is always reasonable to ask of any detail in a literary work what literary or aesthetic function that detail is performing.

The principle applies across all the arts. As Roger Scruton has written: 'Art provides a medium transparent to human intention, a medium for which the question, Why? can be asked of every observable feature, even if it may sometimes prove impossible to answer'.[8] Take the brief but poignant scene near the beginning of *Tess of the d'Urbervilles* when Tess's father's horse Prince is killed in an accident on the road. Tess had fallen asleep when driving her carriage and the mail-cart had rammed into her, piercing the horse's heart. This is how the critic Dorothy Van Ghent describes the passage:

With this accident are concatenated in fatal union Tess's going to 'claim kin' of the d'Urbervilles and all the other links in her tragedy down to the murder of Alec. The symbolism of the detail is naïve and forthright to the point of temerity: the accident occurs in darkness and Tess has fallen asleep—just as the whole system of mischances and cross-purposes in the novel is a function of psychic and cosmic blindness; she 'has put her hand upon the hole'—and the gesture is as absurdly ineffectual as all her effort will be; the only result is that she becomes splashed with blood—as she will be at the end; the shaft pierces Prince's breast 'like a sword'—Alec is stabbed in the heart with a knife; with the arousal and twittering of the birds we are aware of the oblivious manifold of nature stretching infinite and detached beyond the isolated human figure; the iridescence of the coagulating blood is, in its incongruity with the dark human trouble, a note of the same indifferent cosmic chemistry that has brought about the accident; and the smallness of the hole in Prince's chest, that looked 'scarcely large enough to have let out all that had animated him,' is the minor remark of that irony by which Tess's great cruel trial appears as a vanishing incidental in the blind waste of time and space and biological repetition.[9]

---

[8]   R. Scruton, 'Photography and Representation', *Aesthetics and the Philosophy of Art: The Analytic Tradition: an Anthology*, P. Lamarque & S. H. Olsen (eds.) (Oxford: Blackwell, 2003), 368.

[9]   D. Van Ghent, 'On Tess of the d'Ubervilles', Thomas Hardy, *Tess of the d'Ubervilles*, S. Elledge (ed.) (New York: W. W. Norton & Co., 1979), 429–30.

Peter Lamarque

Significantly, Van Ghent completes the paragraph by observing the otherwise naturalness of the scene and its description:

> Nevertheless, there is nothing in this event that has not the natural 'grain' of concrete fact; and what it signifies—of the complicity of doom with the most random occurrence, of the cross-purposing of purpose in a multiple world, of cosmic indifference and of moral desolation—is a local truth of a particular experience and irrefutable as the experience itself.[10]

We are reminded again of the internal and external perspectives. Imaginatively and sympathetically the scene of the accident is pictured to be just what it seems, a terrible accident. From the external critical perspective it serves a narrative function as well, anticipating, with awful foreboding, all the main events to come and assigns weight and significance to them.

Symbolism is a common literary device. The mud and fog at the beginning of *Bleak House*, as every trained reader immediately recognises (Dickens himself rather heavy-handedly spells out the connection with the High Court of Chancery), are more than just passing descriptive detail. Here is how one critic interprets the symbolism:

> The mud and fog of the opening paragraph of the novel are not, we can now see, the primeval stuff out of which all highly developed forms evolve. They are the symptoms of a general return to the primal slime, a return to chaos which is going on everywhere in the novel and is already nearing its final end when the novel begins.

> The human condition of the characters of *Bleak House* is, then, to be thrown into a world which is neither fresh and new nor already highly organised, but is a world which has already gone bad.[11]

The Functionality Principle, though, does not relate exclusively to literary symbolism, at least in the narrow sense of the term. Having symbolic significance is only one kind of function, indeed one kind of significance. Drawing connections across a work is another function of literary detail. The opening scene of *Macbeth* with the contradictions and confusions of the witches ('Fair is foul and foul

[10]   Ibid.
[11]   J. Hillis Miller, 'The World of Bleak House', Charles Dickens, *Bleak House*, Norton Critical Edition, G. Ford and S. Monod (eds.) (New York: W. W. Norton & Co, 1977), 951–952.

is fair') connects with multiple elements throughout the play, developing what L. C. Knights has called 'the themes of the reversal of values and of unnatural disorder'.[12]

An interesting third function of narrative detail is identified by Roland Barthes in what he calls the 'reality effect'. Barthes is intrigued by the way that realist novelists, like Flaubert or Balzac, pile up apparently random descriptive detail. In a somewhat laboured manner, he describes it as follows:

> The truth of this illusion is this: eliminated from the realist speech act as a signified of denotation, the 'real' returns to it as a signified of connotation; for just when these details are reputed to *denote* the real directly, all that they do—without saying so—is *signify* it; Flaubert's barometer, Michelet's little door finally say nothing but this: *we are the real*; it is the category of 'the real' ... which is then signified; in other words, the very absence of the signified, to the advantage of the referent alone, becomes the very signifier of realism ...[13]

The idea, more plainly put, is that the accumulation of seemingly trivial detail in a literary narrative, serves to *signify* (or connote) reality, while failing to denote it. This provides a striking contrast between the use of trivial detail in non-fictional narratives. Where the details actually *do* describe the real, where there is no 'absence of the signifier' or no 'referential illusion', there can be no 'reality effect'. What Barthes sees as definitive of literary realism is, curiously, missing—and impossible—in the case where facts alone are described. The piling up of detail might have the same impact in the two cases—enriching the atmosphere—but they operate, if Barthes is right, under almost exactly opposite narrative constraints.

A fourth principle concerns the kinds of explanation available to incident and action in a literary work. In the real world of fact and action explanation is causal or rational. To explain why something happened we offer causes or an agent's reasons. To the extent that we imagine, from the internal point of view, the events in a literary work these are the explanations we reach for. What caused Tess's accident? The answer, within the fictional world, is that she fell asleep and was run into by the mail-cart. Why did Tess kill Alec

---

[12]   L. C. Knights, 'How Many Children Had Lady Macbeth?' in *Explorations* (Harmondsworth: Penguin, 1964), 29.

[13]   R. Barthes, 'The Reality Effect', *The Rustle of Language*, R. Howard (trans.) (Oxford: Blackwell, 1986), 148.

d'Urberville? The answer, as one critic writes, is that it was 'an act of desperate assertion which places Tess in the line of folk heroines who kill because they can no longer bear outrage'.[14] But there is a literary mode of explanation quite different from the causal and the rational. As the critic just cited goes on to say of the killing: 'it signifies an end to Tess's journey', it is 'traditional, part of the accepted heritage that has come down to us through popular and literary channels'. In other words the killing has a conventional function in the structure of the plot. It happens, we might say, because it has to happen in a story of this kind. That explanation is of a radically different kind from an explanation in terms of agents' reasons.

A principle operates here which I shall call the Teleology Principle, as follows:

> *In literary works the explanation of why an episode occurs as it does and where it does often centres on the contribution the episode makes to the completed artistic structure.*

Thus in the reverse order of normal causal explanation we might explain a prior event in terms of a later event. Oedipus's fateful remark early on in Sophocles's play that those who have brought disaster on Thebes will suffer a terrible fate acquires its literary significance and purpose from the revelations at the end of the play. In a different example, consider how the word 'explains' is used by this critic, speaking of the character Frank Churchill in Jane Austen's *Emma*:

> *Frank is important because he explains Emma herself.* He embodies the vital difference between the artistic principles governing Emma—foolish conduct resulting from faulty judgement, but from motives fundamentally irreproachable, invariably honest and as frank as possible—and his own downright wrong actions causing deliberate and consistent deceit, which produce some of the same effects as Emma's own.[15]

Again, just like the Veneerings in the earlier example, Frank Churchill is not just a person in an imaginary world, he is also an element in a structured plot. His actions and failings gain their

[14] I. Howe, 'The Center of Hardy's Achievement', Thomas Hardy, *Tess of the d'Urbervilles*, S. Elledge (ed.) (New York: W. W. Norton & Co., 1979), 451.

[15] W. A. Craik, 'Emma', Jane Austen, *Emma*, S. M. Parrish (ed.) (New York: W. W. Norton & Co., 1972), 445 (italics added).

significance in contrast to superficially similar failings in Emma herself—tactlessness and lack of self-awareness—though the implied judgements are different. It is characteristic of literary criticism to explain the artistic role of such elements: the explanation is a kind of teleology. Another critic notes the role played by the married pairs at the end of the novel:

> The young generation poses a challenge to the moral order of Highbury, and the book ends when the challenge is fought off, when the young are married and have been assimilated by the mature generation. The story, of course, is first and foremost Emma's story, but she is flanked by important characters. Frank Churchill and Jane Fairfax, Mr Elton and Augusta Hawkins, Harriet Smith and Robert Martin, all these couples form important variations on the theme of assimilation.[16]

The reference to variations on a theme brings me to my final, again familiar, principle, in literary appreciation. The principle concerns literary themes, perhaps the most important factor in characterising the literary realm. Themes are conceptions that bind works together, encapsulating a work's significance and what I called its moral seriousness. They can be identified under different kinds of description, including stand-alone predicates like 'love' or 'despair', or noun phrases like 'the conflict between private and social duty' or whole sentences like 'human life is governed by forces beyond an individual's control'. The presence of sentential characterisations of themes raises questions about literary truth but that is not at issue here. Themes can be of more or less universal interest. Sometimes they are merely local: 'the radicalisation of British universities in the 1960s'. Sometimes they are of more timeless human concern: 'intimations of mortality'. Themes can be stated directly in a work itself, as in King Lear's agonised cry 'As flies to wanton boys are we to the gods; / They kill us for their sport'. Or they are elicited in an interpretation by a critic. In an essay on 'private vision and social order' in Charlotte Bronte's *Jane Eyre*, a critic writes:

> There can be no doubt ... that the reduction of the world to the terms of a single vision, no matter how moral its content or how sanctified its motives, is attended by the most dreadful violence. The power of the 'I' of this novel is secret, undisclosable,

[16] S. H. Olsen, 'Do You Like Emma Woodhouse?', *Critical Quarterly*, 19, No. 4, 1977, 13.

absolute... . The violence with which it simplifies the differences labelled 'inferior,' 'poorer,' 'richer,' 'better,' or 'higher,' the killing and maiming and blinding which are the consequences of its dialectic, tell us as clearly as fiction can that even fantasy must subdue a real world. Jane Eyre's vision masters her world, but the price of her mastery is absolute isolation. When she knows her world completely she is out of it by the most rigorous necessity. I know no other work that so effectively demonstrates the demon of the absolute.[17]

This critic starts his thematic exploration of private visions in *Jane Eyre* from the premise that 'no heroine dreams more often or more successfully than the heroine of this strange romance'.[18] That premise in turn is supported by direct reference to passages where dreams and visions are described.

Thus we can formulate a Thematic Principle:

Appreciation of literary works as literary works is an appreciation of how their subject acquires significance and unity under thematic interpretation.

A theme in a literary work is an organising principle that brings unity and significance to the work's subject. The subject is in effect the material that a reader is invited to imagine. It is a characteristic of literary works that they invite thematic interpretation. A reader looks for internal connectedness through overarching themes. A good literary work is one that both shows a consonance of subject and theme and provides an illuminating development of themes of broad human interest.

III

Such is my all too brief exploration of some salient features of literary works and their content. In this final section we can return to our original question concerning the relation of real-life narratives to literary narratives. I have deliberately quoted frequently in the foregoing discussion from literary critics going about their business. What is notable from these familiar kinds of comments conventionally associated with literary narratives is how

[17]   G. Armour Craig, 'Private Vision and Social Order in Jane Eyre', Charlotte Bronte, *Jane Eyre*, R. J. Dunn (ed.) (New York: W. W. Norton & Co., 1971), 478.
[18]   Op. cit., 472.

utterly inappropriate most of them would be if applied to real-life narratives. What do I mean by real-life narratives? At the most formal extreme would be biographies or autobiographies of real people. These can look most like literary narratives and of course in the broad sense of 'literature', meaning fine writing, they can be classed as literary. They exhibit the same kind of completeness and 'closure' of certain kinds of novels, they often yield broad themes and can be given genre classifications like tragedy or romance. It seems clear, though, that they still differ in significant ways from literary fictional narratives. I will return to them as we proceed. Other real-life narratives are much less formally constructed. Yet these more casual narratives are thought to epitomise those real-life narratives that draw inspiration from the literary realm. These are narratives or narrative fragments that, on familiar accounts, supposedly help structure our lives and ground a coherent sense of ourselves. They might be snatches of memory or summaries of significant events or tales of self-justification.

But as I suggested at the beginning I don't think that these narratives either owe much to literature or are similar to literature, at least literature *taken as literature*. We might well abstract characters and incidents from the great works and hold them up as mirrors to our lives. Indeed it is common to turn the names of iconic characters into general terms: someone can be a Faust or an Oedipus. To be a Faust is merely to be someone who, metaphorically, sells his soul or makes a pact with the devil. But these abstracted and etiolated entities have little to do with the original literary narratives from which they are derived. Just how remote are the humdrum narratives of real life from potential literary antecedents can be shown from the inapplicability of our five principles. I will briefly comment on each.

The Character Identity Principle, which links character identity to character description, immediately shows the gulf between fiction and reality. No real person derives his identity from how he is described, nor is a real person perspectival in the sense outlined earlier. No doubt there is a privileged first person perspective possessed by each individual. But this determines special epistemic access, not a special kind of being; it is epistemological not ontological. Mr and Mrs Veneering, in contrast, are given to us *under a description*. The narrator's perspective on them, including the negative value judgement, is not just one among possible perspectives but is definitive in determining the kind of characters they are. If nothing else this is a simple consequence of the fact that fictional characters are created. It is absurd to suppose that a real person exists 'under a description'. Of course people take on roles so we can say that under the description 'Mayor of Middletown', Smith is the official representative of the city, but no one would suppose that Smith's very identity as a person rests on that description. It can only be a contingent fact that Smith became Mayor. Narratives about people can be true or false, accurate or inaccurate, but there is no limit to the number of possible narratives about any one person. Truth and accuracy are constrained by factors independent of narrative. One of the more obscurantist aspects of narrative theory is the suggestion that even real-life narratives serve an identity-defining function exactly comparable to that applied to fictional characters. The fashionable idea that personal identity resides in the narratives we tell about ourselves—with the implication that without the narratives we would somehow lack identity—is shown to be an absurdity, in its extreme form, when we bring to mind the literary case where strong perspectival identity really does obtain.

The Opacity Principle, whereby attention in literary works is conventionally directed to modes of presentation as much as to the material presented, again distances real-life narratives from literary ones. Simple narratives concerning real life will normally aim for transparency of transmission, even if the story-tellers are not entirely indifferent to narratives modes. With biographies and autobiographies it will not be uncommon for readers to attend, and be invited to attend, to the narrative vehicle. This, though, is largely dictated by broader literary concerns with fine writing and stylistic interest. Like all fact-stating discourses, biographies aim to transmit information and are primarily constrained by 'getting it right'. What this means is that there are natural limits to the opacity desirable or possible in such discourses. Too much opacity will frustrate pragmatic discursive purposes. Therein lies the crucial difference. In literary works opacity is an asset, it is sought, and it enriches character identity, while in referential discourses opacity is a weakness, to be minimised, and merely clouds personal characterisation.

Functionality in literature—the idea that detail bears a functional role—has an analogue in real-life narratives but should not be confused with it. The analogue is a principle of selectivity which operates in all narrative. Of detail in all narrative it can be asked: why was that detail selected? Immediately a difference between fictional and non-fictional narrative is apparent. In non-fictional narrative detail is *selected* from pre-existing facts, in fictional narrative detail is *created*. Among principles of selection are relevance, importance, and significance. Among principles of creation are artistic purpose and internal connectedness. We saw that one artistic purpose might be Barthes's 'reality effect'. The fact that detail can be said to acquire 'significance' in each case should not conceal the difference between significance conceived as importance and significance conceived as bearing meaning. In the literary case, but not the real-life case, detail is significant for conveying meaning. When Tess is first introduced in Hardy's novel, as a young girl in a May-day parade, she, like all the other girls, is wearing white but unlike the others Tess has a red ribbon in her hair. No further reference is made to this ribbon. But in the literary context, according to the Functionality Principle, it is legitimate to ask what function that tiny detail is performing. Here is one suggestion. If the white dresses connote virginity and innocence the redness of the ribbon has other connotations heralding events to come; it is the colour of blood, it connotes sensuousness and sin, in the 17th century the scarlet letter A was pinned to adulterers (a connection with Hawthorne's novel, *The Scarlet Letter*, from 1850), and so forth. If this were a real life narrative what matters primarily is that the detail be accurate. It might be selected in a narrative to suggest the connotations mentioned but the fact itself could bear no such intrinsic meaning.

One serious danger in modelling real-life narratives on literary ones is that a kind of mysticism is encouraged which assigns meanings to facts in the world. A misplaced functionality might encourage this but also, and worse, a misplaced teleology. The Teleology Principle in literature seeks explanations of literary events in their contribution to artistic structure. When real-life narratives take on the appearance of artistic structures—and again biographies and autobiographies sometimes aspire to this—they can easily foster the illusion of seeing lives themselves as works of art. Narratives are dangerous and distorting when they appear to offer false explanations: 'that first meeting was no coincidence, it was meant to happen', 'the seeds of a tragic life were there from the beginning', and so on. Narratives find patterns in people's lives and give structure. There is nothing wrong with that. But the literary model, where patterns are deliberately created and can determine (and thus explain) fictional content, is entirely inappropriate for narratives of real lives. Explanations for non-fictional events must stay in the realm of causes and reasons. Nothing in the real world happens because some structured design determines that it must happen.

Peter Lamarque

Finally, the literary critical search for unifying themes can also find analogues in real-life narratives. After all, biographies can exhibit familiar themes of unrequited love, corrupting power, or unrestrained ambition. But the central point that has been at the heart of all our deliberations on the literary principles applies here too: namely, that literary works are finely wrought artistic structures affording a special kind of internal connectedness. The consonance of subject and theme, which I earlier described as a literary value, is an end in itself in a way that cannot be applicable to narratives that have the further purposes of describing and explaining the lives of real individuals. To think otherwise is to aestheticise, if not fictionalise, real lives. To study someone's life, or one's own, primarily to see how factual detail coheres under some overarching theme is to direct attention away from the underlying explanations of that person's actions. Maybe some biographies or autobiographies aspire to the status of novels and explore literary themes in a comparable manner. But the very eccentricity of this—and the dangers it brings in accuracy and truth-telling—shows that this is not a model that captures the essence of the real-life narrative.

We have come a long way. I hope to have shown by identifying familiar principles of literary narratives how different they are from the narratives we tell about ourselves. If we take, as it is commonly supposed we do take, the great literary works to be models for our self-directed narratives, we are prone to two serious mistakes. The first is the more serious because it is potentially dangerous: that is to suppose that our own life narratives are mini-works of literature, complying with the principles of literary appreciation. It is not the hubris of this that matters but the false image of ourselves as kinds of fictional characters, whose identity rests on narrative description and whose actions are explicable in functional, teleological or thematic ways. The second mistake moves in the opposite direction: to suppose that literary works are simply stories about people like you and me, a species of real life narratives. Under this tendency we think of fictional characters as our 'friends' and we sometimes model ourselves on them. But literary characters, as our principles show, are quite different from us, both ontologically and epistemically. They move in a world of artifice and structure and their actions and very identity are subject to principles that, again, have no application to the world the rest of us inhabit. In being swept up in narrative fever we must beware of running radically different kinds of narratives together.

Reasons to be Fearful: Strawson, Death and Narrative

KATHY BEHRENDT

When attempting to face the prospect of one's own death, it has been said that 'the mind blanks at the glare'.[1] Perhaps we should not treat our attitude towards our death as rational or reflective of our views on the self and on life. But to exempt views on death from the scrutiny of rational discourse seems to be a last resort (albeit one we may need recourse to in the end). There is a general tendency to neglect death within those discussions of the self that fall outside the confines of a certain strain of continental thought roughly construed, or at best to treat it as a topic that resides beyond the borders of the rational. I do not aim to rectify this situation here, nor do I think it obvious that death is something that can be clearly and consistently dealt with by those theories of persons and selves that primarily represent, to use Thomas Nagel's words, 'an internal view that sees only this side of death—that includes only the finitude of [one's] expected future consciousness'.[2] But I do believe that those who have spent a good deal of time thinking about the life of the self ought to spare a thought or two for its demise, and that such thoughts may contribute to our over-all assessment of their view.

I will compare and assess what two significant and opposing approaches to the self have to say about death. By death here, I am speaking only of one's own death—not grieving, or the death of others, or even one's own dying and the pain and fear that that process may involve. I take death to mean, minimally, the permanent end of life, on the understanding that we can grasp and accept this conception of death independent of resolving the more vexed question of what the criteria for death are, i.e. what

---

[1]   P. Larkin, 'Aubade', originally published in *Times Literary Supplement* Dec. 23, 1977, reprinted in *Philip Larkin: Collected Poems*, A. Thwaite (ed.) (London: Faber and Faber, 1988), 208–209.
[2]   T. Nagel, *The View From Nowhere* (Oxford: Oxford University Press, 1986), 225.

conditions must be met in order for the end of life to obtain.[3] The two approaches in question are those of the episodic anti-narrativist, as articulated by Galen Strawson, and the narrativist, as somewhat synthetically pieced together from a variety of accounts.[4] As we shall see, neither party fares particularly well on the matter of death, both unable to point towards a view of death that is clearly consistent with their views on the self. In the case of the narrative view, this inconsistency, while not as explicit, is particularly entrenched.

II

Galen Strawson offers a view of the self that is both anti-diachronic and anti-narrative. He holds an anti-diachronic or 'episodic' view of the self in that he does not think that he himself as an inner mental self—as opposed to a biological entity or human being—continues over time for any significant duration. His self in this sense is not 'something that was there in the (further) past and will be there in the (further) future'.[5] While he is perfectly aware that Galen Strawson the human being has endured for some time and will probably carry on for some time to come, and he has from-the-inside memories of Galen Strawson's experiences, and expectations and practical concerns for Galen Strawson's future, he does not identify his present self with those past or future subjects. His self as a mental entity is largely bound to the 'present, brief, hiatus-free stretch of consciousness'.[6] He sometimes calls this anti-diachronic stance the 'Pearl view' of the self, meaning that 'many mental selves exist, one at a time and one after another, like pearls on a string' in the life of a human being.[7]

---

[3] For this concept/criteria distinction, see J.M. Fischer, 'Introduction: Death, Metaphysics, and Morality', *The Metaphysics of Death*, J.M. Fischer (ed.) (Stanford: Stanford University Press, 1993), 3–30, 3–6.

[4] As there is no single narrativist group or movement I will speak freely of 'the narrativist view' or 'narrativist views', on the understanding that I am primarily concerned with those views as they pertain to the self and involve some alleged reflexive application of conventional narrative structures to one's own life, descriptively and/or normatively.

[5] G. Strawson, 'Against Narrativity', *Ratio* 17, 2004, 430. Cf. ' "The Self" ', in *Models of the Self*, S. Gallagher and J. Shear (eds.) (Thorverton: Imprint Academic, 1999), 1–24.

[6] ' "The Self" ', op. cit. note 5, 14.

[7] Ibid., 20.

As for the narrative view, Strawson defines this as, minimally, involving the deliberate application of a story-like unifying or form-finding construction to the various events that compose one's life, in the sense of 'conceiving of one's life ...as some sort of ethical-historical-characterological developmental unity, or in terms of a story, a *Bildung* or 'quest'', which fits 'the form of some recognized narrative genre'.[8] He attacks the narrative view of the self both as construed descriptively, as offering an account of how we in fact live and view our lives, and normatively, as a prescription for how we ought to live our lives.

The anti-diachronic and anti-narrative views, while they may influence one another, are distinct and do not depend upon one another, according to Strawson.[9] One does not need to be anti-diachronic in order to be anti-narrative, though it seems clear that it helps; if one does not view the self as diachronically extended, it is easier to reject the view that the self is and/or ought to be the subject of a certain developmental progress.[10] It is evident that in Strawson's own case the presence of the anti-diachronic and anti-narrative views reinforce one another and each forms part of what is intended to be an over-all account of the nature of the self, which he has been developing for some time. I therefore consider the implications of his view of death for both his anti-diachronic and his anti-narrative stance. The problems that arise in each case are separate, though, and it may be that in the end the anti-diachronic and anti-narrative positions would benefit from being fully divorced from each other, at least as far as dealing with death is concerned.

III

As Strawson himself acknowledges, what he says about death seems, at least on the face of it, decidedly to contradict his anti-diachronic stance. He says that when he thinks of his death at some unspecified future time, he thinks that it is he, *qua* inner mental self, who will die and, what is more, that he fears this death. 'This seems odd', he admits, 'given that my death necessarily

---

[8] 'Against Narrativity', op. cit. note 5, 441, 442.
[9] Ibid., sect. 6.
[10] This is especially clear in ' "The Self" ', op. cit. note 5, sect. VIII, in which anti-diachronicity and anti-narrative are largely treated as of a piece.

Kathy Behrendt

comes after any future events in my life' and, granting his anti-diachronic Pearl view of the self, he doesn't think he continues to exist for these future events in life.[11] How then can it be he himself who dies and whose death is the intentional object of his fear? He has an explanation, namely that relative to the eternity of non-existence that is death, his whole life as a human being is so short as to condense it to a moment in which, it seems, he *qua* the same mental entity (or 'Me*', to use Strawson's notation) still exists at the end of it: 'When eternity—eternal nonexistence—is in question, the gap between Me* and death that is created by the fact that I still have an indefinite amount of life to live approximates to nothing (like any finite number compared with infinity). So death—nonexistence for ever—presents itself as having direct relevance for Me* now even if Me* has no clear future in life—not even tomorrow'.[12] This is an explanation of how Strawson manages to over-ride his anti-diachronic stance and thereby to be entitled to a view on his (distant future) death. Is it a satisfactory explanation?

There are several reasons for being less than satisfied with it, in so far as the explanation seems to presuppose a dubious view of death, and one that has problematic consequences. This can be drawn out by means of some standard Epicurean criticisms of the fear of death. The first of these is something I'll call the 'temporal fallacy', according to which death is mistakenly treated either explicitly or implicitly as an ongoing state of affairs comparable to an 'event in life'.[13] The temporal fallacy is a more general form of what we might call the 'experiential fallacy' that Lucretius identified, according to which the man who fears death, unconsciously 'infects [the corpse] with his own perception', covertly believing himself to continue after death and experience its disadvantages.[14] Strawson's explanation as to why he views death as something that will happen to Me*, is that my death unlike my life is eternal, 'eternity' being equated with 'eternal nonexistence', and an 'eternity of nonexistence' being what he fears.[15] A finite duration, however long, shrinks to a pin-point when contrasted

---

[11] ' "The Self" ', op. cit. note 5, 16.

[12] Ibid. Cf. 'Against Narrativity', op. cit. note 5, 430–431.

[13] To borrow from Wittgenstein, *Tractatus Logico-Philosophicus*, D. Pears and B. McGuinness (trans.) (London: Routledge & Keegan Paul, 1961), 6.4311.

[14] Lucretius, *De Rerum Natura* 3.883. Cf 3.870–83. All translations of Lucretius are by J. Warren, *Facing Death: Epicurus and his Critics* (Oxford: Clarendon Press, 2004).

[15] ' "The Self" ', op. cit. note 5, 16, 17.

with an infinite duration, and the temporally-extended succession of Strawsonian mental selves is compressed into a seemingly single unit in the face of posthumous infinite temporal duration.

But the fact that one is dead by a certain point on a standard B series time-scale, and for all points later than that point, is quite different from the suggestion that one's death is eternal, in the sense of having an infinite temporal duration. As Nagel points out, we don't object to death on grounds of quantity, in the way in which we might feel compelled to value life quantitatively; we may say Bach reaped more of the benefits of life than Schubert, but we don't by the same token say that Shakespeare has received a larger portion of the evil of death than has Proust.[16] Whilst Nagel doesn't go on to explore this in depth, I think the reason for the disparity is that 'infinity' in the case of death is not infinite duration but timelessness.[17] The thing in question is removed from time altogether by being removed from existence. Yet infinite duration seems to be how Strawson is and must be viewing death in order that he compare it to the finite duration of life. The result of this comparison is indeed cause for distress. As Tom Stoppard's re-imagined Guildenstern remarks: 'Death followed by eternity ...the worst of both worlds. It *is* a terrible thought'.[18] But if Strawson were to treat death not as a state of eternal duration but as something ex-temporal, it would no longer be commensurable with the temporal nature of life and the basis for his explanation—the prospect of a future of eternal non-existence—would be lost.

A further reason for finding Strawson's explanation problematic lies in another Epicurean-identified complication, namely the well-known symmetry argument, according to which our attitude towards our post-natal non-existence—our death—ought to be consistent with our attitude towards our pre-natal non-existence, or the time before our birth, the situation for us in both cases being the same. Strawson is particularly vulnerable to the implications of the symmetry argument. If the thought of eternal non-existence provokes the belief that it is he who will die, then contemplation of the infinite duration of time prior to his birth ought to prompt the view that it is he who was born (on whatever date Galen Strawson the human being was born), and if he fears the time after death

---

[16] T. Nagel, 'Death', in *Mortal Questions* (Cambridge: Cambridge University Press, 1979), 1–10, at 3.

[17] Again, borrowing from Wittgenstein, op. cit. note 13.

[18] T. Stoppard, *Rosencrantz and Guildenstern are Dead* (New York: Grove Weidenfeld, 1967), act 2, 72.

then he ought also to fear the time before birth. But we have no reason to think he does fear his pre-natal non-existence; it is in any case a highly unlikely and uncommon view.[19] Assuming he does not in fact fear the time before his birth, he is, like most of us, guilty of an asymmetrical attitude towards pre-and post-natal non-existence. There are many worthy objections to the symmetry argument, but the bulk of them tend to appeal to our general evaluative bias towards the future, in order to justify our widespread tendency to negative attitudes towards post-natal non-existence and indifference towards pre-natal non-existence. It is unclear whether Strawson could reasonably uphold and sustain such a bias, in light of his express claims to the effect that his self-interest does not extend to the past *or* the future (more of which below). Given these claims, and assuming Strawson does not in fact fear the time before his birth, he may belong to what Derek Parfit presented as the wholly hypothetical class of those 'who both lack the bias towards the future, and do not regret their past non-existence'. Such a view is the only one against which the symmetry argument has genuine force; for someone in this position cannot appeal to the point that it is non-existence in general—pre- and post-natal—that they fear, nor can they cite future bias as the reason for fearing only the latter.[20]

IV

Even apart from these criticisms, we still have to be aware of the limits of Strawson's explanation as to why he fears his death. It is an explanation of how he over-rides his anti-diachronic view in order to arrive at the thought that he, who does not endure in life, nevertheless will suffer death. It therefore allows him to fulfil a necessary condition of fearing death, namely having the thought that it is *he* who will die. Even if it is or can be made acceptable, therefore, his explanation only entitles him to *an* attitude towards his death. It does not justify or account for why that attitude is one

[19] Though a compelling example of anxiety concerning pre-natal non-existence can be found in the opening of V. Nabokov, *Speak Memory* (Harmondsworth: Penguin, 1967), 17.

[20] D. Parfit, *Reasons and Persons*, rev. ed. (Oxford: Clarendon Press, 1987), 175. Parfit attributes the symmetry argument to Epicurus, but it is more commonly ascribed to Lucretius, *De Rerum Natura* 3.832–42 and 3.972–5. Cf. Warren, op. cit. note 14, ch. 3.

of fear, nor is it intended to do so. Indeed, his explanation of why he feels it is he who will die appears to presuppose rather than account for his fear; as he writes, 'the thought of eternity ...has an emotional force that makes it seem plain that death faces Me*'[21]—as though the emotion precedes and prompts his diachronic lapse. In so far as his explanation of his attitude towards death does not seek to account for the particular nature of the attitude—fear—my criticisms of his explanation do not touch on that particular attitude.

In order to get at fear of death and its appropriateness within the framework of a Strawsonian view of the self, we must turn from anti-diachronicity to that other key aspect of Strawson's view, namely his anti-narrative stance. Here we're not just faced with the absence of explanations. We are also in possession of an overwhelming body of evidence, in the form of his anti-narrative view of life, that would lead us to expect Strawson to possess a much more dispassionate attitude towards death than he does. As said, though, Strawson does not present his particular attitude towards death as rationally justified. But—and especially in an age in which we are coming increasingly to recognise that emotions are at least in part cognitive—it is still worthwhile asking whether the fear of death can be rationally accounted for by someone who advocates Strawson's anti-narrative stance while at the same time does wish to claim her fear or abhorrence of death is consistent with her anti-narrative position. This, I will argue, is none too easy to do. The philosopher concerned to align her view of death with her anti-narrative stance will find her options constrained if she constructs that stance on the Strawsonian model.

V

The *locus classicus* of the anti-narrative position is, arguably, Epicureanism. The Epicureans did not deny that they, *qua* enduring mental and physical beings, would die, so any strain of anti-narrativism here is not influenced (for worse or for better) by an anti-diachronic view of the nature of the self. The crucial point of comparison is that the Epicureans did not place value on kinetic or time-dependent pleasure, but on katastematic, or static, pleasure. It is this that underlies Epicurus' controversial pronouncement that

---

[21]   ' "The Self" ', op. cit. note 5, 16.

'the infinite time has as much pleasure as the finite'.[22] Here is Stephen Rosenbaum's gloss on this key aspect of the Epicurean outlook:

> ... the Epicurean view of the significance of projects for human life lies in the way they may or may not engage the natural capacities of the human, not in their completion. Completeness thus lies in a certain time-independent quality of one's activities, not in whether the activities produce specific (future) results ...It is not that the completion of projects in the future is unimportant, but rather that being unimpededly engaged in the activity of completing them is the only essential aspect of their contribution to one's well-being ...[This is] better said to be the idea of complete living, rather than that of a complete life.[23]

Compare this with Strawson's articulation of a strong anti-narrative stance: 'I'm completely uninterested in the answer to the question 'What has GS made of his life?', or 'What have I made of my life?' I'm living it, and this sort of thinking about it is no part of it. This does not mean that I am in any way irresponsible. It is just that what I care about, in so far as I care about myself and my life, is how I am now'.[24] Such a sentiment is echoed throughout Strawson's attack on the narrativist view, and is crucial to it. In keeping with Rosenbaum's gloss on the Epicurean stance, he claims to be able to maintain a basic, practical awareness of and attention to the future of GS. But in his case, as in the Epicurean case, this does not amount to subordinating the present to any larger, explicitly-articulated purpose or future result. Trajectory, vocation, development, project, and quest are all terms that Strawson associates with the narrative view, and in rejecting that view he rejects a long-term interest in the self over time and any picture of life as deliberately moving towards a conclusion whose nature will be determined by the pattern of living that precedes it. It is worth noting that, aside from this fundamental similarity with respect to katastematic values, Strawson also shares the Epicureans' concerns about the negative influence of religious beliefs amongst those who

---

[22] Epicurus, *Kyria Doxa* 19. All translations of Epicurus are by Warren, op. cit. note 14.

[23] S. Rosenbaum, 'Epicurus on Pleasure and the Complete Life', *Monist* 73, 1990, 37.

[24] 'Against Narrativity', op. cit. note 5, 438; cf. ' "The Self" ', op. cit. note 5, 15.

espouse kinetic values,[25] and levies Epicurean or neo-Epicurean charges of parochialism and cultural imposition against his opponents.[26]

Thus it appears that Strawson the anti-narrativist shares certain key values with the Epicurean, especially concerning the interest in one's self as it exists in the present or, at the very least, as something not bound by concerns for the future. Yet strongly related to their view of complete living as a present-tense endeavour is the Epicureans' notorious indifference to death. According to that view, death is not to be feared because there is no actual perceiving subject of it, and there is no possible subject of it:[27] 'death, the most terrifying of evils, is nothing to us, since for the time when we are, death is not present; and for the time when death is present, we are not'.[28] What is the relation between the Epicurean view of life and the Epicurean view of death? Much is assumed but certain passages are explicit:

> The mind, taking the calculation of the goal and limit of the flesh and, banishing the fears brought on by eternity, makes life complete and no longer in need of an infinite time. But the mind does not flee from pleasure nor, when things bring about a departure from life, does it depart as if lacking something from the best life. The man who knows the limits of life knows how easy it is to produce the removal of pain caused by want and to make one's whole life complete. As a result, there is no need for competitive behaviour.[29]

Katastematic pleasure is founded on the absence of pain for the Epicurean, as this (and other) texts indicate, and so does not require

[25] Cf. 'Against Narrativity', op. cit. note 5, 436–37.

[26] Cf. ibid., 429, 437. For an Epicurean position on this, see Rosenbaum, 'Epicurus on Pleasure and the Complete Life', op. cit. note 23, 36: 'There is no goal or type of goal, the objective achievement of which is necessary for a person to live a complete life. The requirement that a person achieve such goals in order to have a complete life would be, for Epicurus, an abstract, unjustifiable, and anxiety-producing cultural imposition on human thriving.'

[27] For the significance of the difference between these two strands of arguments see: Nagel, op. cit. note 16; M. Nussbaum, 'Mortal Immortals: Lucretius on Death and the Voice of Nature', *Philosophy and Phenomenological Research* 50, 1989, n. 5; and Warren, op. cit. note 14, ch. 2.

[28] Epicurus, *Letter to Menoeceus*, 125. Cf. *Kyria Doxa*, 2.

[29] Epicurus, *Kyriai Doxai*, 20–21.

Kathy Behrendt

a diachronically extended series of actions or experiences in order to be attained. It seems that ridding oneself of fear of death is part of recognising that a good life is not contingent upon kinetic, time-bound pleasures or goals and does not require an interest in the persisting self's progress over time. Indifference to death and the acceptance of katastematic values are mutually supporting: by abandoning interest in a persisting self not subject to mortality, we clear the ground for the appreciation of katastematic pleasure; at the same time, realising that pleasure does not require persistence makes it possible to accept mortality. Normally adherence to the Epicurean view of death requires a therapeutic re-examination of one's ordinary values which, it is expected, will be time-bound and so will run contrary to it; but in so far as the Strawsonian anti-narrativist is largely bereft of the time-bound values that commonly hinder progress towards Epicurean enlightenment, she ought to be a prime contestant for immediate indoctrination into the Epicurean indifference to death.

It may be retorted that the anti-narrativist concerned with the rational explanation of her emotions is still entitled to fear death. She just needs to account for it in such a way as to address the Epicurean argument that death is nothing to us—an argument that is notoriously unconvincing, it must be said. Perhaps she could avail herself of some of the standard criticisms of Epicureanism here. Unfortunately for her, these criticisms tend to affiliate their proponents with the narrative camp. The rejection of Epicurean equanimity towards death is traditionally tied (explicitly or otherwise) to a rejection of the Epicurean view of life, through the promotion of time-bound pleasures and values. Take the examples of two of the best-known arguments, variations of which continue to inundate the philosophical literature on death. The desire-frustration account (primary advocate: Bernard Williams) proclaims death an evil (and a unique evil) because it frustrates certain categorical desires to live—these tend to be egocentric long-term desires involving deep interest in one's further future, and are linked by Williams to his commitment to determinate diachronic personal identity.[30] The deprivation theory (primary advocate: Nagel) says death is bad because it deprives a person of the goods in life. A person, on this theory, is not merely an actual subject of experience at a given moment, but 'a person identified by his

[30] B. Williams, 'The Makropulos Case', in *Problems of the Self* (Cambridge: Cambridge University Press, 1973), 82–100.

history and his possibilities';[31] we must consider not just who the present subject is but what he was and could be in order to address difficult questions of when and for whom the badness of death applies. As Martha Nussbaum interprets Nagel, death is 'a termination of something that was under way, projecting towards a future'.[32] By treating the person as a temporally-extended being with an on-going concern for, or identity enshrouded in, his past history and/or future possibilities, both the desire-frustration account and the deprivation theory seem to presuppose or tacitly endorse crucial aspects of the narrative view (or at least something incompatible with an anti-narrative view),[33] and so it is not advisable for the anti-narrativist to look towards these sorts of arguments in order rationally to sustain her fear of death in the face of the Epicurean insistence upon equanimity.

Of course we could fall back on the claim that no rational explanation of fear of death is in order here. I've said that that sort of approach is a last resort, but in this case it may be a welcome refuge. Perhaps fear of death does not admit of rational explanation within the confines of the anti-narrativist account of the self. But on the other hand, nothing else in that account depends upon holding the view of death that Strawson does; his fear of death is not a product of his anti-narrativism. It is possible that he, or at the very least a follower of his view, could come to divest himself of this fear without thereby doing violence to the rest of his view. But if this cannot be achieved, and fear of death prevails, then it is perhaps best treated as a-rational, standing apart from the account, and neither the outcome nor the source of rational influence. As we shall see, this would still place the Strawsonian anti-narrativist in a superior position to the narrativist, who may not be at liberty to deal so perfunctorily with the problems that death creates for his account—problems that are arguably borne of elements intrinsic and essential to it.

[31] Nagel, op. cit. note 16, 5.
[32] Nussbaum, 'Mortal Immortals', op. cit. note 27, 315.
[33] Note that Nagel's remarks, elsewhere in the same article, concerning the desirability of eternal life, may place him in opposition to another crucial aspect or implication of the narrativist view of the self (see n. 41 below); nevertheless, his emphasis on viewing a person in terms of his history and possibilities is sufficient to render him at odds with aspects of Strawson's anti-narrative stance, in particular Strawson's lack of concern for questions of the sort, 'What has GS made of his life?' ('Against Narrativity', op. cit. note 5, 438).

Kathy Behrendt

VI

So far I've been contrasting the narrative view with the Epicurean attitude towards life. It is hardly surprising to learn that narrativism is antithetical to a view that proclaims that the value of life is not kinetically-based—is not time-dependent. Following Strawson's broad characterisation of the narrative approach to the self as involving a deliberate unifying or form-finding tendency modelled on recognised narrative genres, it is clear that the life of the self upon the narrative view is essentially time-dependent. It requires concern for one's past and future self, in so far as the self has an ongoing engagement in the realisation of the non-immediate achievements, goals, and possibilities that form and contribute to the narrative construct. But while time is important for the narrativist, the point of contrast between the narrativist and the Epicurean does not merely concern the duration of life. Gisela Striker attacks the Epicurean view from an overtly narrativist position, arguing that although Epicurus may have been right to imply that an infinitely long life is not desirable (as we shall see, the narrativist and the Epicurean are in agreement on this point), he wrongly focused on the duration of life and neglected the issue of the completeness of life. Death is bad when one has not completed one's life, says Striker, and Epicurus with his focus upon katastematic pleasures cannot accommodate this point.[34] The Epicurean goal, in so far as we can speak of one, being katastematic and essentially negative in form (the absence of pain), can theoretically be achieved at any point in a life and does not require the playing out of certain patterns of living over time.[35] In contrast, Striker reveals her time-dependent understanding of complete and incomplete lives through comparison of life with the

[34] G. Striker, 'Commentary on Mitsis', *Proceedings of the Boston Area Colloquium on Ancient Philosophy* 4, 1988, 325–326. Cf. Rosenbaum, op. cit. note 23, and Warren, op. cit. note 14, 115 ff.

[35] Cf. Warren, op. cit. note 14, ch. 4: he offers two possible interpretations of the Epicurean notion of a complete life—one which, in keeping with the narrative view eschews only premature death, and the other which sees the good life as obtainable no matter what a person's age or stage in life. He rallies strong textual evidence in support of the latter view (focusing on the Epicurean rejection of Solon's dictum, 'call no man happy until he is dead', and the claim that katastematic pleasure is not at all improved by duration), and concludes that Epicureanism is incompatible with the narrative outlook.

viewing of an opera; one does not want to be made to leave after the first act, but to experience the whole spectacle—its progress and vicissitudes.[36]

Note that death *per se* is not being identified as bad here; we need only fear premature death. This is because the time that the narrativist depends upon for completeness cannot be unlimited. Other narrativist sympathisers such as Williams, Nussbaum, and Richard Wollheim all corroborate this point,[37] each agreeing in one way or another that a complete life takes considerable time and so death before a certain point is an evil, but that 'immortality is not the answer to death'[38]—after a certain point death is desirable or at least necessary. Why is so-called non-premature death desirable or necessary upon narrative views of the self? The answer is encapsulated in Jeff Malpas' rhetorical query, 'How could one conceive of a life without end as constituting a whole?'.[39] It is not just its duration or diachronic extension but its finitude that permits our lives to be structured along conventional narrative lines, which in turn allows us to partake of the benefits that narrativity putatively confers, be it unity and completeness, authenticity, participation in fulfilling human relationships, self-understanding, ethical character, or achievement of the status of personhood. In the case of lived narratives, the ending is secured and indeed constituted by death, as Alasdair MacIntyre makes explicit; faced with the objection that life, unlike stories, has no beginnings, middles or ends, he responds, 'Have you never heard of death?'[40] Therefore while the narrativist eschews the Epicurean's indifference to life's duration, there is a sense in which he is not wholly at odds with the Epicurean; he can accept death at least on

---

[36]   Striker, op. cit. note 34, 325–326.
[37]   See: Williams, op. cit. note 30; Nussbaum, op. cit. note 27; and R. Wollheim, *The Thread of Life* (Cambridge, MS: Harvard University Press, 1984), ch. IX.
[38]   Wollheim, ibid., 267.
[39]   J. Malpas, 'Death and the Unity of a Life', in *Death and Philosophy*, J. Malpas and R. Solomon (eds.) (London: Routledge, 1998), 120–134, 131.
[40]   A. MacIntyre, *After Virtue*, 2nd ed. (Notre Dame: University of Notre Dame Press, 1984), 212.

certain terms.[41] Nussbaum even goes so far as to suggest that such a narrativist-driven acceptance of (non-premature) death is neo-Epicurean.[42]

VII

There are several things that concern me about the place of death in the narrativist view. The first two concerns pertain to the suggestion that non-premature death is acceptable to the narrativist. As Steven Luper-Foy proclaims, 'any reason for living is an excellent reason for not dying',[43] and while this is a point that the Epicurean can reject, it is much harder for the narrativist to deny. If we see life as 'projecting towards a future', in which certain possibilities may be realised in accordance with a certain narrative trajectory or structure, it seems hard to avoid the view that death at any time is abhorrent, because it deprives us of the fulfilment of all possibilities.[44] This is where the Epicureans have the advantage over the narrativists; by dissociating the complete life from the attainment of goals over time and instead restricting the highest achievement to *ataraxia* or the absence of pain or disturbance, the value of which does not increase with its duration, completeness such as it is for the Epicurean can clearly be obtained within a life.[45] In answer to this, it might be said that the narrativist view allows us to curtail death's potential for deprivation by providing us with a prescription for securing a complete life; comparison of lives to novels or stories suggests that completion is both imperative and

[41]   This is where Nagel may diverge from narrativist accounts; despite his emphasis on a life judged in terms of its history and possibilities, he is careful to observe that 'a man's sense of his own experience ...does not embody this idea of a natural limit' and that, furthermore, there may be 'no limit to the amount of life that it would be good to have' (op. cit. note 16, 9–10). This does not exclude Nagel from the official narrativist view, because there is no such official view. But I believe it betrays the spirit of many narrativist accounts; I take the limit or finitude of life to be a necessary adjunct, in light of what the more overt narrative advocates say or imply in their writings with respect to both the shape and the completeness of a life.

[42]   Nussbaum, op. cit. note 27. Cf. S. Luper-Foy, 'Annihilation', in *The Metaphysics of Death*, op. cit. note 3, 269–290.

[43]   Luper-Foy, ibid., 278.

[44]   Cf. Nagel, op. cit. note 16, 9–10.

[45]   Cf. Warren, op. cit. note 14, ch. 4.

obtainable. Were we to achieve it, we would thereby cheat death, leaving nothing for it to deprive us of. But if one has a kinetic-based view of life's structure and value, is it possible to obtain complete satisfaction with one's life (a possibility that Italo Calvino describes as a 'too uninteresting to make it worth investigating')?[46] Only in fiction is it even arguably the case that there are no possibilities outside the confines of the given narrative (thus we view with deep suspicion questions to the effect of where Elizabeth Bennet and Darcy might spend their honeymoon). There will always be, up until the time of our death, further possibilities for us that death will eradicate, some if not many of which could otherwise stand as reasons to go on, upon a kinetic-based set of values.[47] So I greet with some suspicion any allegedly neo-Epicurean gesture on the narrativist's part to embrace so-called non-premature death.

Relatedly, the reduction of concern with death to concern with premature death just seems descriptively false. There is a form of dread of death that stands apart from any and all concerns we may have with our lives and their completeness or lack thereof. 'The mind blanks at the glare', says Philip Larkin, 'not in remorse' for 'the good not done, the love not given, time / Torn off unused ...', but 'at the total emptiness for ever'.[48] This dread of the 'total emptiness forever', which some philosophers have attempted to deny or downgrade in light of other possible death-related fears, undeniably exists and is deeply felt by some.[49] Amélie Rorty calls it the fear of death 'as such', and Nagel, the 'unmistakable experience' of the 'expectation of nothingness'.[50] I'm inclined to

---

[46] I. Calvino, 'Learning to be Dead', in *Mr. Palomar*, W. Weaver (trans.) (Toronto: Lester & Orpen Dennys Ltd., 1985), 121–126, 124. He adds: 'This is the most difficult step in learning how to be dead: to become convinced that your own life is a closed whole, all in the past, to which you can add nothing and can alter none of the relationships among the various elements' (ibid., 125).

[47] Cf. Rosenbaum, op. cit. note 23, 34–35.

[48] Larkin, op. cit. note 1.

[49] Deniers and downgraders include: R. Rorty, *Contingency, Irony, and Solidarity* (Cambridge: Cambridge University Press, 1989), ch. 2.; R. Solomon, 'Death Fetishism, Morbid Solipsism', in *Death and Philosophy*, op. cit. note 39,152–176; and Warren, op. cit. note 14, 4.

[50] A. Rorty, 'Fearing Death', in *Mind in Action* (Boston: Beacon Press, 1988), 197–211, at 200, and Nagel, op. cit. note 2, 225. In keeping with Larkin, both Rorty and Nagel distinguish this unique and objectless dread of death from various death-related concerns, both personal and social, which, as Rorty notes, 'attend other conditions as well as death' (A. Rorty,

think that this is the sort of fear of death to which Strawson was referring. If, as Larkin conveys, it stands apart from the many varieties of remorse and regret to which we are so susceptible, so likewise it stands independent of and impervious to the rewards of life, including the completion of our long-term life projects, and therefore even the committed narrativist ought to remain susceptible to it.

My final concern—and the most serious one, I think—is about the role of death more generally within the narrativist account. Here the narrativist seems to commit a variation upon the temporal and experiential fallacies discussed earlier in connection with Strawson. The narrativist (implicitly or explicitly) treats death as an event in life, when he of necessity attempts to incorporate death into the story of his life as its final occurrence. But death is not an event in life. Death is not lived through. It can't form part of one's self-narrative. It can only interrupt such a narrative. Only from the spectator or reader's point of view does death contribute to the narrative of a life. Not so for the subject herself, so there is something like a category error being committed when one tries to incorporate one's own death within one's life story. If our lives are stories they are necessarily incomplete ones from the point of view of ourselves, which is the only point of view we're concerned with here. The narrativist thus ends up with a paradox at the heart of his view: he needs mortality for meaning, completeness, unity, yet his death deprives him of completion of his self-narrative.[51]

VIII

The response to this final criticism may be that it overstates the problem. MacIntyre says of Kafka that 'it is no accident that Kafka could not end his novels, for the notion of an ending like that of a

---

ibid). Note also the discrepancy between the 'expectation of nothingness' and Nagel's earlier, more widely accredited discussion of what we fear in fearing death (op. cit. note 16); his later discussion places him at further remove from the narrativist view.

[51]   Cf. S. Mulhall, 'The Enigma of Individuality: Identity, Narrative and Truth in Biography, Autobiography and Fiction', in *Oxford Handbook of Philosophy and Literature*, R. Eldridge (ed.) (Oxford: Oxford University Press, forthcoming).

beginning has its sense only in terms of intelligible narrative'.[52] But MacIntyre does not here explicitly make the converse claim that I am making on behalf of the narrativist, namely that narratives only make sense if they have endings (as well as beginnings). The fact that Dickens' *The Mystery of Edwin Drood* was unfinished doesn't make what we have of it read like Kafka, and something similar could be said for self-narratives; our inability to complete them doesn't undermine their narrative credentials as a whole. There may be something to this. But I would suggest that we grasp the narrative arc of incomplete novels or stories (whether their incompletion be due to accident or deliberate irony or subversion) in light of complete ones, which constitute the norm, and my point is that there is no such norm available when it comes to self-narratives; they are all necessarily incomplete, unlike novels or stories, which are occasionally unfinished but are nevertheless embedded in a tradition of finished ones. This discrepancy between the incomplete story and the incomplete life may put intolerable pressure on the attempt to treat one's own life as a story, especially in light of the fact that the comparison when made is often between self-narratives and conventional or traditional, linear, usually literary, narratives,[53] which tend to have (to repeat MacIntyre's description) beginnings, middles and ends.

A related but more substantial response to my concern might be to say that the mistake of treating one's death as the end of one's narrative stems from what Peter Goldie has identified as an overly-literal conception of the narrativist endeavour—one in which 'life is a narrative, of which the person living the life is the author'.[54] As Goldie rightly notes, 'to elide the notion of narrative and the notion of what a narrative is about is to lose the distinction between language (and thought) and the world—between represen-tation and what is represented'.[55] On my argument, the pitfalls of failing to separate the story from the subject of a self-narrative become especially apparent and unavoidable when it comes to writing the final sentence. But as Goldie suggests, we do not need

[52] MacIntyre, op. cit. note 40, 213.
[53] Cf. for instance: MacIntyre, op. cit. note 40, ch. 15; Nussbaum, op. cit. note 27; O. Flanagan, *Varieties of Moral Personality* (Cambridge, MS.: Harvard University Press, 1991); M. Schechtman, *The Constitution of Selves* (Ithaca: Cornell University Press, 1996), ch. 5.
[54] P. Goldie, 'One's Remembered Past: Narrative Thinking, Emotion, and the External Perspective', *Philosophical Papers* 32 (2003), 303.
[55] Ibid.

to buy into the overly-literal reading of the narrativist endeavour. Even if some narrativists are themselves guilty of a literalist approach (Goldie identifies MacIntyre as the prime offender) others are not, or needn't be. The narrativist can reject the literal reading while sustaining what is important about his view:

> the denial that we are *literally* authors of our own lives does not imply that narratives are not central to how we lead our lives. We think, talk and write *about* our lives as narratives, and our doing this can profoundly affect our lives as such, in our engagement with, and response to, our past lives, and in our practical reasoning about what to do in the future. Narrative thought and talk about our lives, or segments of our lives, can thus be embedded in, and profoundly influence, the lives that we lead, even though those lives are not themselves narratives.[56]

This sounds eminently sensible. Will it be acceptable to narrativists in general? Not in so far as many of them are literalists (along with MacIntyre, Strawson identifies Jerome Bruner, Daniel Dennett, Marya Schechtman, Charles Taylor, and Paul Ricoeur all as possible culprits).[57] Even setting this aside, will the non-literal version of the narrative outlook avoid the pitfalls of the narrativist view, when it comes to death? It ought to, if the allegation of those pitfalls was itself a result of presupposing the literalist reading of the narrative position; if one is not literally the author of one's own story, if the life of the self is not literally the product of one's own narration, then it is no great criticism to note that one cannot ever deliver on the final draft.

I welcome a less literal construal of the narrative endeavour, but I suspect that the upshot of opting for a non-literal narrativist view will be to remove oneself to the periphery of many narrativists' concerns and alleged insights, and that the confrontation with death will exacerbate this marginalisation. Narrative risks becoming a conceit upon a non-literal approach—something we can take or leave, as circumstance or temperament warrants. This plays into

[56] Ibid., 303–304.

[57] Strawson, 'Against Narrativity', op. cit. note 5, 435 ff. I would also add Owen Flanagan to the list. He writes: narrative is the 'essential genre of self-representation, and not merely ...one normative ideal among others. A self is just a kind of life that has a beginning, a middle, and an end that are connected in a traditional storylike manner' (Flanagan, op. cit. note 53, 148–149). Cf. D. Jopling, *Self-Knowledge and the Self* (London: Routledge, 2000), 48–49 for discussion of this passage and of essentialism in the narrative view.

the hands of the Strawsonian excoriation of narrativists on the grounds that they are 'really just talking about themselves ...saying [what] is true for them', but not true in a more strict sense.[58] Why? Because in abandoning the literalist reading one thereby abandons the descriptive thesis, according to which the narrative view reflects facts about the way persons are and, some will claim, *essentially* are.[59] All one is then left with is at best an ungrounded normativity—a set of claims about how one ought to view one's life—claims which have no obvious application beyond one's own case and are not grounded in general truths about our nature. Even in one's own case they do not represent the literal truth of the matter and may serve to obscure it: 'the more you recall, retell, narrate yourself, the further you risk moving away from accurate self-understanding, from the truth of your being'.[60] Nothing makes the dichotomy between narrative and reality more perspicuous than confrontation with one's death, which permanently resists the application of narrative thought. Deprived, therefore, even of the pretence of ever being able to apprehend of the whole of one's life as narratively complete, the value of the entire enterprise up until that point may be cast into doubt, or retroactively downgraded. In contrast, there is something heroic perhaps about the literalist narrativist who is able to forge ahead upon the assumption that we are all authors of our own story, and life as narrative is somehow literally true, and who may not be disabused of these beliefs up until the point of his death (at which point he may be too preoccupied to take note). But the non-literalist narrativist with her admission that narrative is something that we—or she, anyway—superimposes on reality leaves herself all the more exposed to the limitations of the enterprise, including if not especially the impossibility of closure and completeness.

IX

Where does all this leave us? Death places a limit on the narrative view by exposing a significant point of discrepancy between conventional narrative and so-called lived narrative, both by casting doubt on the possibility and the value of a closed, complete life, and

[58] Strawson, ibid., 437.
[59] Cf., for instance, Flanagan's claims, note 57 above, and also MacIntyre, op. cit. note 40, ch. 15, and Schechtman, op. cit. note 53, ch. 5.
[60] Strawson, ibid., 447. Cf. Jopling, op. cit. note 57, 47–55.

by paradoxically demanding and being debarred from narrative closure. Just how serious this is, is a matter for further debate and may depend on whether or not narrativists are and ought to be committed to a literal construal of the narrative view of the self.[61] By the same turn, death remains a concern for Strawson's view as well, for two reasons. First, his explanation of how he over rides his episodic view of the self in order to be entitled to any attitude towards death of the self is unsatisfactory. This is not a serious problem for a death-conscious anti-narrativist who does not share Strawson's anti-diachronic stance. She will not be subject to the difficulties anti-diachronicity creates in entitling her to any attitude towards her own death. Though at the same time, she will not benefit from the circumstantial support that anti-diachronicity otherwise lends anti-narrativity. Second, the particular attitude towards death that Strawson displays, fear, is out of keeping with the anti-narrative view of life. The anti-narrativist who fears death but strives for an attitude that is rationally consistent with the rest of her view will be disturbed by this. If so, she could perhaps place her hopes in the possibility of an Epicurean transformation of attitude, which would render her view of death consistent with her anti-narrative stance. This remains at least a theoretical possibility, because fear of death is not built into the nature of the Strawsonian view of the self. This is in contrast with the aforementioned paradox, which may be intrinsic to the narrativist account, and which leaves the narrativist no option but to treat his death as playing a role that is simultaneously necessary and unfulfillable according to the dictates of a narrativist view of the self. To be fair to all parties, it is worth noting that even the Epicureans, who presented themselves as paradigms of consistent thinking about human life and death, have been accused of failing in this regard, specifically of overcoming fear of death at the cost of their professed humanity.[62] Death continues to create obstacles for those who are especially concerned to work out consistent views of the

---

[61] With respect to the paradox, Stephen Mulhall, for one, sees the need only for qualification rather than rejection or fundamental over-haul of the narrativist view, and is not in any case threatened by the implication of a paradox ('The Enigma of Individuality', op. cit. note 51)

[62] Cf. Nussbaum, op. cit. note 27, who claims their view ultimately promotes abhorrence of rather than indifference to mortality, and accuses the Epicureans of denying their humanity and wanting to live like gods.

life of a self. It may be the ultimate test case for measuring the resilience of those views. It may be the stumbling block on which all are bound to falter.[63]

[63] Thanks to Daniel Hutto, Randy Metcalfe, Stephen Mulhall, and Galen Strawson, for discussion and support. Research for this paper was undertaken during my tenure as Junior Research Associate at New College, Oxford.

Stories, Lives, and Basic Survival: A Refinement and Defense of the Narrative View

MARYA SCHECHTMAN

Everyone loves a good story. But does everyone live a good story? It has frequently been asserted by philosophers, psychologists and others interested in understanding the distinctive nature of human existence that our lives do, or should, take a narrative form. Over the last few decades there has been a steady and growing focus on this narrative approach within philosophical discussions of personal identity, resulting in a wide range of narrative identity theories. While the narrative approach has shown great promise as a tool for addressing longstanding and intractable problems of personal identity, it has also given rise to much suspicion. Opponents of this approach charge it with overstating or distorting the structure of actual lives.

I have defended a narrative account of personal identity in the past, and am still inclined to do so. I am, however, also sensitive to the complaints that have been leveled against this approach. In particular, the considerations raised by Galen Strawson in his *Against Narrativity* seem to me challenges that must be met. Strawson points to many real deficiencies in existing narrative approaches. The existence of these deficiencies does not, however, entail that the narrative approach should be rejected outright, as Strawson claims. Rather, it suggests that this approach needs to be clarified and refined. The more hyperbolic assertions must be weeded out, and claims about what work a narrative account of identity can accomplish must be made more modest and specific.

My goal here is to begin this refinement by amending and expanding my own narrative account in response to some of Strawson's challenges. When my view is clarified, it will turn out that Strawson and I disagree on far less than we may seem to at first. Most of my modified narrative view is, though still narrative, immune from the challenges Strawson raises. There is, however, still some disagreement between us, at least at the level of basic sensibility. Clarifying the view I wish to defend, and the points where its disagreements with Strawson are superficial, will be immensely valuable in finding where the real points of contention lie, and in outlining the genuine challenges for a narrative approach.

In section one I offer a brief review of some of the salient features of Strawson's reading of the narrative approach, and his objections to it. Strawson's argument is against narrative views in general. Although he describes a great many different versions of this approach, he rejects them all. With respect to many of these views I essentially accept Strawson's arguments, and wish only to defend a very particular narrative account. In section two I thus offer a rough taxonomy of narrative accounts of identity, and carve out the space within which I wish to locate my own view. In section three I begin to develop this view in more detail, offering a brief description of the narrative view as I originally presented it and the issues it was developed to address. In section four I explain how Strawson's arguments have made me rethink the details of my view. Strawson's objections help me to see that what I had put forth as a single view is really two distinct strands of insight about identity and narrative, employing somewhat different conceptions of narrative and aiming to answer somewhat different questions. In section five I show that once these strands have been distinguished each can be seen as a narrative view that avoids Strawson's objections. Finally in section six I consider where Strawson would still be likely to object to my newly described narrative view(s). The point of contention will lie in the relation between the two insights I have extracted from my original view. Strawson will, I think, be able to accept both strands so long as they are kept really separate. Implicit in my view, however, is an understanding that the two are intimately interconnected. Further development of my account would involve working out these relations, and it is here where my sensibility about these matters and Strawson's are likely to diverge.

1. A brief review of Strawson's objections

Strawson's case against the narrative approach is very intricate, and I cannot reproduce it in its entirety here. Instead I limit myself to reviewing a few of the points that will be particularly important in what follows. I begin with three distinctions Strawson draws. First, he distinguishes between the '*psychological Narrativity thesis,*' which holds as a 'straightforwardly empirical, descriptive thesis' that ordinary humans experience their lives in narrative form, and the '*ethical Narrativity thesis,*' which holds that it is a good thing to experience one's life as a narrative—'essential to a well-lived life, to true or full personhood.'[1] As Strawson points out, this distinction leaves us with four positions on narrativity depending on the value ascribed to each thesis. These range from the most strongly narrative views that endorse both the psychological and ethical theses (holding that we do narrate our lives and it is a good thing that we do) to the most strongly anti-narrative (holding that we do not (or at least do not all) narrate our lives, and that it generally is (or at least can be) a good thing not to do so). Strawson tells us that the first of these is the dominant view in the academy; while the latter is the view he wishes to defend.[2] The psychological Narrativity thesis, he argues, is false, and the ethical Narrativity thesis is not only false, but pernicious.

The next important distinction Strawson draws is between 'one's experience of oneself when one is considering oneself principally as a human being taken as a whole, and one's experience of oneself when one is considering oneself principally as an inner mental entity or 'self' of some sort.'[3] To illustrate the difference here he provides the example of Henry James claiming that he thinks of one of his earlier works as the work of 'quite another person than myself.' Obviously James is aware that he is the human being who authored this earlier work, but he experiences himself as, in Strawson's terms, another *self*. I will return to this example later. For now what is important is to be clear on Strawson's distinction between human and self. 'One of the most important ways in which people tend to think of themselves (quite independently of religious belief) is as things whose persistence conditions are not obviously or automatically the same as the persistence conditions of a human being considered as a whole.'[4] It is with respect to the *self*—the inner, mental entity whose persistence conditions can differ from those of the human—that Strawson denies the narrativity thesis. To disambiguate pronouns which might apply either to humans or to selves he adopts the convention of asterisking pronouns meant to apply to the self—e.g. I*, me*.

The final important distinction we need to understand is the distinction Strawson draws between Diachronic and Episodic self-experience. In Diachronic self-experience 'one naturally figures oneself, considered as a self, as something that was there in

---

[1] Strawson, 'Against Narrativity', *Ratio XVII*, No. 4, 2004, 428.
[2] Ibid., 429–430.
[3] Ibid., 429.
[4] Ibid., 430.

Marya Schechtman

the (further) past and will be there in the (further) future.'[5] In Episodic self-experience, by contrast, 'one does not figure oneself, considered as a self, as something that was there in the (further) past and will be there in the (further) future.'[6]

With these distinctions in hand, Strawson is able to lay out his case against both the psychological and ethical narrative theses. There are many different understandings of what a narrative is, and hence what it is to have narrative self-experience. Minimally, says Strawson, it would seem that to have a narrative self-conception one's self-understanding would have to be Diachronic—without this, he thinks, there could be no meaningful sense in which one thought of oneself in narrative terms. In addition Strawson lists three other features that might be added to a Diachronic self-experience to make it a narrative one. One is 'form-finding,' the tendency to seek patterns, unity, or coherence. In addition one might (and some narrative theorists do) require that one think of one's life-trajectory as a story in the sense of taking the form of a standard literary genera, and/or that one revise and edit the past in one's self-understanding.[7] To be a narrative view at all Strawson surmises, a view must thus require us to have Diachronic self-experience with form-finding. Different narrative views will then differ depending upon their requirements with respect to having a story-telling tendency and revising the past.

The differences between these different versions of the narrative view are not, however, deeply important to Strawson's general point. He rejects all versions of the narrative approach—both psychological and ethical—because he denies that it is either necessary or especially desirable for a person to experience himself* diachronically. There are wide variations both in the way that people do experience themselves* and in the ways of experiencing themselves* that will lead to their flourishing. Strawson offers himself as one example of an Episodic who lives a perfectly rich and fulfilling life. He tells us that he has 'absolutely no sense of [his] life as a narrative with form, or indeed as a narrative without form. Absolutely none.' And he goes on to add 'nor do I have any great or special interest in my past. Nor do I have a great deal of concern for my future.'[8] As for those who find the episodic life

[5] Ibid.
[6] Ibid.
[7] Ibid., 442–444.
[8] Ibid., 433.

'chilling, empty, and deficient,'[9] he suspects that they are simply assuming that what is true for them—they may well be Diachronic by nature or need narrative structure to make their lives meaningful—is true for everyone. Views that demand that everyone strive for a narrative self-experience, he says, 'close down important avenues of thought, impoverish our grasp of ethical possibilities, needlessly and wrongly distress those who do not fit their model, and are potentially destructive in psychotherapeutic contexts.'[10] He adds that his guess is that 'aspiration to explicit, Narrative, self-articulation ...almost always does more harm than good'[11], and that his 'own conviction is that the best lives almost never involve this kind of self-telling ...'[12] He concludes, therefore, that 'the ethical Narrativity thesis is false, and that the psychological Narrativity thesis is also false in any non-trivial sense.'[13]

2. An initial narrowing of the topic: different kinds of narrative account

Although the distinctions between different types of narrative account are of limited importance for Strawson's purposes, they will play a role in my support of the narrative approach. My defense is not a defense of narrativity generally, but rather of a specific cluster of narrative views, and I am in substantial agreement with Strawson about many versions of this approach. As a precursor to describing the details of my own view, it will thus be useful to provide a rough sketch of the landscape of narrative approaches and to signal my general position within it. There are three basic questions for a narrative theorist: (1) What counts as a life-narrative? (2) What counts as *having* a narrative? and (3) What are the practical implications of having (or failing to have) a narrative? For each of these questions there is a range of possible answers.

Consider first the question of what constitutes a life-narrative. At one end of the spectrum, a life-narrative can be conceived as nothing more than a sequential listing of the events in one's history. Here 'narrative' would be used in something like the sense in which

[9] Ibid., 431.
[10] Ibid., 429.
[11] Ibid., 447.
[12] Ibid., 437.
[13] Ibid., 438–439.

it is used in the context of police reports, or in the narrative of a medical procedure. Toward the middle of the spectrum are conceptions of a life-narrative that involve not just a sequential listing of life events, but also an account of the explanatory relations among them—a story of how the events in one's history lead to other events in that history. At the far end of the spectrum is the idea of a life-narrative as an account of a life that approximates as much as possible a story created by a gifted author and edited by a talented editor. On this understanding there should be a unifying theme and direction to a life-narrative, and extraneous material should be left out.

A similar range of possibilities can be found in answers to the question of what it is to have a narrative. At one end of this spectrum is the rather weak requirement that a person's narrative must somehow operate to impact his current experience. According to this understanding a person's narrative need not be in any way accessible to consciousness in order for her to be said to have a self-narrative. In the middle range, having a narrative would require that a person be able, at least sometimes, to become conscious of her narrative and make it explicit. At the extreme end of the spectrum would be the view that in order to have a narrative in the relevant sense a person must actively and consciously undertake to understand and live her life in narrative form.

Finally there is a similar spectrum of answers concerning the implications of having a self-narrative. Here possible answers range from very basic benefits of a narrative self-conception to much higher-order benefits. At the basic end of the spectrum is the claim that having a narrative is necessary to function at all. In the middle is the claim that having a self-narrative is necessary for engaging in certain sorts of complex, person-specific activities—that it is necessary, for instance, for autonomy, moral agency, prudential reasoning or other kinds of higher-order capacities. At the far end is the claim that a narrative self-conception is essential to leading a good or meaningful life.

In theory, a narrative view could combine claims anywhere along these three spectra, but combinations of answers that fall at roughly the same point along the relevant continua are the most natural. To a first approximation, we can thus think of a range of narrative views moving from what I will call the 'weak narrative views' through the 'middle-range narrative views' to the 'strong narrative views.' The weak narrative views hold that someone must be able to organize her life according to a fundamental implicit knowledge of the events in her history, or she will not be able to function well at even the most basic level. More concretely, it is the idea that someone with severe cognitive deficits of the sort caused by Korsakoff syndrome or advanced dementia will need some help to get by. The middle-range views will say that someone needs a certain understanding of how the events in her history hang together, an understanding that is mostly implicit but that she can access locally where appropriate, if she is to be able to engage in person-specific activities on which we place great importance. The strong narrative views say that a person must actively and consciously undertake to live and understand her life as a story in the strong sense—with a unified theme and little or no extraneous material—if that life is to be meaningful.

Strawson, I take it, would find the weak narrative views trivial, the middle-range views false, and the strong views dangerous. About the weak and strong views, I am mainly in agreement with him. I am not certain that I think weak narrative views are entirely trivial, but this is not an important point of contention. About the fact that some mechanism for keeping track of and deploying information about one's history is essential to effective functioning there is little disagreement. Likewise, I do not have as clearly developed views as Strawson does on the evils of strong narrative views. I am largely convinced, however, by his discussion of the ways in which the requirements of such views can be repressive, thwarting spontaneity and self-understanding and causing great unhappiness for some individuals. At the very least I agree that this view in its strongest form is false. I see no reason to believe that one must see one's life as a 'quest' or as having an 'overall ethical character' or a grand *telos* or unifying theme to be fully a person. I do not think that all, or even most, people have such a clear sense of the structure or direction of their lives, and I do not think that having one is necessary for life to be meaningful, good, or worth living.

I am therefore happy to concede to Strawson, and to critics of the narrative account more generally, that the strong views are too strong. I think the weak views are true, and interesting, but I am willing to allow that some might find it a stretch to call such views *narrative* views. In any event they do not represent the form of narrative view I will defend. The narrative view I am interested in developing thus lies in the middle ranges. I turn now to a description of that view.

Marya Schechtman

3. The Narrative Self-Constitution View and its successors

I call the narrative view I endorse the 'narrative self-constitution view.'[14] Its most basic claim is that we constitute ourselves as persons by forming a narrative self-conception according to which we experience and organize our lives. This self-conception and its operations are largely implicit and automatic. As we are socialized into human culture, we are taught to operate with a background conception of ourselves as continuing individuals, leading the lives of persons. What this means more specifically is that we experience the present in the context of a larger life-narrative. In order to have a narrative self-conception in the relevant sense, the experienced past and anticipated future must condition the character and significance of present experiences and actions. When I have a self-constituting narrative, what happens to me is not interpreted as an isolated incident, but as part of an ongoing story.

There are, of course, a great many ways in which the larger narrative context can impact and condition experience. This impact can be seen, for instance, in the difference between the way someone experiences a period of intensely hard work when she knows that once the project is off her desk her promotion is assured and she can leave on vacation, and the way she experiences it if it is part of a life of grindingly difficult labor with no foreseeable relief. It is also seen in the differences between what someone experiences and does walking up to the door of *his* house rather than to the door of *a* house. Or of walking up to the door of his *new* house rather than to the door of the house he has lived in for many years; or to the door of a house in which his loving family waits rather than to the door of an empty house after a bitter breakup—even if it is the same house and the same door in each case. These are, of course, just a few examples of how the present can be understood through the lens of a narrative self-conception, but it should be sufficient to provide the general idea.

The narrative self-constitution view says that in developing and operating with such a narrative one constitutes one's identity as a person, and that the actions and experiences included in someone's narrative are, for that reason, her own actions and experiences. This view does, however, place two constraints on an identity-constituting narrative. In order to successfully constitute oneself as a person one's narrative self-conception must meet what I call the

---

[14] I develop this view in M. Schechtman, *The Constitution of Selves* (Ithaca: Cornell University Press, 1996), 93–135.

'reality constraint' and the 'articulation constraint.' The reality constraint requires that a person's narrative conform to what we are generally accepted to know about the basic character of reality and about the nature of persons. A narrative must, for instance, respect the fact that, at least given what we know now, physical beings cannot be in two places at one time, that humans do not typically live much more than one hundred years, and similar facts.

The articulation constraint requires that a person be able to articulate her narrative locally when appropriate, or at least to recognize the legitimacy of certain questions. Basically this constraint requires that confronted with questions like 'how did you come to be in this place?' or 'why did you choose that course of action?' or 'what is your educational background and how has it helped you in your current job?' or 'where do you think you'll go next?' a person has something to say. She does not need to have a clearly thought-out plan or an elaborate explanation. Sometimes, even often, the answer to such questions may be 'because I felt like it' or 'it seemed like a good idea at the time, though I can't recall why now.' The point is that one should not simply be at a loss, or fail to understand the sense of such questions. The requirement here is thus not that one must have a perfectly worked-out and explicit account of why everything in her life is as it is, but rather that she must recognize a certain kind of explanatory obligation, and be able to meet it for the most part.

The narrative self-constitution view sits in the middle of the range of possible answers to each of the three questions described above, and hence is a middle-range view. The conception of narrative it employs is more than a mere chronology of events in one's history, but there is no requirement that an identity-constituting narrative have a unifying theme, or represent a quest or have a well-defined plot arc that fits a distinct literary genera. The articulation constraint demands that self-narration be more than the subpersonal, background operation of knowledge about one's past or projections of one's future, but constructing a self-narrative is also not conceived as something that must be undertaken as a conscious and active project. This view also sits in the middle range of the spectrum with respect to the question of the implications of having or not having a narrative. It focuses on the way in which possessing a self-constituting narrative supports person-specific capacities. To understand more fully what the view has to say on this issue, and to set up some of the discussion of the next few sections, it will be helpful to provide a bit of background about the context in which the narrative self-constitution view is developed.

Marya Schechtman

This view is, in the first instance, meant to address difficulties encountered in the discussion of philosophical problems about the persistence conditions for persons. For many decades the idea that the identity and persistence of persons should be defined in psychological rather than biological terms has been, if not *the* dominant view on these matters, at least among the most dominant. The main arguments for this position rest on the observation that facts about personal identity carry immense significance, and the claim that this practical significance attaches to psychological rather than biological continuity. I identify four features of personhood in particular that are frequently invoked to support psychological theories of identity. They are: moral responsibility (a person is rightly held responsible for only her own actions), prudential concern (there is a particular kind of concern that we have for only our own future states), compensation (justice demands that the person who makes a sacrifice and the person receiving compensation be the same person), and survival (there is a basic interest a person has in her own survival).

Arguments for psychological accounts of identity typically take the form of thought experiments in which psychological and biological continuation diverge (replication, teleportation, brain transplants and the like). It is assumed that in considering these cases we will judge that the four features follow the psychological rather than the biological life. If, for instance, Mr. Smith's brain, with all of Mr. Smith's memories, beliefs, desires, values and affections, were transplanted into Mr. Jones' body (and Mr. Jones' brain thrown away), it is assumed that the resulting person would be rightly held accountable for Mr. Smith's and not Mr. Jones' prior actions; that he would be rightly compensated for Mr. Smith's labors; that Mr. Smith should take a prudential interest in the well-being of the resulting person but Mr. Jones need not; and that Mr. Smith, but not Mr. Jones, would survive in the relevant sense.

A satisfying psychological account should thus define identity in such a way that the relation that constitutes identity supports the four features. My basic argument for the narrative self-constitution view rests on the claim that standard psychological accounts of identity cannot do so, but my narrative account can. To see the gist of the argument for this claim, it will help to have just a bit more of the history of the psychological approach to personal identity before us. Although it is a bit of a digression, this history will also be useful in the analysis that follows, so it is worth spending a few moments on it.

At the core of the psychological account is a distinction between persons and human beings closely related to Strawson's distinction between *selves* and human beings. The psychological theorist's *person,* like Strawson's *self,* is a psychological entity with persistence conditions distinct from those of human beings. One of the main tasks of the psychological theorist is thus to describe in more detail the psychological continuity that constitutes the persistence of a person. John Locke, considered by many to be the originator of the modern psychological account of identity, defines this continuity in terms of the continuation of *consciousness.* What makes a person at one time the same person as someone at another time is that they have the same consciousness. Locke's argument for this view is essentially the one described above. He offers hypothetical cases and shows that the four features of personhood—moral responsibility, prudential concern, compensation, and survival—follow consciousness rather than either the body or the soul (assuming that this latter can, as seems logically possible, separate from a particular consciousness).[15]

While there is something very intuitively appealing about this idea, it is also not immediately evident just what continuity of consciousness consists in. Locke makes it clear that the sort of continuity of consciousness he is imagining can survive interruption.[16] So some account must be given of how consciousness can be unified across hiatuses of this sort to allow for the continuity of a single psychological entity, viz., a single person, who survives sleep and short periods of forgetfulness. The standard reading of Locke is that he proposes memory as the force which unifies consciousness across such breaks, and hence holds a view where memory connections between present and past unify diachronic consciousness into a single person. It becomes clear quite quickly however that a simple memory theory—where some past action or

---

[15]   J. Locke, *An Essay Concerning Human Understanding*, P. H. Nidditch (ed.) (Oxford: Clarendon Press, 1975), 338–348.

[16]   In arguing that a single consciousness does not always imply a single soul he says '... this consciousness, being interrupted always by forgetfulness, there being no moment of our Lives wherein we have the whole train of all our past Actions before our Eyes in one view [we cannot be assured that the soul remembering an experience is the same soul that had the experience]'(Locke, *Essay Concerning Human Understanding*, 336). These interruptions are not, however, taken to undermine sameness of consciousness. As I shall discuss below, Strawson does not believe that the ontological/metaphysical self can survive such interruptions of consciousness.

experience is mine just because I remember it from a first-person perspective—is untenable for many reasons. There is no clear way to make a non-circular distinction between genuine, identity-creating memories and delusional pseudomemories, and the memory theory threatens to make identity intransitive, to name just a few difficulties.

Neo-Lockean psychological continuity theorists of the past five decades or so have tried to overcome the deficiencies of the memory theory while retaining the basic insight that personal identity consists in the continuity of consciousness. They therefore amend and develop the standard memory theory in a variety of ways. To memory connections they add other psychological connections, such as those between intentions and actions, or the different temporal stages of persisting beliefs, values and desires. In addition, they often require that these connections have some specific cause, usually the continued functioning of the same brain. In the end, the standard psychological continuity theory offers a view where the continuity of consciousness is defined roughly in terms of similarity between contents of consciousness from moment to moment that is appropriately caused.

While this development of Locke's view does solve many of the original problems, it has difficulties of its own. In particular, the picture of personal continuity spelled out in terms of similarity of psychological contents does not seem to yield a deep enough connection between experience at different times to support the four features. It is not because I am *like* someone who took an action or worked some number of hours that I am responsible for that action or entitled to compensation; it is because the experiencing subject suffering the consequences (or enjoying the rewards) is the *same* subject who took the relevant action. It is not because someone in the future will be *like* me that I care in a particular way about her experiences, but because I expect to experience them myself. And survival is not guaranteed by someone quite *like* me having experience in the future; *I* must have experience. The unity of consciousness that sounded so plausible as an account of personal identity in Locke's view is a deep, phenomenological relation between different portions of a life, and the relation psychological continuity theorists offer does not seem deep enough to provide the connection we seek.

This is where the narrative self-constitution view comes in. The connections it provides, I argue, can account for the four features and their role in our lives in a way that ordinary psychological accounts cannot. At its strongest, Locke's view does not read as a simple memory theory. Rather, he says, we make past actions and experiences ours by *appropriating* them. In my reading of Locke, this requires not just remembering those actions and experiences in the first person, but being affected by them in the way the narrative self-constitution view requires. There must be not only cognitive but affective and practical relations to an action or experience remote in time if it is to be appropriated. In other words, it must be woven into one's narrative.

This detour brings us back to the narrative self-constitution view's stance on the third of the questions a narrative account must answer. The implications of having a narrative, on this view, are that it provides the phenomenological unity of consciousness over time that constitutes personal survival and generates person-specific capacities such as moral agency, the ability to engage in prudential reasoning and in relations of compensation.

4. Revising the Narrative Self-Constitution View

Strawson's objections, at least in his estimation, apply to the narrative self-constitution view. In describing himself as an Episodic he denies having the kind of appropriative connections to his past and future that I say are required for an identity-constituting self-narrative. He says, you will recall, that he does not have any 'great or special' interest in his past or 'a great deal of concern for [his] future.'[17] Expanding on this later he says, 'I'm well aware that my past is mine in so far as I am a human being, and I fully accept that there is a sense in which it has special relevance to me* now. At the same time I have no sense that I* was there in the past, and think it is obvious that I* was not there, as a matter of metaphysical fact.'[18] He makes it clear that being Episodic does not keep him from being responsible to either his past or future; nor does it interfere with his capacity for loyalty, friendship or ethical behavior.[19] In other words, Strawson reports that he possesses the capacities connected to the four features without conceiving of his life as a narrative. This report is completely plausible, and I do not doubt it for a moment. On the surface, however, this seems to imply that a self-narrative is not necessary to provide a basis for the four

---

[17] Strawson, 'Against Narrativity' op. cit. p. 433.
[18] Ibid., 434.
[19] Ibid., 450.

features, and this in turn implies that the central claim of the narrative self-constitution view is false.

Despite appearances, however, I think that the basic idea behind my view is actually compatible with everything Strawson reports about Episodic existence. There are two ways in which I could respond to Strawson's analysis on behalf of the narrative self-constitution view. One is to say that he has misunderstood what a narrative is on this view. Strawson acknowledges quite a strong relation among the temporal parts of his human life taken as a whole. He recognizes that he* has a special relation to other parts of the life of Galen Strawson, that these are of special emotional significance, and that he has certain responsibilities with respect to them. All that he lacks is an identification of those other parts of Strawson's life as him*. The relations within his human existence, however, contain much of what is involved in having a self-narrative of the sort I have been describing.

A second possibility focuses not on issues concerning the strength of the required narrative, but rather on its duration. Much of Strawson's argument against the narrative view is based on the fact that he does not experience his entire human life in narrative terms—that there are different *selves* within his human existence. Since the narrative self-constitution view is devised as a means of expressing the intuitions behind the psychological approach to identity, however, it does not and should not insist that the duration of an identity-constituting self-narrative must be the same as the duration of a human life. *Persons*, after all, are distinguished from human beings on this view; that is its main impetus. The fact that Strawson does not view his entire human life as a narrative thus does not serve as an objection to the narrative view if each self* is constituted by a narrative internal to it (as I shall suggest in a moment they are).

Both of these responses seem to me promising, and both seem legitimate expressions of the basic ideas behind the narrative self-constitution view. The problem is that they are in some tension with one another. The first response implies that a self-narrative should, under ordinary circumstances, correspond approximately to the chronology of a single human life, and also that a self-narrative does not require that one identify in any deep way with all of the phases of one's life-narrative. The second response, on the other hand, seems to leave it open that a very ordinary form of self-narration would involve narratively created selves of much shorter duration than a human life, and that strong identification with other phases of the narrative self *is* required for identity-constituting self-narration.

I have come to believe that this tension between the two possible responses to Strawson's objections represents a pre-existing tension in the narrative self-constitution view. There are really two different questions of identity at issue in this view, and each is answered with a slightly different narrative theory. This distinction is obscured in the original view, and the pressure placed on the view by Strawson's challenge reveals this ambiguity. Perhaps the clearest way to get at the basic idea here is to draw a distinction between persons and selves. In discussing the history of the psychological approach I said that the 'persons' that interest philosophers of personal identity are basically the same as Strawson's 'selves.' While this is true to a rough approximation, I am increasingly convinced that the concept of person as used by psychological theorists mixes together two components. One is Strawson's notion of the self; the other is a practical notion that is more intimately connected to social context. On the one hand a person is conceived as the subject of experiences, the 'I' that we experience as a psychological entity with persistence conditions distinct from human beings. On the other hand, a person is conceived as the bearer of certain complex social capacities that carry important practical implications. A person is a moral agent who can be held responsible for her actions, a reasoning creature who can be held to be irrational when she acts against her interests, and a creature capable of a range of complex relationships with other persons.

It is not immediately obvious that the self and the person must be coextensive. Locke thinks that they are. He sees the kind of continuity of experiencing subject that defines the persistence of the self as the precondition for the capacities that make someone a person[20], and Lynne Rudder Baker makes a similar claim.[21] The psychological tradition more broadly tends to use 'person' and 'self' more or less interchangeably, and in the original statement of my narrative self-constituition view I do the same. What the tension between my two proposed responses to Strawson's objections suggests, however, is that the connection between these two concepts may be more complicated than Locke suggests and psychological theorists assume. An account of the persistence

[20]   Locke, op. cit. note 16, 338–348.
[21]   See, for instance, L. Rudder Baker, *Persons and Bodies: a Constitution View* (Cambridge: Cambridge University Press, 2000), 147.

conditions for a self and an account of the persistence conditions for a person are not automatically the same. Although both may be distinguished from human beings, they should also be distinguished from each other. Within the narrative self-constitution view is a narrative account of selves and a narrative account of persons, and the question of how strong a narrative is required or how long it must endure will depend, at least to some extent, on which is receiving emphasis. As I will explain later, I think there are important connections between person and self that must be described in a complete account of our identity. To get to the point where such description is possible, however, we need first to look at what the narrative self-constitution view has to say about each, individually.

The tension between the two possible lines of response to Strawson can thus be resolved by distinguishing between a narrative account of persons and a narrative account of selves. The narrative account of *persons* (PN) says that in order to constitute oneself as a person—a being capable of the sorts of interpersonal interactions described above—one must recognize oneself as continuing, see past actions and experiences as having implications for one's current rights and responsibilities, and recognize a future that will be impacted by the past and present. One need not deeply identify with past or future actions and experiences, care about them, or take an interest in them, but one does need to recognize them as relevant to one's options in certain fundamental ways. I need not identify with the self who decided to buy the sports car, but if I signed the loan I need to recognize that it is mine to pay, and that my credit will be impacted if I do not. The strength of a person-constituting narrative is thus the weaker of the two possibilities described above, but the duration is the longer.

What one considers one's own actions and experiences in this weaker sense will have to correspond for the most part to what is in one's human history. The reason for this is simple. Since this kind of self-narrative is supposed to constitute one as fit for certain sorts of social interactions, one's own conception of who one is (in this sense) will need to mostly jibe with others' assessments of who one is. Otherwise the person-defining interactions will be impossible. Since we mostly reidentify each other by reidentifying human bodies, the person that one is will have to be closely connected to the human that one is. The narrative self-constitution view does allow for exceptions to this rule, but they will be, at least in our world, highly unusual.

The narrative account of *selves* (SN) says that one's continuation as a self is constituted by the stronger kind of narrative described above. For an action or experience to belong to my*self* I do need to identify with it or care about or take an interest in it. Temporally remote actions and experiences that are appropriated into one's *self* narrative must impact the present in a more fundamental sense than just constraining options or having caused one's current situation and outlook. These events must condition the quality of present experience in the strongest sense, unifying consciousness over time through affective connections and identification. To include these actions and experiences in my narrative I will need to have what I have elsewhere called 'empathic access' to them.[22] In *this* sense of narrative, actions and experiences from which I am alienated, or in which I have none of the interest that I have in my current life, are not part of my narrative.

The narrative self-constitution view can thus be separated into two distinct claims. First is the claim that in order to constitute oneself as a *person*—someone with the capacity for moral responsibility, prudential interest, relations of compensation and related person-specific activities—one must implicitly organize one's experience according to a narrative that recognizes past and future experiences as one's own in the sense that one sees the past as having implications for one's present situation and choices, and the present as having similar implications for the future. Second is the claim that in order to constitute oneself as a *self*, one must have a narrative in which one experiences the past and future as one's own in the strong sense of experiencing the present as part of the whole narrative.

5. Strawson's objections and the Revised Narrative Self-Constitution View

Many of Strawson's objections to the narrative self-constitution view apply only because of the conflation of the account of persons and the account of selves in the original statement of that view. Placing emphasis on the account of persons can make the narrative connections this view requires sound too strong, while placing emphasis on the account of selves can make the duration of narrative it requires sound too long. When these two strands of the

[22]   M. Schechtman, 'Empathic Access: The Missing Ingredient in Personal Persistence', *Philosophical Explorations* 2, 2001, 94–110.

account are distinguished, however, each builds in a context that makes it, for the most part, compatible with Strawson's reports of the nature of Episodic existence, and so immune from his main objections.

Consider first the narrative account of the persistence of persons described above (PN), which holds that in order to be capable of engaging in person-specific activities one needs to recognize past and future actions as one's own in the sense of acknowledging some level of responsibility for and to them. Strawson's description of his own Episodic existence includes exactly this kind of relation to his own human past and future, and so the existence of Episodics poses no obvious counterexample to this view. Nonetheless, I can imagine two ways in which an anti-narrative challenge in the spirit of Strawson's might be raised against PN. First, it might be argued that the sense of 'narrative' involved is strained or trivial. If all that is required to have a *narrative* self-conception is to recognize one's human history as one's own and accept certain implications of that fact, it might be argued, then this narrative view doesn't say anything very startling. Strawson rejects the narrative view in any 'non-trivial' version. He describes triviality in this context as follows: 'if someone says, as some do, that making coffee is a narrative that involves Narrativity, because you have to think ahead, do things in the right order, and so on, and that everyday life involves many such narratives, then I take it the claim is trivial'[23]. If the kind of narrative that constitutes the identity of a person on my view is relevantly like a coffee-making narrative Strawson will reject it on the grounds of triviality.

I would argue, however, that there really are significant differences between the narrative of coffee making and a person-constituting narrative as I have defined it, because a person-constituting narrative is genuinely a kind of story we tell ourselves about ourselves, and not just sequence of events. It is not a story that needs to build to a climax and provide a satisfying resolution of the loose ends; nor does it need to have a moral or a theme. But it is an explanatory account of how actions and events lead to other actions and events, how we come to be in the position we are in and where that position is likely to lead us. Moreover, my narrative view of persons involves the substantive claim that having this kind of story is necessary to engage in certain kinds of distinctive activities and interactions. This part of the view is not

---

[23] Strawson 'Against Narrativity' op. cit. p. 438–439.

trivial in the way that the claim that one must do things in the proper order to make coffee is. In the case of person-constituting narratives new capacities are claimed to arise as the result of self-narration.

In light of this analysis, however, the critic of PN, the person-narrative view, might charge that in fact the kind of self-narrative required is not necessary for the person-specific capacities. Strawson, after all, makes a point of insisting that the Episodic can be capable of all of the relevant person-specific activities. 'A gift for friendship,' he says, 'does not require any ability to recall past shared experiences in detail, nor any tendency to value them. It is shown in how one is in the present.'[24] 'Diachronicity,' he adds, 'is not a necessary condition of a properly moral existence, nor of a proper sense of responsibility.'[25] But Strawson's remarks in this regard only deny the need for a stronger sense of narrative, which the separation between the PN and the self-narrative view (SN) allows me to agree is not required for these capacities. A good friend need not have any interest in reminiscing or spending the evening with a stack of old photos. Still, someone who did not take the fact of a lengthy history together as in any way relevant to settling the question of whether he should come to your aid when he does not feel like doing so right at the moment of your need, would not seem a terribly gifted friend. Someone might indeed be a friendly person and generally willing to come to the aid of the people in her life. While this is admirable, it is not the same as being a true and loyal friend to a particular person or set of people. A similar point applies to Strawson's claims about moral responsibility. I agree it is possible to have a sense of responsibility with no clear consciousness of one's entire life unfolding according to a theme. It is considerably less plausible, however, that one could act responsibly without the sense that present options were constrained by past choices and that present choices have implications for the future. PN thus seems compatible with all of Strawson's observations about Episodic life, and hence avoids his objections to the narrative approach.

The relation of Strawson's position to the narrative view of *self* offered above is somewhat more complicated. It depends upon exactly how Strawson is thinking about the episodes that make up an Episodic life. Throughout his work on the self, Strawson distinguishes between the metaphysical/ontological question of

---

[24] Strawson, op. cit. note 1, 450.
[25] Ibid.

what actually constitutes a single self, and the phenomenological question of what we experience as self. The self, he argues, is a subject of experience, and the answer to the metaphysical/ ontological question is that a self is the subject of a hiatus-free stretch of consciousness. Given our best psychological theory, this means that a single self in fact lasts no more than three seconds. But there is also a phenomenological sense of self, the length of time one* perceives oneself* as enduring.

Since the argument of *Against Narrativity* is about how we do and should experience ourselves, it must be the phenomenological notion of self that is relevant here. Our question, then, becomes the definition and duration of the phenomenological notion of self for Strawson. There seem to me two possibilities. Sometimes he seems to imply that the self lasts as long as a stretch of consciousness that is *experienced as* hiatus-free –for instance when he suggests half an hour as a possible candidate for the typical duration of experience of self.[26] More often, however, it seems that the limits of the phenomenological sense of self are set by the extent to which one identifies with temporally removed experiences and takes them to be strongly one's own. This is suggested by the claim that how long an episodic's experience of self endures will depend upon 'what one is thinking about.'[27] It is also suggested by the fact that 'there are certain things in the future—such as my death—and equally certain things in the past—such as embarrassment that I can experience—as involving Me*.[28] And that 'there is no reason why some Episodics may not sometimes apprehend some of their past dubious actions as involving their Me*, and accordingly feel remorse or contrition.'[29] Here it seems that there can be interruptions of the flow of consciousness that do not undermine the unity of the phenomenological Me*. It is to be expected that there were, for instance, intervals of sleep between the past embarrassing experience and the present experience of embarrassment, and between the present fear of death and death itself.

One understanding of the phenomenological self, then, is that it is defined in very much the same way the self is defined on my narrative view. This understanding seems, moreover, more coherent

---

[26]   G. Strawson, 'The Self and the SESMET', *Journal of Consciousness Studies* 6, No.4, 1999, 111.

[27]   Ibid.; See also G. Strawson, 'The Self', *Journal of Consciousness Studies* 4, No. 5/6, 1997, 419–421.

[28]   Strawson, op. cit. note 26, 111.

[29]   Ibid.

overall with Strawson's discussion of the self in *Against Narrativity*. Consider the example he gives to illustrate the distinction between the self and the human being—Henry James claiming that one of his past works seems to him to have been written by someone else. Clearly what is expressed here is a certain feeling of affective and intellectual distance from the earlier author, not simply an interruption of consciousness. We would not expect James, hard at work on his latest novel, to say the same thing about the pages he wrote the day before or before lunch. What is at issue here is not a break in the stream of consciousness, but rather a sense of alienation or indifference with respect to part of one's human past. So it seems that the sense of self described by Strawson here is precisely about a phenomenolgical experience of a unity of self across breaks in the stream of consciousness—just the sort of thing Locke was seeking to define. As Strawson describes it, this unity seems to be found in the subject's strong identification with past and future phases of his life, and this is precisely what SN requires. Here, too, there seems to be ultimate compatibility between Strawson's description of Episodic psychology and the narrative view I propose.

When the narrative view of person and the narrative view of self are distinguished from one another and the sense of narrative relevant to each carefully specified, each is compatible with what Strawson describes of the Episodic lifestyle, and his challenges no longer apply. This does not mean, however, that there is no space for disagreement, as we will see in the next and final section.

6. Remaining disagreements

While Strawson might be able to accept my narrative view of the person and my narrative view of the self when each is taken individually, there is likely to be somewhat less agreement when we consider the connection between these two strands of the newly bifurcated narrative self-constitution. In the original statement of the view, the difference in narrative strength that turns into the difference between a person-narrative and a self-narrative was described in terms of degrees of attribution. A person, I noted, will relate to different elements of her narrative in different ways. She will identify more strongly with some than with others, and feel more of an affective connection to them. Those narrative elements that a person more strongly appropriates, I said, are more fully or completely her own than those from which she is more distanced.

Marya Schechtman

In addition, I strongly implied that it is desirable for a person to be as strongly identified as possible with the whole of her narrative, a tightly woven self-narrative making for a stronger person than a weaker one.

Something of this sentiment remains in my revised theory. Here it turns into the idea that there are advantages to making one's self-narrative coincide as far as possible with one's person-narrative. Person-narratives, we have seen, need to be of fairly long duration if they are to do the work of allowing us to engage in the kinds of complex practical and social activities definitive of personhood. Self-narratives, on the other hand, can be quite short and still produce a phenomenological subject; there can, as Strawson points out, be a succession of many different self-narratives within the life of a single person. I maintain, however, that we can influence the duration of our self-narratives and that there are reasons to try to do so in a way that makes the duration of the self and of the person largely coincide. I do not insist that it is *always* desirable to have an extended self-narrative. There may be circumstances in which it is better for a life to include radical affective breaks within it. Sometimes it can be a good idea to put the past behind us or the future out of play. I do maintain, however, that there are strong *prima facie* advantages to extending the self-narrative that apply independent of personal style.

First let me give an idea of what I mean when I say that we can influence the duration of our self-narrative, focusing in particular on the ways in which such a narrative can be extended. What I have in mind here are the familiar ways in which people seek to re-evoke emotions and interests that no longer occur spontaneously. We look at photographs, go to reunions, take second honeymoons, maintain holiday traditions, listen to oldies stations, re-read our favorite novels, and in various other ways stock up on the madeleines and tea that aid in recovering lost time. These attempts do not always work of course—sometimes there is no way to get a feeling back no matter what one does—and they do not work in the same way for all people—some of us are more susceptible to these cues than others. I am committed, however, to the view that there is value in seeking to maintain affective connection to as much of our (person) lives as we can. This does not mean that we must consciously undertake a project of self-recovery, or that people who keep scrapbooks and listen to nostalgia radio have better lives than those who just get on with the business of enjoying the present. It also does not mean (as I shall explain in a moment) that those who are less successful at extending their narratives necessarily have worse lives. It does mean, however, that lives that encourage affective and emotional identification with the past and future instead of resting with mere cognitive awareness of what one did and projections of what one might do are often made richer and smoother through this effort. This is something I suspect Strawson would vehemently deny.

I cannot here offer arguments for my claim that it is desirable to try to bring person and self into coincidence, but let me offer two of the guiding ideas behind it. The first has to do with the practical significance of personal identity. The situation of a self depends a great deal on its situation in the life of a person. Rights, responsibilities, options and obligations stem from one's past as a person, and one has particular kinds of responsibilities to one's future as a person. If the connection of the self to its personal past and future is merely a cold acknowledgement of being part of the same person-life, with all the rights and privileges that implies, this seems a recipe for alienation. It is like acknowledging that one's children are one's children, and one is therefore obligated to do certain things for them, but feeling no affection for them or interest in their well-being. The force of this consideration as it stands is admittedly somewhat questionable. It is always open to an Episodic to simply claim that he feels no such alienation, and it does not distress him at all to have obligations and responsibilities that connect to motives and experiences with which he cannot identify—just as someone might say that it does not distress him at all to parent children to whom he has no emotional attachment. If what is at issue is an empirical claim about what makes people unhappy the Episodic's introspective report will surely carry the day. To develop my idea into an argument for the desirability of making person and self coextensive, then, it will be necessary to develop a notion of alienation that is not strictly psychological in the way an introspective report could reveal.

The second consideration in favor of an extended self is linked to the idea that selves are not as tidy and distinct as Strawson would imply. In 'The Self' he designates his view of metaphysical/ontological self the 'Pearl view, because it suggests that many mental selves exist, one at a time, and one after another, like pearls on a string, in the case of something like a human being.'[30] It is not entirely clear whether Strawson would urge a similar view of the phenomenological self, but it is hard to make such a picture stand up. Phenomenological selves are more fluid and amorphous than metaphysical selves as Strawson defines them. They can expand

---

[30] Strawson, op. cit. note 27.

and shrink, their duration depending on our state of health, our interests, and 'what we are thinking about.'[31] What is part of the phenomenological self can shift, the same element being included at one time and not at another. Phenomenological selves are not as neatly successive as pearls on a string, or not usually; we do not often get past one and on to the next, certain that the first is over and done. Instead we find frequently that feelings and identifications we thought long gone reemerge to our great surprise.

This means that it is not always obvious what is really no longer part of the self and what is, in some respect at least, a part of the self that is lying dormant or unexpressed. Selves can plausibly be thought to contain not only the motivations and identifications I am experiencing right now, but those that sit just below the surface, waiting to be reignited by the right context. If this is so, there seems a real value in giving those aspects of the self a chance to flourish and find expression. This also explains the claim I made a bit earlier, that despite the value of encouraging the extension of the self, those in whom the encouragement bears no fruit are not necessarily worse off. If one actively endeavors to reconnect with affect and emotion from time past and cannot do so, that may be evidence that those features are not latent parts of the self but have become truly external. In that case the advantage of giving them expression does not apply, and what advantage there is attaches to the considerations offered above about the practical implications of personal identity. Nonetheless, there is still a reason to encourage these connections since this is the way we discover what is still part of the self.

Both of these considerations need much more clarification and development before they constitute anything like arguments for the desirability of making one's personal narrative and one's self-narrative co-extensive. What I have done here is mostly just express a conviction and describe a plan for the development of the revised narrative self-constitution view. There is much work to be done in producing a satisfying narrative account of our identities. Strawson's challenges have, however, shown what parameters such a view would have to have, and where the real disagreements with anti-narrative theorists lie.

---

[31] See note 25.

Self and Other: The Limits of Narrative Understanding

DAN ZAHAVI

If the self—as a popular view has it—is a narrative construction, if it arises out of discursive practices, it is reasonable to assume that the best possible avenue to self-understanding will be provided by those very narratives. If I want to know what it means to be a self, I should look closely at the stories that I and others tell about myself, since these stories constitute who I am. In the following I wish to question this train of thought. I will argue that we need to operate with a more primitive and fundamental notion of self; a notion of self that cannot be captured in terms of narrative structures. In a parallel move, I will argue that there is a crucial dimension of what it means to be other that is equally missed by the narrative approach. I will consequently defend the view that there are limits to the kind of understanding of self and others that narratives can provide.

1. The narrative account of self

Let me start out by presenting the narrative account of the self in some detail. A central starting point is the assumption that we need to distinguish between merely being conscious or sentient, and being a self. The requirements that must be met in order to qualify for the latter are higher. More precisely, being a self is an achievement rather than a given. How is selfhood achieved? In and through narrative self-interpretation. Some creatures weave stories of their lives, they organize their experiences and actions according to narrative structures thereby situating them in the context of a unifying story, and this is what constitutes them as selves. This is why being a self is quite different from being slim, 38-years old or black-haired. Who I am is not something given, but something evolving, something that is realized through my projects. There is no such thing as who (in contrast to what) I am independently of how I understand and interpret myself. To put it differently, no account of who one is can afford to ignore the issue of one's self-interpretation, since the former is (at least partially) consti- tuted by the latter.

Dan Zahavi

It is important to understand that the emphasis on narratives is not merely to be understood as an epistemological thesis. I attain insight into who I am by situating my character traits, the values I endorse, the goals I pursue, etc. within a life story that traces their origin and development; a life story that tells where I am coming from and where I am heading. In a similar manner, I get to know who you are by learning your life story. But the reason why narratives constitute a privileged way to obtain knowledge about the self is precisely because they constitute it. As Bruner puts it, 'A self is probably the most impressive work of art we ever produce, surely the most intricate'.[1] Thus, narratives do not merely capture aspects of an already existing self, since there is no such thing as a pre-existing self, one that just awaits being portrayed in words. To believe in such a pre-linguistic given is quite literally to have been misled by stories.

When it is being claimed that the self is a product of a narratively structured life, that it is constructed in and through narration, the claim is obviously not that selfhood requires the actual composition of an autobiography. Autobiographies are merely the literary expressions of the kind of narrative self-interpretation that we continuously engage in. We consequently need to distinguish the kind of narratives that characterize our ongoing lives from consciously worked-up narratives. For my self-interpretation to count as narrative is simply, according to Schechtman, for me to understand the different life episodes in terms of their place in an unfolding story.[2] It is a question of organizing my experiences and actions in a way that presupposes an implicit understanding of me as an evolving protagonist.

The narrative account is quite explicit in emphasizing both the *temporal* and *social dimension* of selfhood. As Ricoeur has argued, the time of human existence is neither the subjective time of consciousness nor the objective time of the cosmos. Rather, human time bridges the gap between phenomenological and cosmological time. Human time is the time of our life stories; a time structured and articulated by the symbolic mediations of narratives.[3] Events and experiences that occur at different times are united by being

---

[1]   J. Bruner, *Making Stories: Law, Literature, Life* (Cambridge, MA: Harvard University Press, 2002), 14.

[2]   M. Schechtman, *The Constitution of Selves* (Ithaca: Cornell University Press, 1996), 97.

[3]   P. Ricoeur, *Temps et Récit III: Le Temps Raconté* (Paris: Éditions du Seuil 1985), 439.

incorporated into a single narrative. Whether or not a particular action, experience or characteristic counts as mine is a question of whether or not it is included in my self-narrative.[4] In fact, according to MacIntyre, the unity of the self 'resides in the unity of a narrative which links birth to life to death as narrative beginning to middle to end'[5]; or as Husserl—a thinker not customarily associated with the narrative approach—puts it, 'The ego constitutes itself for itself in the unity of a (his)story [*Geschichte*]'.[6] Narration is a social process that starts in early childhood and which continues for the rest of our lives. Who one is depends on the values, ideals and goals one has; it is a question of what has significance and meaning for one, and this, of course, is conditioned by the community of which one is part. The concepts I use to express the salient features of whom I take myself to be are concepts derived from tradition and theory and will vary widely from one historical period to the next and across social class and culture. As Bruner points out, our self-making stories are not made up from scratch; they pattern themselves on conventional genres. When talking about myself, my selfhood becomes part of the public domain, and its shape and nature is guided by cultural models of what selfhood should and shouldn't be.[7] Furthermore, others are called upon to hear and to accept the narrative accounts we give of our actions and experiences. To come to know oneself as a person with a particular life history and particular character traits is, consequently, both more complicated than knowing one's immediate beliefs and desires and less private than it might initially seem.[8] When I interpret myself in terms of a life story, I might be both the narrator and the main character, but I am not the sole author. The beginning of my own story has always already been made for me by others and the way the story unfolds is only in part determined by my own choices and decisions. In fact, the story of any individual life is not only interwoven with the stories of others (parents, siblings, friends etc.), it is also embedded in a larger historical and

---

[4]   Op. cit. note 2, 94.

[5]   A. MacIntyre, *After Virtue: A Study in Moral Theory* (London: Duckworth, 1985), 205.

[6]   E. Husserl, *Cartesianische Meditationen und Pariser Vorträge* (Den Haag: Martinus Nijhoff, 1950), 109.

[7]   Op. cit. note 1, 65.

[8]   D. A. Jopling, *Self-Knowledge and the Self* (London: Routledge, 2000), 137.

Dan Zahavi

communal meaning-giving structure.[9] I understand myself as the inheritor and continuer of a tradition, or to quote Husserl:

I am a member of a we-community in the broadest sense—a community that has its tradition and that, for its part, is connected in a novel manner with the generative subjects, the closest and the most distant ancestors. And these have 'influenced' me: I am what I am as an heir.[10]

Ricoeur, who has frequently been regarded as one of the main proponents of a narrative approach to the self, has occasionally presented his own notion of narrative identity as a solution to the traditional dilemma of having to choose between the Cartesian notion of the self as a principle of identity that remains the same throughout the diversity of its different states and the positions of Hume and Nietzsche, who held an identical subject to be nothing but a substantialist illusion.[11] Ricoeur suggests that we can avoid this dilemma if we replace the notion of identity that they respectively defend and reject with the concept of narrative identity. The identity of the narrative self rests upon narrative configurations. Unlike the abstract identity of the same, the narrative identity can include changes and mutations within the cohesion of a lifetime. The story of a life continues to be reconfigured by all the truthful or fictive stories a subject tells about him- or herself. It is this constant reconfiguration that makes 'life itself a cloth woven of stories told'.[12] However, although it is undeniable that Ricoeur has made decisive contributions to the discussion, Ricoeur himself has also pointed to some of the limitations of this approach. As he states in *Temps et récit*, narrative identity is the name of a problem at least as much as it is that of a solution.[13]

Like most interesting accounts, the narrative approach certainly does face some problems. To tell a story about one's own life is not simply a recounting of the brute facts, rather it is, as Bruner puts it, an interpretative feat.[14] Stories are not simply records of what happened, but continuing interpretations and reinterpretations of our lived lives. They are essentially constructive and reconstructive

[9] Op. cit. note 5, 221.
[10] E. Husserl, *Zur Phänomenologie der Intersubjektivität II* (Den Haag: Martinus Nijhoff, 1973), 223.
[11] Op. cit. note 3, 443.
[12] Ibid, 443.
[13] Ibid, 446.
[14] Op. cit. note 1, 12–13.

phenomena that involve deletions, abridgments, and reorderings. A storyteller will typically impose more coherence, integrity, fullness and closure on the life events than they possessed while simply being lived. To put it differently, a narrative necessarily favours a certain perspective on one's experiences and actions to the exclusion of others. But insofar as there is no straightforward one-to-one correlation between the life as it is led and the life as it is told, one is immediately confronted with the question concerning to what extent one can talk about the truth and falsity of self-narratives. It seems misguided to suggest that self-narratives are constitutionally self-fulfilling and therefore infallibly true. We can be mistaken about who we are, and it should be obvious that a person's sincere propagation of a specific life story does not guarantee its truth. In fact, in some cases the stability of our self-identity might be inversely proportional to the fixed stories we tell about ourselves. Elaborate storytelling might serve a compensatory function; it might be an attempt to make up for the lack of a fragile self-identity. But given that our self-narratives are fallible, are they only constrained by the narratives of others, or can we also appeal to narrative-transcendent facts? This question is, of course, related to the controversy over whether the narrative conception of self commits one to a realist or fictionalist take on the self. Some defenders of a narrative approach to selfhood have argued that the self is nothing but a fictional centre of narrative gravity. It is merely the abstract point where various stories intersect.[15] In a parallel move, it has been argued that narratives merely reflect our need for a satisfying coherence, and that they distort reality by imposing fictional configurations on a life that in and of itself has no beginning, middle and end.[16] By contrast, others have claimed that the narrative self has reality insofar as it is a *real* social construction. It has also been argued that although there are obvious differences between fictional narratives and real life ones—in life we have to take things as they come, we are in the middle of events, and are denied the authoritative retrospective

[15]   D. C. Dennett, *Consciousness Explained* (Boston: Little, Brown and Company, 1991), 418; D. C. Dennett, 'The Self as the Center of Narrative Gravity.' *Self and Consciousness: Multiple Perspectives*, F. S. Kessel, P. M. Cole and D. L. Johnson (eds.) (Hillsdale, NJ: Erlbaum, 1992), 103–115.
[16]   L. O. Mink, 'History and Fiction as Modes of Comprehension', *New Literary History* 1, 1970, 558.

Dan Zahavi

point of view of the story-teller or historian[17]—narrative beginning-middle-end structures can be seen as an extension and enrichment of configurations already found in experience and action.[18] Lived time already has a quasi-narrative character, which is why it is not amenable to just any telling. What is dreamlike or fanciful is consequently not the belief that our lives have coherence, but the belief that they have none.[19]

It would lead too far to attempt to tackle all of these questions in the following. So what I intend to do is to focus on the underlying issue that really seems to be at stake in all the different questions: Self-narratives may capture something important about who we are, but is the narrative model capable of delivering an exhaustive account of what it means to be a self? Is it really legitimate to reduce our selfhood to that which can be narrated? Is it possible to resist fictionalism as long as the self is taken to be nothing but a narrative construction? In its dominant version, the narrative approach combines an epistemological and an ontological thesis. Per se, I don't have a problem with neither thesis, nor with their conjunction. I do think the stories we tell are a central means by which we come to know ourselves and others. I do think such stories reflect how we view ourselves and that these stories come to shape our self-understanding and thereby also who we are. Thus, I would readily concede that narratives play an important role in the constitution of a certain dimension or aspect of selfhood. However, I would oppose the exclusivity claim, that is, the claim that *the* self is a narratively constructed entity and that *every* access to self and other are mediated by narratives. These are the kind of radical claims that one can find among many of the defenders of the narrative account. As Wilhelm Schapp, for instance, writes in his classical work *In Geschichten Verstrickt:* Human life is a life that is caught up in stories, it is nothing apart from these stories, and such stories provide the only possible access to oneself and to others.[20]

---

[17]   D. Carr, *Time, Narrative, and History* (Bloomington: Indiana University Press, 1986), 59.

[18]   D. Carr, 'Discussion: Ricoeur on Narrative,' *On Paul Ricoeur: Narrative and Interpretation*, D. Wood (ed.) (London: Routledge, 1991), 162.

[19]   Op. cit. note 17, 90.

[20]   W. Schapp, *In Geschichten Verstrickt* (Frankfurt am Main: Vittorio Klostermann, 1953/2004), 123, 126, 136, 160.

2. The experiential self

In my view, it is an unacceptable oversimplification to assume that the self is a univocal concept, as if there is only one type or level or aspect of self to reckon with. The first step in my argumentation will be to show that we need to operate with a different dimension or level of selfhood than the one addressed by the narrative account.

This is *per se* not a new idea. In recent years, Damasio and Metzinger have both argued in a similar fashion. In *The Feeling of What Happens*, Damasio claims that a sense of self is an indispensable part of the conscious mind. As he writes: 'If 'self-consciousness' is taken to mean 'consciousness with a sense of self,' then all human consciousness is necessarily covered by the term—there is just no other kind of consciousness'.[21] When I think of the moon, read a text, perceive a windowsill, a red book, or a steaming teacup, I automatically and implicitly sense that I, rather than anyone else, am doing it. I sense that the objects I now perceive are being apprehended from my perspective and that the thoughts formed in my mind are mine and not anyone else's. Thus, as Damasio puts it, my conscious life is characterized by a constant, but quiet and subtle, presence of self.[22]

Consciousness is not a monolith, however, and Damasio finds it reasonable to distinguish the simple, foundational kind, which he calls *core consciousness*, from a more complex kind, which he calls *extended consciousness*. Core consciousness has a single level of organization and remains stable across the lifetime of the organism. It is not exclusively human and does not depend upon memory, reasoning, or language. In contrast, extended consciousness has several levels of organization. It evolves across the lifetime of the organism and depends upon both conventional and working memory. It can be found in a basic form in some nonhumans, but only attains its highest peak in language-using humans. According to Damasio, these two kinds of consciousness correspond to two kinds of self. He calls the sense of self that emerges in core consciousness *core self* and refers to the more elaborate sense of self provided by extended consciousness as *autobiographical self*.[23] From a developmental perspective, there are little more than simple states

---

[21]   A. Damasio, *The Feeling of What Happens* (San Diego: Harcourt, 1999), 19.

[22]   Ibid, 7, 10, 127.

[23]   Ibid, 16–17, 127.

Dan Zahavi

of core self in the beginning, but as experience accrues, memory grows and the autobiographical self can be deployed.[24]

There is, superficially at least, a rather striking overlap between Damasio's position and the view recently defended by Metzinger in his book *Being No One*. Metzinger also argues for a close link between selfhood, self-experience, and the first-person perspective. As he puts it, during conscious experience, human beings experience themselves as being someone. But the phenomenology of being someone is essentially connected to the phenomenology of perspectivalness, to the experiential perspectivity of one's own consciousness. Our experiential life possesses a focus of experience, a point of view. It is a first-person perspective in the sense of being tied to a self. Thus, it doesn't make sense to speak of a first-person perspective without speaking of a self.[25] But what does this experiential selfhood amount to? Metzinger writes that there seems to be a primitive and pre-reflective form of phenomenal self-consciousness that underlies all higher-order and conceptually mediated forms of self-consciousness, and in which these have to be anchored, if an infinite regress is to be avoided. What this pre-reflective self-intimacy amounts to, is a very basic and seemingly spontaneous, effortless way of inner acquaintance, of 'being in touch with oneself,' of being 'infinitely close to oneself.' It can also be articulated in terms of a pre-reflective and non-conceptual sense of ownership or consciously experienced 'mine-ness' that accompanies bodily sensations, emotional states and cognitive contents. In non-pathological cases, all these mental states are pre-attentively and automatically experienced subjectively as one's own states, as part of one's own stream of consciousness. This consciously experienced selfhood—which precedes any thinking about the self—differs from all other forms of experiential content by its highly invariant nature. Excepting pathological cases, and contrary to, say, the scent of crushed mint leaves or the taste of buttermilk, it is always there. Frequently it will recede into the background of phenomenal experience. It will be attentionally available, but will often not be attended to at all, but merely be expressed as a subtle background presence.[26]

From a purely descriptive point of view, however, there is nothing new in the analyses offered by Damasio and Metzinger. In

[24]   Ibid, 175.
[25]   T. Metzinger, *Being No One* (Cambridge, MA: MIT Press, 2003), 5, 157, 303.
[26]   Ibid, 158, 267, 291, 626.

186

both cases, we are dealing with a reformulation and (unintended) repetition of ideas already found in classical phenomenology. To put it differently, the most explicit defence and analysis of what might be called the *experiential dimension of selfhood* is precisely to be found in classical phenomenology, i.e., in thinkers like Husserl, Heidegger, Sartre, Merleau-Ponty and Michel Henry. Let me give a few examples.

In *L'être et le néant*, Sartre argues that consciousness is at bottom characterized by a fundamental self-givenness or self-referentiality which Sartre terms *ipseity* (selfhood, from the Latin *ipse*).[27] When Sartre speaks of self, he is referring to something very basic, something characterizing (phenomenal) consciousness as such, and although it is something I can fail to articulate, it is not something I can fail to be. As he also writes, 'pre-reflective consciousness is self-consciousness. It is this same notion of *self* which must be studied, for it defines the very being of consciousness'.[28]

In *Phénoménologie de la perception*, Merleau-Ponty occasionally speaks of the subject as realizing its *ipseity* in its embodied being-in-the-world.[29] However, he also refers to Husserl's investigations of inner time-consciousness and writes that the original temporal flow must count as the archetypical relationship of self to self and that it traces out an interiority or *ipseity*. One page later, Merleau-Ponty writes that consciousness is always affected by itself and that the word 'consciousness' has no meaning independently of this fundamental self-givenness.[30]

In the beginning of the recently published *Bernauer Manuskripte über das Zeitbewusstsein*, Husserl writes that consciousness exists, it exists as a stream, and it appears to itself as a stream. But how the stream of consciousness is capable of being conscious of itself; how it is possible and comprehensible that the very being of the stream is a form of self-consciousness, is the enduring question.[31] Husserl's investigation of temporality is to a large extent motivated by his interest in the question of how consciousness is given to itself, how it manifests itself. His analysis of what he calls the

---

[27] J.-P. Sartre, *L'Être et le Néant* (Paris: Tel Gallimard, 1943/1976), 142.

[28] Ibid, 114.

[29] M. Merleau-Ponty, *Phénoménologie de la Perception* (Paris: Éditions Gallimard, 1945), 467.

[30] Ibid, 487–488.

[31] E. Husserl, *Die Bernauer Manuskripte über das Zeitbewusstsein (1917–18)* (Dordrecht: Kluwer Academic Publishers, 2001), 44, 46.

Dan Zahavi

structure of inner time-consciousness (protention-primal impression-retention) is precisely to be understood as an analysis of the (micro)structure of the pre-reflective self-givenness of our experiences.[32] What we find in Husserl is consequently a sustained investigation of the relationship between selfhood, experiential self-givenness, and temporality.

To mention just one further example, Michel Henry has repeatedly characterized selfhood in terms of an interior self-affection.[33] Insofar as subjectivity reveals itself to itself, it is a self.[34] It is because consciousness is as such characterized by a primitive, tacit, self-consciousness, that it is appropriate to ascribe a fundamental type of *ipseity* to the experiential phenomena. More precisely, Henry links a basic notion of selfhood to the first-personal givenness of experiential life, and writes that the most basic sense of self is the one constituted by the very self-givenness of experience.[35]

The crucial idea propounded by all of these phenomenologists is that an understanding of what it means to be a self calls for an examination of the structure of experience, and vice versa. Thus, the self is not something that stands opposed to the stream of consciousness, but is, rather, immersed in conscious life; it is an integral part of its structure. More precisely, the (minimal or core) self is claimed to possess experiential reality, it is taken to be closely linked to the first-person perspective, and is in fact identified with the first-personal *givenness* of the experiential phenomena. This first-personal givenness of experiential phenomena is not something quite incidental to their being, a mere varnish that the experiences could lack without ceasing to be experiences. On the contrary, this first-personal givenness makes the experiences *subjective*.

Let me try to unpack this idea. Self-experience—at its most primitive—is simply taken to be a question of having first-personal access to one's own consciousness; it is a question of the first-personal givenness or manifestation of experiential life. Most

[32] E. Husserl, *Ideen zu einer Reinen Phänomenologie und Phäno–menologischen Philosophie II* (Den Haag: Martinus Nijhoff, 1952), 118; E. Husserl, *Formale und Transzendentale Logik* (Den Haag: Martinus Nijhoff, 1974), 279–280.

[33] M. Henry, *L'Essence de la Manifestation* (Paris: PUF, 1963), 581, 584, 585.

[34] M. Henry, *De la Subjectivité* (Paris: PUF, 2003), 52.

[35] Op. cit. note 33, 581.

people are prepared to concede that there is something 'it is like' for a subject to undergo a conscious experience (to taste single malt whiskey, to have the blues, to remember a swim in the North Sea). But insofar as there is something it is like for the subject to have the experience, the subject must in some way have access to and be acquainted with the experience. Moreover, although conscious experiences differ from one another—what it is like to smell crushed basil leaves is different from what it is like to see the full moon or to hear Bartok's *Music for Strings, Percussion & Celesta*—they also share certain features. One commonality is the quality of *mineness* (or to use Heidegger's term '*Jemeinigkeit*'), i.e., the fact that the experiences are characterized by first-personal givenness. That is, the experiences are given (at least tacitly) as *my* experiences, as experiences *I* am undergoing or living through. To put it differently, experiences are not merely characterized by certain qualitative features, they are also characterized by the fact that they necessarily exist for a subject or a self; they necessarily feel like something for *somebody*. The first-personal givenness of experiences consequently entails a primitive form of intrinsic self-reference. I do not first experience a neutral or unowned toothache or taste of cauliflower in order then in a subsequent move to have to ask the question 'Whose experience is this actually?' And whether the experience in question is experienced as mine or not does not depend on something apart from the experience, but on the givenness of the experience. If the experience is given in a first-personal mode of presentation, it is experienced as my experience, otherwise not. In short, the self is conceived as the invariant dimension of first-personal givenness in the multitude of changing experiences.

Incidentally, this view makes it clear that self-experience, on this view, is not to be understood as an experience of an isolated, worldless self. To have a self-experience is not to interrupt the experiential interaction with the world in order to turn one's gaze inwards; on the contrary, self-experience is the self-experience of a world-immersed self. It would, consequently, be a decisive mistake to interpret the phenomenological notion of a minimal experiential core self as some kind of Cartesian-style mental residuum, that is, as some kind of self-enclosed and self-sufficient interiority. The phenomenological notion of self is fully compatible with a strong emphasis on the fundamental intentionality, or being-in-the-world, of consciousness. It is no coincidence that even Heidegger employed such a minimal notion of self.[36]

On a purely descriptive level, there is a striking similarity between the views espoused by Damasio, Metzinger, and the phenomenologists. But this is also where the agreement ends. Whereas Damasio claims that the sense of self is an indispensable part of the conscious mind and considers the conscious mind and its constituent properties to be real entities, not illusions,[37] and whereas the phenomenologists would argue that the self is real if it has experiential reality, and that the validity of our account of the self is to be measured by its ability to be faithful to experience, by its ability to capture and articulate (invariant) experiential structures, Metzinger defends the view that it would be a fallacy (what he calls the error of phenomenological reification) to conclude from the content and structure of phenomenal self-experience to the literal properties of an internal and non-physical object, which is what Metzinger takes the self to be.[38] In Metzinger's view, a phenomenological account of selfhood has no metaphysical impact. Our self-experience, our primitive pre-reflective feeling of conscious selfhood, is never truthful in that it does not correspond to any single entity inside or outside of the self-representing system. This is why Metzinger can write that the central ontological claim of his position is that no such things as selves exist.[39]

But why should the reality of the self depend upon whether it faithfully mirrors either subpersonal mechanisms or external (mind independent) entities? If we were wholeheartedly to endorse such a restrictive metaphysical principle, we would declare the entire life-world, the world we live in, and know and care about, illusory. Metzinger argues that the central ontological claim of his position is that no such things as selves exist. But considering Metzinger's repeated claim that phenomenal content cannot count as epistemically justified content—at one point he explicitly characterizes our phenomenal experience during waking state as an online

---

[36] M. Heidegger, *Zur Bestimmung der Philosophie* (Frankfurt am Main: Vittorio Klostermann, 1999).

[37] Op. cit. note 21, 7, 308.

[38] Op. cit. note 25, 271. Since the phenomenologists would typically deny that the self is an object (be it an internal or an external one) one might wonder whether it is Metzinger himself who is engaged in a process of reification.

[39] Ibid, 563–565.

hallucination[40]—couldn't one by using the very same arguments show that there is no such 'thing' as phenomenal consciousness itself?[41] And what about the cultural and historical world, is that also fictitious? If there are no I, you, and we, how can there then be 'a rich social reality'?[42] Given Metzinger's view, would the truly consistent position not be to argue that there are in fact no such things as chairs, playing cards, operas, marriage ceremonies and civil wars?

But let me return to my main questions: Is *the* self a narrative construction? Are narratives the primary access to self? I think at this stage it should be obvious why I want to take exception to both claims. The experiential core self is an integral part of the structure of phenomenal consciousness and must be regarded as a pre-linguistic presupposition for any narrative practice. Only a being with a first-person perspective could consider her own aims, ideals and aspirations *as* her own and tell a story about them. When speaking of a first-person perspective one should consequently distinguish between having such a perspective and being able to articulate it linguistically (eventually to be labelled as a weak and strong first-person perspective, respectively). Whereas the former is simply a question of enjoying first-personal access to one's own experiential life, the latter obviously presupposes mastery of the first-person pronoun.

Some of the narrativists seem to recognize the existence of the former, but they fail to recognize its full significance and to draw the requisite conclusion, namely that even this primitive and foundational structure merits the name of self. In *Time, Narrative, and History*, for instance, Carr grants that experiences and actions must already be given as mine if I am to worry about how they hang together or make up a coherent life-story, but he then claims that such unity is merely a necessary and not a sufficient condition for selfhood.[43] In *Narrative and the Self*, Kerby insists that the attempt to explain the phenomenon of selfhood by appealing to the primitive structures of (time-)consciousness is like the attempt to describe a house only in terms of its framework or underlying structure. In his view the reality of the human self is not as easily

---

40 Ibid, 51.
41 Ibid, 401, 404.
42 Ibid, 590.
43 Op. cit. note 17, 97.

Dan Zahavi

accounted for.[44] One might readily agree that there is more to human existence than the possession of a first-person perspective, but on the other hand, who would want to live in a house that lacked a stable foundation? Finally, to mention just one further example, in *Making Stories,* Bruner admits that certain features of selfhood are innate and that we need to recognize the existence of a primitive, pre-conceptual self, but at the same time, he maintains that dysnarrativia (which we for instance encounter in Korsakoff's syndrome or Alzheimer's disease) is deadly for selfhood and that there would be nothing like selfhood if we lacked narrative capacities.[45] Apart from wondering why Bruner doesn't make the obvious move and concede that it is necessary to operate with different complementary notions of self, one might also ask whether his allusion to neuropathology is really to the point. Alzheimer's disease is a progressive, degenerative brain disorder that results in profound memory loss, changes in behaviour, thinking, and reasoning as well as a significant decline in overall functioning.[46] The person suffering from Alzheimer's will consequently have a wide range of cognitive impairments; the comprehension and expression of speech (and narratives) will only be one of the areas affected. So even *if* no self remains in the advanced stages of Alzheimer's, one cannot without further ado conclude that dysnarrativia was the cause of its death. (If one were on the lookout for a disorder that specifically targeted narrative capacities, global aphasia might be a better choice—but then again, who would want to claim that those struck by global aphasia cease being selves?). Furthermore, there is a big if. It is by no means obvious that Alzheimer's disease brings about a destruction of the first-person perspective, a complete annihilation of the dimension of mineness and that any experience that remains is merely an anonymous and unowned experiential episode, so that the 'subject' no longer feels pain or discomfort as his or her own. In fact, it is hardly insignificant that experienced clinicians report that no person with Alzheimer's disease is exactly like another.[47] But if this is true, and if Alzheimer's disease does in fact constitute a severe case of dysnarrativia, we should draw the exact opposite conclusion

[44]   A. P. Kerby, *Narrative and the Self* (Bloomington: Indiana University Press, 1991), 32.
[45]   Op. cit. note 1, 86, 119.
[46]   L. Snyder, *Speaking our Minds: Personal Reflections from Individuals with Alzheimer's* (New York: W.H. Freeman, 2000), 44.
[47]   Ibid, 72.

Self and Other: The limits of narrative understanding

from Bruner. We would be forced to concede that there must be more to being a self than what is addressed by the narrative account. This is in fact the conclusion drawn by Damasio, who explicitly argues that neuropathology provides empirical evidence in support of the distinction between core self and autobiographical self. Neuropathology reveals that core consciousness can remain intact even when extended consciousness is severely impaired or completely absent, whereas a loss of core consciousness will cause extended consciousness to collapse as well.[48]

One option is to distinguish between a minimal experiential self and an extended narrative self. Another option is the following: When dealing with the experiential self, one might retain the term 'self', since we are dealing precisely with a primitive form of self-givenness or self-referentiality. By contrast, it may be helpful to speak not of the self, but of the *person* as a narrative construction. After all, what is being addressed by a narrative account is the nature of my personal character or personality; a personality that evolves through time and is shaped by the values I endorse and by my moral and intellectual convictions and decisions. It might also be worthwhile to consider the etymology of the concept of person. The Latin *persona* refers to masks worn by actors and is related to the expression *dramatis personae*, which designates the characters in a play or a story.[49]

The fact that the person (i.e., the narrative self) presupposes the experiential self (but not vice versa) does not diminish the significance of the former. Due to the first-personal givenness of experience, our experiential life might be inherently individuated. It remains, however, a purely formal kind of individuation. A description of my experiential self will not differ in any significant way from a description of your experiential self, except, of course, in so far as the first is a description of me, the second a description of you. By contrast, a more tangible kind of individuality manifests itself in my personal history, in my convictions and decisions. It is through such acts that I define who I am, thereby distinguishing myself from others; they have a character-shaping effect. I remain the same as long as I adhere to my convictions; when they change, *I*

[48] Op. cit. note 21, 17, 115–119.
[49] This is neither to suggest that persons are after all mere fictions or that they are masks that somehow conceal the primitive core self. My point is merely that there is an etymological link between narratives and the original concept of persons.

change.[50] Thus, ideals can be identity defining; acting against one's ideals can mean the disintegration (in the sense of a dis-integrity) of one's wholeness as a person.[51]

Persons do not exist in a social vacuum. To exist as a person is to exist socialized into a communal horizon, where one's bearing to oneself is appropriated from the others. I become a person through my life with others in our communal world. As Husserl, a remarkably versatile thinker, observes:

> The origin of personality lies in empathy and in the social acts which are rooted in the latter. To acquire a personality it is not enough that the subject becomes aware of itself as the center of its acts: personality is rather constituted only when the subject establishes social relations with others.[52]

Usually, the self under consideration is already personalized or at least in the process of developing into a full-blown person. But although a narrow focus on the experiential core self might, therefore, be said to involve a certain amount of abstraction, there is no reason to question its reality, it is not a *mere* abstraction. Not only does it play a foundational role, but, the notion of an experiential core self has also found resonance in empirical science. There are for instance pathological limit situations where this minimal self might, arguably, be encountered in its purity.[53]

3. Narratives and otherness

So far I have considered the relation between narratives and selfhood. What about our encounter with others? Isn't it the case that we make sense of the actions of others by placing them in narrative frameworks? Isn't it the case, as both Hutto and Bruner have argued, that our ability to understand others is greatly

[50] J. G. Hart, *The Person and the Common Life* (Dordrecht: Kluwer Academic Publishers, 1992), 52–54.

[51] Cf. L. L. Moland, 'Ideals, Ethics, and Personhood.' *Personhood,* H. Ikäheimo, J. Kotkavirta, A. Laitinen and P. Lyyra (eds.) (Jyväskylä: University of Jyväskylä Press, 2004), 178–184.

[52] Op. cit. note 10, 175.

[53] Cf. J. Parnas, 'Self and Schizophrenia: A Phenomenological Perspective.' *The Self in Neuroscience and Psychiatry,* T. Kircher and A. David (eds.) (Cambridge: Cambridge University Press, 2003), 217–241.

enhanced by our shared narratives and by our understanding of how a manifold of character types will react in various narrative scenarios?[54]

I think there is a truth to these claims, and I think that the *Narrative Practice Hypothesis* constitutes a promising alternative to the standard positions in the Theory of Mind debate,[55] but I also think there is a limit to how far narratives can get us. Let me mention two of my reservations.

The first one is rather trivial. From a developmental point of view, it just will not do to make narratives the basis and foundation of intersubjectivity. Children only acquire narrative skills at a relatively late stage, but already from birth onwards, they engage in increasingly sophisticated forms of social interaction. Eye-contact and facial expressions are of paramount importance to the young infant, who already shortly after birth is able to distinguish its mother's face from the faces of strangers. When a mother mirrors a two to three-month-old infant's affects, the infant will reciprocate and show sensitivity to the affective mirroring of the mother. In fact, infants clearly expect people to communicate reciprocally with them in face-to-face interactions, and to work actively with them in order to sustain and regulate the interaction. If the mother is asked to remain immobile and unresponsive, the infant will react by ceasing to smile, and will exhibit distress and attempt to regain her participation.[56]

From around nine months of age, infants can follow the eye-gaze or pointing finger of another person and, when they do so, they often look back at the person and appear to use the feedback from his or her face to confirm that they have, in fact, reached the right target. In other words, they seek to validate whether joint *attention* has been achieved. Similarly, they might show objects to others, often looking to the other person's eyes, to check whether he or she is attending.

---

[54] D.D. Hutto, 'The Story of the Self: The Narrative Basis of Self-Development.' *Critical Studies: Ethics and the Subject,* K. Simms (ed.) (Amsterdam: Rodopi, 1997); Op. cit. note 1, 16.

[55] Cf. D. D. Hutto, 'The Narrative Practice Hypothesis.' *Narrative and Understanding Persons*, D.D. Hutto (ed.) (Cambridge: Cambridge University Press, 2007).

[56] E. Fivaz-Depeursinge, N. Favez and F. Frascarolo, 'Threesome Intersubjectivity In infancy.' *The Structure and Development of Self-Consciousness: Interdisciplinary Perspectives*, D. Zahavi, T. Grünbaum and J. Parnas (eds.) (Amsterdam: John Benjamins, 2004), 221–34.

Dan Zahavi

From early on children can recognize when they are being attended to by others. This is evident from their display of affective forms of self-consciousness (shyness, coyness, embarrassment, etc.) when looked at. Fourteen-month-olds are even able to recognize that they are being imitated by adults. In one experimental setup, an infant and two experimenters would be sitting across each other. One of the experimenters would be imitating the actions of the infant, whereas the other experimenter would perform other non-matching actions from within the same repertoire of movements. The infant would consistently look, smile and direct more testing behaviour at the imitating adult.[57]

All of these cases—and there are many more—exemplify forms of intersubjectivity that precede narratively based interactions.

One possible retort might be that even if these forms do not comprise full-fledged narratives, they still contain what might be called micro-narratives; the exchanges are still structured as meaningful sequences with a beginning and an end. This reply is, of course, part of a strategy that we have already come across. Remember that several of the narrativists in order to increase the plausibility of their own positions found it necessary to distinguish consciously worked out narratives from pre- or quasi-narratives, which they claimed characterize our ongoing lives. Similarly, in order to ward off the accusation of fictionalism, several of them argued that the narrative beginning-middle-end structures should be seen as extensions and enrichment of temporal configurations already found in experience and action.[58] The problem with this type of retort, however, is that by severing the link between language and narrative, it stretches the latter notion beyond breaking point. The term threatens to become all-inclusive and consequently vacuous—in the end everything meaningful involves narratives—and this is surely a sign of bankruptcy.

Another objection might be that none of the examples mentioned above demonstrate that the infant is in possession of a proper understanding of the self-other distinction, and that such an understanding—which is a prerequisite for any real intersubjectivity—only enters the stage through language-use and

[57] A. Gopnik and A.N. Meltzoff, 'Minds, Bodies and Persons: Young Children's Understanding of the Self and Others as Reflected in Imitation and 'Theory of Mind' Research.' *Self-Awareness in Animals and Humans*, S. Parker and R. Mitchell (eds.) (New York: Cambridge University Press, 1994), 166–186.

[58] Op. cit. note 18, 162.

narratives. It would lead too far to discuss this objection in detail, so I will simply refer to the work of developmental psychologists like Daniel Stern and Philippe Rochat, who in my view have argued convincingly for the presence of a basic self-other differentiation in young infants.[59]

Let me pass on to my second reservation, which I want to discuss in slightly more detail. Contrary to what seems to be the prevalent view within the contemporary theory of mind debate, most phenomenologists would claim that it is possible to experience the feelings, desires, and beliefs of others in their expressive behaviour.[60] That I can have an actual *experience* of another conscious subject—and do not have to rely on theoretical inferences or internal simulations—does not imply, however, that I can experience the other in the same way as she herself does, nor that the other's consciousness is accessible to me in the same way as my own is. The second- (and third-) person access to psychological states differ from the first-person access, but this difference is not an imperfection or a shortcoming; rather, it is constitutional. It makes the experience in question an experience of another, rather than a self-experience. As Husserl would put it, had I had the same access to the consciousness of the other as I have to my own, the other would cease being an other and instead become a part of myself.[61] To demand more, to claim that I would have a real experience of the other only if I experienced her feelings or thoughts in the same way as she herself does, is nonsensical. It would imply that I would only experience another if I experienced her in the same way that I experience myself, i.e., it would lead to an abolition of the difference between self and other. Thus, the givenness of the other is of a rather peculiar kind. We experience the meaningful behaviour of others as expressive of mental states that transcend the behaviour that expresses them. As both Sartre and Lévinas famously argued, the otherness of the other is exactly *manifest* in this transcendence.

According to Sartre, any convincing account of intersubjectivity must respect the irreducible difference between self and other, must respect the *transcendence* of the other. Whereas a standard approach

---

[59] D. N. Stern, *The Interpersonal World of the Infant* (New York: Basic Books, 1985); P. Rochat, *The Infant's World* (Cambridge, MA: Harvard University Press, 2001).

[60] Cf. D. Zahavi, 'Expression and Empathy.' *Folk Psychology Reassessed*, D. Hutto and M. Ratcliffe (eds.) (Dordrecht: Springer, 2007).

[61] Op. cit. note 6, 139.

to the problem of other minds has been by way of asking how it is possible to experience others, Sartre took this line to be misguided, and instead proposed a reversal of the traditional direction of inquiry. According to Sartre, it is crucial to distinguish between the other, whom I perceive, and the other, who perceives me, that is, it is crucial to distinguish between the other as object, and the other as subject. What is truly peculiar and exceptional about the other is not that I am experiencing a *cogitatum cogitans*, but that I am encountering somebody who transcends my grasp, and who in turn is able to perceive and objectify *me*. Thus, rather than focusing upon the other as a specific object of empathy, or as somebody that can be grasped and fixed by means of narratives, Sartre argued that the true other, the other-as-subject, is exactly the being for whom *I* can appear as an object, and that it is when I have the painful experience of my own objecthood, for and before a foreign subject, that I have experiential evidence for the presence of the other-as-subject.[62]

In his analysis of intersubjectivity, Sartre emphasized the transcendent, ineffable and elusive character of the other, and rejected any attempt to bridge or downplay the difference between self and other. A similar approach was adopted by Lévinas who also took the problem of intersubjectivity to be primarily a problem of the encounter with radical otherness. As long as we are conceiving of the other as something that can be absorbed by or integrated into a totality, we have not yet reached a proper understanding of the other as other: 'If one could possess, grasp, and know the other, it would not be other'.[63] Lévinas consequently argued that a true encounter with the other is an encounter with that which cannot be conceptualized or categorized. It is an encounter with an ineffable and radical exteriority. The other is not conditioned by anything in my power, but can only offer itself from without, independently of all systems, contexts, and horizons as a kind of epiphanic visitation or revelation.[64] In *Totalité et infini* Lévinas explicitly criticized traditional philosophy for being a totalizing enterprise. In his view, it was a philosophy of power characterized by a relentless movement of absorption and reduction. It absorbed the foreign and different into the familiar and identical. It reduced the other to the

---

[62] Op. cit. note 27, 302–3, 317.

[63] E. Lévinas, *Le Temps et l'Autre* (Paris: Fata Morgana, 1979), 83.

[64] E. Lévinas, *Totalité et Infini* (Dordrecht: Kluwer Academic Publishers, 1961/1990), 70.

same.[65] Needless to say, this is also a criticism that one could direct at the attempt to understand others by ensnaring them in unifying narratives. To put it differently, the narrative approach to others might be criticized for entailing what could be called a *domestication of otherness*: You reduce the other to that which can be captured by narratives.

Sartre's and Lévinas's accounts of intersubjectivity can be criticized in various ways. The most obvious objection is that I never encounter others in isolation, but always in a context. I meet others in the situational framework of a history with a beginning and a direction. But although both Sartre and Lévinas might, more generally speaking, be said to miss out on important aspects of sociality and interpersonal co-existence, I also think they call attention to a crucial aspect of what it means to encounter others; an aspect or dimension that I fear is lost by the narrative approach. Thus, once again, Schapp goes too far. In his book *In Geschichten Verstrickt*, he claims that what is essential about others are their stories. The encounter with the other in flesh and blood, the concrete face-to-face encounter, doesn't add anything significant, doesn't point beyond the narrative. In fact, and sticking to the metaphor, Schapp argues that the face also tells stories, and that meeting somebody face-to-face is like reading a book. It is when we know these stories that we know the other person. To know or meet somebody in person is merely to encounter new stories or have the old stories confirmed.[66] But as I have suggested, this take fails to realize that the other is precisely characterized by an otherness which resists or exceeds whatever narratives we bring to bear on him or her.

4. Conclusion

A full appraisal of the narrative account of self must resolve some issues that to a large extent have shaped the ongoing dispute between phenomenology and hermeneutics. These issues include 1) the relation between experience and language, 2) the relation between temporality and historicity, and 3) perhaps most importantly, the question concerning to what extent self-experience is necessarily mediated through signs, symbols and cultural works; a question that has found a vivid articulation in Ricoeur's discussion

---

[65] Ibid, 33, 38.
[66] Op. cit. note 20, 105–106.

of what he calls the wounded cogito (*cogito blessé*). I don't take myself to have addressed any of these issues exhaustively, but I hope it is clear that I reject the claim that phenomenology and hermeneutics are excluding alternatives. In my view, the two approaches complement each other, though it is probably also obvious that I would grant a certain priority to the phenomenological approach, and take issue with the kind of position that has been espoused by, for instance, Charles Taylor. According to Taylor, the self is a kind of being that can only exist within a normative space and he therefore claims that any attempt to define selfhood through some minimal or formal form of self-awareness must fail, since such a self is either non-existent or insignificant.[67] But, as I have argued, an account of self which disregards the fundamental structures and features of our experiential life is a non-starter, and a correct description and account of the experiential dimension must necessarily do justice to the first-person perspective and to the primitive form of self-reference that it entails. None of the narrative theories that I am familiar with have—in so far as they are at all aware of the problem—even come near to being able to explain how first-personal givenness could be brought about by narrative structures. But this failure is not really surprising, since the reverse happens to be the case. In order to tell stories about one's own experiences and actions, one must already be in possession of a first-person perspective. To claim that an experience is only appropriated as my own the moment I tell a story about it is simply wrong.[68]

I do have some sympathy for the narrative approach, and for the general idea that who I am is a question of what matters to me, and therefore something that cannot be settled independently of my own self-understanding, but I don't think this approach can stand alone. It needs to be supplemented by an account that does more justice to the first-person perspective. This is why I have argued that it is mandatory to operate with a more primitive and fundamental notion of self than the one endorsed by the narrativists; a notion that cannot be captured in terms of narrative

---

[67] C. Taylor, *Sources of the Self* (Cambridge, MA: Harvard University Press, 1989), 49.

[68] It also flies in the face of many recent important insights concerning the function of first-person indexicals (the fact that 'I,' 'me,' 'my,' 'mine' cannot without loss be replaced by definite descriptions) and ascription-less self-reference (the fact that one can be self-conscious without identifying oneself via specific properties).

structures. In a parallel move, I have argued that there is a crucial dimension of what it means to be other that is bound to be missed by the narrative approach. In short, I have defended the view that there are limits to the kind of understanding of self and others that narratives can provide. One of the obvious questions that so far remain unanswered is whether there is a systematic link between the two limitations. The answer seems straightforward. The reason why the other is characterized by a certain dimension of inaccessibility and transcendence, the reason why the other is an other is precisely because he or she is also a self, with his or her own irreplaceable first-person perspective.[69]

[69] For a further discussion of the issues presented in this paper, cf. D. Zahavi, *Self-awareness and Alterity* (Evanston: Northwestern University Press, 1999) and D. Zahavi, *Subjectivity and Selfhood: Investigating the first-person perspective* (Cambridge, MA: MIT Press, 2005). This study has been funded by the Danish National Research Foundation.

Pathologies in Narrative Structures[1]

SHAUN GALLAGHER

Per Aage Brandt, commenting on a passage from Merlin Donald, suggests that there is 'a narrative aesthetics built into our mind.'[2] In Donald, one can find an evolutionary account of this narrative aesthetics.[3] If there is something like an innate narrative disposition, it is also surely the case that there is a process of development involved in narrative practice. In this paper I will assume something closer to the developmental account provided by Jerome Bruner in various works,[4] and Dan Hutto's account of how we learn narrative practices,[5] and I'll refer to this narrative aesthetics as a narrative competency that we come to have through a developmental process. I will take narrative in a wide sense, to include oral and written communications and self-reports on experience. In this regard narrative is more basic than story, and not necessarily characterized by the formal plot structure of a story. A story may be told in many different ways, but always via narrative discourse.[6] Also, having narrative competency includes not just abilities for understanding narratives, but also for narrative

[1]   An earlier version of this paper was originally presented as 'The Success and Failure of Narrative,' a plenary lecture at the conference *Language Culture And Mind: Integrating Perspectives And Methodologies In The Study of Language*, Paris, 18 July 2006.
[2]   P. A. Brandt, 'Narrative models and meaning'. *p.o.v.* Number 18, December 2004 (http://pov.imv.au.dk/Issue_18/section_1/artc3A.html).
[3]   M. Donald, *Origins of the Modern mind: Three Stages in the Evolution of Culture and Cognition* (Cambridge, MA: Harvard University Press, 1991).
[4]   E.g. J. Bruner, *Actual Minds, Possible Worlds* (Cambridge, MA: Harvard University Press,1986).
[5]   D. D. Hutto, 'Narrative Practice and Understanding Reasons: Reply to Gallagher.' *Consciousness and Emotion: Special Issue on Radical Enactivism*, R. Menary (ed.) (2006); D. D. Hutto, 'Folk Psychology without Theory or Simulation', *Folk Psychology Reassessed*, D. D. Hutto and M. Ratcliffe (eds.) (Dordrecht: Springer, 2007).
[6]   P. Abbott, 'Narrative and the Evolution of Intelligence', paper presented at Department of English, University of California Santa Barbara, April 17, 1998, http://www.anth.ucsb.edu/projects/esm/PorterAbbott.html

understanding, which allows us to form narratives about things, events and other people. To be capable of narrative understanding means to be capable of seeing events in a narrative framework.

The questions that I want to explore are these: what are the cognitive elements that contribute to the development of narrative competency? What do we gain from the deployment of this narrative competency? And what do we lose if something goes wrong with it? In regard to the latter question I will focus on problems found in schizophrenic narratives.[7] Of course, the attempt to understand how narrative competency goes wrong in schizophrenia can only be one piece of the large and complex task involved in understanding schizophrenia. Furthermore, I do not mean to suggest that narrative analysis is something like a key to this full understanding; rather, it is only one approach that must be combined with others.

Let me also note that my focus will be on self-narratives. Developmentally self-narratives are initiated and shaped by others. Two-year-olds may be working more from scripts established by others than from full-fledged narratives. Indeed, their autobiographical memories have to be elicited by questions and prompts.[8] This means that 'the child's own experience ... is forecast and rehearsed with him or her by parents ... children of 2–4 years often 'appropriate' someone else's story as their own'.[9] It is important to see that self-narrative is always already shaped by others, and by those kinds of narratives that are common and possible in the culture surrounding the child. This developmental fact allows us to understand the importance of the role played by self-narrative in our understanding of others, and other-narratives, which include the self-narratives told by others. Pragmatically, in our narrative understanding of others, we make use of our own self-narrative as a repository of experience and, at the same time, as a way to differentiate between self and other. There are other larger narratives available; narratives that help to constitute the shared

[7] For recent work on narratives in depression and anxiety, see J. Zinken, C. Blakemore, L. Butler, T.C. Skinner, 'Emotions in Syntax: Relations between Narrative Structure and Emotional State', paper presented at *Language Culture and Mind* Conference, Paris, 2006.

[8] M. L. Howe, *The Fate of Early Memories: Developmental Science and the Retention of Childhood Experiences* (Cambridge, MA: MIT Press, 2000).

[9] K. Nelson, 'Narrative and the Emergence of a Consciousness of Self', *Narrative and Consciousness*, G. Fireman, T. McVay, and O. Flanagan (eds.) (Oxford: Oxford University Press, 2003), 31.

normative practices[10] that inform our cultural and common sense understandings. Together, with these narrative understandings, we go on to invent important institutions, create laws, and engage in complex social practices. This intersubjective setting is something that we need to keep in mind as a balance to what in the following might seem an overly cognitive account of narrative competency.

What are the cognitive elements that contribute to the development of narrative competency? There are four important contributories that act as necessary conditions for its proper (non-pathological) development: the capacity for temporal ordering, the capacity for minimal self-reference, episodic and autobiographical memory, and the capacity for metacognition.[11] I'll discuss each of these in turn.

The cognitive capacities for narrative competency

Capacity for temporal ordering

Narrative involves a twofold temporal structure. First, there is a timeframe that is internal to the narrative itself, a serial order in which one event follows another. This internal timeframe contributes to the composition of narrative structure. Paul Ricoeur notes a dialectic of 'discordance' and 'concordance' in the process of narrative.[12] In some way each event in the narrative is something new and different ('discordance'); yet in another way each event is part of a series ('concordance'), determined by what came before and constraining what is to come. Configurations of concordance and discordance compose the basic structure of plot in stories. Even if there is no plot, however, there is always a serial order in the narrative.

One can think of the internal order of the narrative as the serial order of what McTaggart called a B-series, in which one event

10 Cf. R. B. Brandom, *Making It Explicit* (Cambridge, MA: Harvard University Press, 1994).
11 See S. Gallagher, 'Self-Narrative in Schizophrenia', *The Self in Neuroscience and Psychiatry*, A. S. David and T. Kircher (eds.) (Cambridge: Cambridge University Press, 2003), 336–357.
12 P. Ricoeur, *Oneself as Another*, (trans. K. Blamey) (Chicago: University of Chicago Press, 1992).

Shaun Gallagher

follows another.[13] Once established, this is an unchanging order. That is, if event X predates event Y, then it always does so. The American revolutionary war happened before the French revolution, and this fact does not depend on how long ago these events happened. Within narrative, however, a series of events that have a certain objective order may be presented out of order, and this may happen in several ways. First, a narrator may want to create a dramatic effect by presenting event Y first, and then moving back (flashing back) to event X. Events are presented as having the proper serial order, but the order of their presentation is different from the order of their objective happening. Second, it may be the case that the narrator simply does not know the objective order of events and thinks that event Y did happen before event X—a simple mistake rather than a dramatic effect. This has no effect on the internal structure of the narrative, as long as the order is consistently maintained. If the narrative references real events in this way, then it does so in a non-veridical way. Third, it may also happen that a narrator does know the objective order of events but unwittingly confuses the order, sometimes presenting event X as prior to event Y, and other times presenting event Y as prior to event X. This kind of inconsistency is a mark of irrationality.

In contrast to the internal time frame, there is an external temporality that defines the narrator's temporal relation to the events of the narrative. We can think of this as what McTaggart calls the A-series, which is a perspectival or relative time frame. That is, from the narrator's current perspective (the present), the narrated events happen either in the past, the present, or the future. Even if this relation is left unspecified ('Once upon a time ...') it is usually open to specification that these events happened in the past, or will happen in the future, relative to the narrator's present. In the case of fictional events, of course, the events may never have happened and never will happen. We might think of them precisely as not having a specifiable place in time relative to the narrator. With respect to self-narrative, however, this cannot be the case. Even if the event in question never did happen (for example, an event falsely remembered) or never will happen (for example, a planned event that never comes to be actualized) in self-narrative it is still set in a temporal relation to the narrator.

By the capacity for temporal ordering I mean simply the ability to work in these time frames without serious confusion. These are

[13] J. M. E. McTaggart, 'The Unreality of Time'. *Mind* 17 (New Series, no. 68), 1908, 457–474.

learned capacities that are based on a more fundamental temporal ordering of experience. I experience event X, and then I experience event Y; I also experience X-followed-by-Y receding into the past and as forming part of my past experience. When I experience X as occurring, I may at the same moment anticipate Y, or perhaps something other than Y. What is unavoidable is that when I am conscious I always anticipate something. Husserl shows that this anticipatory aspect (or 'protention') directed at what is just about to happen is part of the very structure of experience, as is the 'retention' of what has just occurred.[14] Each moment of consciousness has a retention-primal (now) impression-protention structure which allows us to experience the world in an orderly way, characterized with certain degrees of continuity and discontinuity. At every moment I am pre-reflectively aware of what I am experiencing just now, of what I have just experienced (in the previous now), and of what I expect to happen in the next second or so. If this were not so, I would never experience a melody; nor could I form a sentence, or make sense of a sentence that I am reading or hearing. This basic temporal structure of experience is not only a prerequisite for the proper temporal ordering found in narrative, its proper functioning is also a necessary condition for the development of a minimal sense of self, for our ability to remember our experience, and for our ability to reflect on our experience.

Capacity for minimal self-reference

I retain the just-past content of my experience by retaining my just-past experience. What Husserl shows in his analysis of this basic temporal structure of consciousness is that the retentional function retains not only an intentional sense of the just-past note of a melody (or whatever content one is experiencing) but it does so only by retaining the consciousness-of-the-passing-melody. That is, experience always involves a retention of consciousness itself so that we have not only an experience of the melody, but at the same time an experience of ourselves experiencing the melody. This is what phenomenologists call the sense of ipseity, which is a pre-reflective (proprioceptive, ecological) sense of self that contributes to the basic differentiation between self and non-self.

---

[14]   E. Husserl, *Zur Phänomenologie des Inneren Zeitbewusstseins (1893–1917),* R. Boehm (ed.) (den Haag: Martinus Nijhoff, 1966).

Shaun Gallagher

Ipseity is the sense that this experience is my experience. It is the 'mineness' of experience—a minimal sense of self that is an immediate and present self-consciousness. As such it is the ground for my use of the first-person pronoun, and the basis for my ability to issue reports about my experience.

To begin to form a self-narrative one must be able to refer to oneself by using the first-person pronoun. Without the basic sense of differentiation between self and non-self I would not be able to refer to myself with any specification, and self-narrative would have no starting point. The minimal sense of self is what gets extended and enhanced in the self-narrative.

Certain forms of access that I have to my minimal self (as Wittgenstein says, '*as subject*') cannot be mistaken, and as a result certain uses of the first-person pronoun in self-reference are immune to error through misidentification.[15] For example, if I say 'I think it is going to rain today,' I may be entirely wrong about the rain, but I cannot be wrong about the I. I cannot say 'I' and mean to identify someone else by that word. If I say 'I see that John is at his desk,' I can be wrong about it being a desk; I can be wrong about it being John; and I can even be wrong about my cognitive act (it may be hallucination rather than visual perception). It would be nonsensical, however, to ask me 'Are you sure that *you* are the one who sees that John is at his desk?'

Importantly, even in cases where I do *objectively* misidentify myself (e.g., if I mistakenly claim that I am the one who hit the target, when in fact it was somebody else who hit the target), my use of the first-person pronoun has a guaranteed self-reference.[16] When I say 'I', I am referring to myself, even though I may be wrong about who hit the target. Indeed, I can misidentify myself ('*as object*') in this respect only because I have correctly self-referred. In such cases, it is precisely myself about whom I am wrong. This makes the minimal self an extremely secure anchor for self-narratives.

In a self-narrative I may report what I feel in terms of emotional state, but I often report what I am doing or what I did, or what I plan to do. In other words, action is central to self-narrative. My experience of action may be specified further to include both a sense of ownership for movement (that is, a sense that I am

[15] S. Shoemaker, 'Self-Reference and Self-Awareness.' *The Journal of Philosophy* 65, 1968, 555–567.

[16] P. F. Strawson, 'The First Person—and Others.' *Self-Knowledge*, Q. Cassam (ed.) (Oxford: Oxford University Press, 1994).

moving) and a sense of agency (that is, a sense that I am the one causing the movement), both of these still on a pre-reflective level.[17] For the construction of self-narrative the sense of agency is the basis for the attribution of action to oneself. In my self-narrative I am either (or alternatively) an agent or a sufferer,[18] and my construal of myself as such depends on my ability to self-attribute action. Thus, even if other aspects of the minimal self are intact a lack of a sense of agency will be disruptive to self-narrative. As we will see, this has importance in considerations of schizophrenia.

Episodic and autobiographical memory

Both the capacity for temporal ordering and the capacity for minimal self-reference are necessary for the proper working of episodic and autobiographical memory, which involves the recollection of a past event and when it took place, and self-attribution, the specification that the past event involved the person who is remembering it. Building on a long philosophical tradition, starting with Locke,[19] which holds that just such memories form the basis of personal identity, narrative theorists contend that personal identity is primarily constituted in narratives that recount past autobiographical events. If there is any degree of unity to my life, it is the product of an interpretation of my past actions and of events in the past that happened to me, all of which constitute my life history.[20] If I were unable to form memories of my life history, or were unable to access such memories, then I have nothing to interpret, nothing to narrate sufficient for the formation of self-identity.

Maguire et al. point out that the coherence of narrative depends on two factors: that the story makes sense, and that the person who hears the story has access to prior knowledge.[21] In the construction

[17]   See S. Gallagher, 'Philosophical Conceptions of the Self: Implications for Cognitive Science', *Trends in Cognitive Sciences* 4, 2000, 14–21.

[18]   Op. cit. note 12.

[19]   J. Locke, *An Essay Concerning Human Understanding*. A. C. Fraser (ed.) (New York: Dover, (1690, second edition 1694), 1959).

[20]   Op. cit. note 12.

[21]   E. A. Maguire, C. D. Frith, and R. G. Morris, 'The Functional Neuroanatomy of Comprehension and Memory: the Importance of Prior Knowledge', *Brain* 122, No. 10, 1999, 1839–1850.

of self-narrative, autobiographical memory provides the prior knowledge out of which the coherent narrative is formed.[22] Likewise, the narrative (and self-narrative) process is not simply something that depends on the proper functioning of episodic (and autobiographical) memory, but in fact contributes to the functioning of that memory. Just to the extent that the current contextual and semantic requirements of narrative construction motivate the recollection of a certain event, that recollection will be shaped, interpreted and reconstructed in the light of those requirements.

In addition, autobiographical memory depends on, but also reinforces a more objective sense of self. One can see this in terms of development. Around the same time as autobiographical memory starts to form, 18 months to 24 months, the child gains capability in mirror self-recognition, which generates an objective sense of self, as well as capability in language, which is essential for the construction of narrative.

> By 18–24 months of age infants have a concept of themselves that is sufficiently viable to serve as a referent around which personally experienced events can be organized in memory ... the self at 18–24 months of age achieves whatever 'critical mass' is necessary to serve as an organizer and regulator of experience ... this achievement in self-awareness (recognition) is followed shortly by the onset of autobiographical memory ... [23]

Capacity for metacognition

Another important cognitive capacity required for narrative compentency is an ability to gain a reflective distance from one's own experience. The process of interpretation that ordinarily shapes episodic memories into a narrative structure depends on this capacity for reflective metacognition or metarepresentation. To form a self-narrative, one needs to do more than simply remember life events. One needs to reflectively consider them, deliberate on their meaning, and decide how they fit together semantically. A life

---

[22]   K. Vogeley, M. Kurthen, P. Falkai, and W. Maier, 'The Human Self Construct and Prefrontal Cortex in Schizophrenia', *The Association for the Scientific Study of Consciousness: Electronic Seminar* (1999), (http://www.phil.vt.edu/assc/esem.html).

[23]   Op. cit. note 8, 91–92.

event is not meaningful in itself; rather it depends on a narrative structure that lends it context and sees in it significance that goes beyond the event itself.

Metacognition is clearly essential for the interpretive process that produces the self-narrative. As Merlin Donald puts it, metacognition provides the 'cognitive governance' that allows for disambiguating and differentiating events within the narrative.[24] It not only allows for reporting on one's experience, but also for an enhancement of that experience. It is possible, for the sake of a unified or coherent meaning, to construe certain events in a way that they did not in fact happen. To some degree, and for the sake of creating a coherency to life, it is normal to confabulate and to enhance one's story. As Ricoeur points out, narrative identity 'must be seen as an unstable mixture of fabulation and actual experience'.[25] Self-deception is not unusual; false memories are frequent.

What do we gain from the deployment of this narrative competency?

The narrative self

There is a growing consensus, across a number of disciplines, including philosophy, psychology, and neuroscience, that narrative competency provides important structure for the development of something more than a minimal (momentary and immediate sense of) self.[26] In contrast to the minimal (proprioceptive and ecological) self, the narrative self involves a diachronic and complex structure that depends on reflective experience and on factors that are

[24] M. Donald, 'An Evolutionary Rationale for the Emergence of Language from Mimetic Representation', plenary paper presented at *Language Culture and Mind Conference*, Paris, 17–20 July 2006.

[25] Op. cit. note 12, 162.

[26] Op. cit. note 12; A. MacIntyre, *After Virtue*, 2nd ed. (Notre Dame, IN: University of Notre Dame Press, 1984); Op. cit. note 4; D. Dennett, *Consciousness Explained* (Boston: Little, Brown, and Company, 1991); A. Damasio, *The Feeling of What Happens: Body and Emotion in the Making of Consciousness.* (New York: Harcourt Brace and Co, 1999); M. Schechtman, *The Constitution of Selves* (Ithaca: Cornell University Press, 1996); C. Taylor, *Sources of the Self: The Making of the Modern Identity* (Cambridge MA: Harvard University Press, 1989); R. Wollheim, *The Thread of Life* (New Haven and London: Yale University Press, 1984).

conceptual, emotional, and socially embedded. We conceive of ourselves as extended over time in a narrativized fashion, 'situated in a present that bears the past and projects itself imaginatively into the future'.[27]

Dennett has proposed a version of narrative theory consistent with recent developments in neuroscience.[28] He finds in the brain something analogous to what Hume had found in the mind, a collection of distributed processes with no central theater, no real, neurological center of experience.[29] Importantly, however, the brain is capable of generating virtual connections that loop through the human social environment. That is, the brain generates language. Language allows us to weave stories that trace our experiences in relatively coherent plots over extended time periods. In these stories we extend our biological identities through the use of words like 'I' and 'you'.

The narrative self, however, has no substantial reality. Rather, on Dennett's account, the narrative self is an empty abstraction—an abstract 'center of narrative gravity.' A narrative self is an abstract and movable point where various fictional or biographical stories about ourselves, told by ourselves or by others, intersect.

In contrast to Dennett, Ricoeur conceives of the narrative self not as an abstract point at the intersection of various narratives, but as something richer and more concrete.[30] He emphasizes the fact that one's own self-narrative is always entangled in the narratives of others, and that out of this entanglement comes a unified life narrative that helps to shape the individual's continuing behavior.

The narrative self may be more than a simple abstract point of intersecting narratives, but also less than a unified product of a

---

[27] J. Phillips, 'Schizophrenia and the Narrative Self.' *The Self in Neuroscience and Psychiatry* T. Kircher and A. David (eds.) (Cambridge: Cambridge University Press, 2003), 319–335.

[28] D. Dennett, 'Why Everyone is a Novelist.' *Times Literary Supplement*, 4459 (September 16–22, 1988), 1016, 1028–29; D. Dennett, op. cit. note 26.

[29] Hume had used the metaphor of the theater, but immediately set it aside: 'The mind is a kind of theatre, where several perceptions successively make their appearance ... The comparison of the theatre must not mislead us. They are the successive perceptions only, that constitute the mind; nor have we the most distant notion of the place, where these scenes are represented ...'. D. Hume, *A Treatise of Human Nature*, A. Selby-Bigge (ed.) (Oxford: Oxford University Press, 1888/1975), 253. Dennett (1991) rejects the notion of a Cartesian theater.

[30] Op. cit. note 12.

consistent narrative. It is possible to conceive of the narrative self as a complex product that is not fully unified—a product of incomplete summation and selective subtraction, imperfect memories and multiple reiterations. The self so conceived can provide a good model to explain the various equivocations, contradictions, and struggles that find expression within an individual's personal life. On a psychological level, a narrative model like this could account for conflict, moral indecision and self-deception, in a way that would be difficult to work out in terms of more traditional theories of self-identity. At certain extremes, however, broken narratives may be reflective of certain psychopathologies.

Furthermore, as Ricoeur notes, my own self-narrative is greatly influenced by what others say about me, and is more generally constrained by the kinds of things that can be said, and that are said about persons in my culture. What others say can have an effect on my self-identity from a first-person perspective insofar as it can be related, positively or negatively, with my own self-narrative. What someone else says about me *matters* only so far as it fits or fails to fit into my own self-narrative. The connection between myself and others in the framework of narrative, however, is deeper than this.

Narrative and intersubjectivity

In contrast to standard theory of mind (TOM) accounts of social cognition, based on theoretical stances or simulation models, there is good developmental, neuroscientific, and phenomenological evidence for an interactive-narrative approach. I want to focus on the narrative component involved in this approach, but narrative competency doesn't arise *ex nihilo*. It normally depends on capacities for human interaction and intersubjective understanding that develop in certain embodied practices in early infancy— practices that are emotional, sensory-motor, perceptual, and nonconceptual. These embodied practices constitute our primary access for understanding others, and they continue to do so even after we attain our more advanced abilities for social understanding.[31]

In most intersubjective situations we have a direct understanding of another person's intentions because their intentions are

[31] See S. Gallagher, 'The Practice of mind: Theory, Simulation or Primary Interaction?' *Journal of Consciousness Studies* 8, No. 5–7, 2001, 83–108.

explicitly expressed in their embodied actions and their expressive behaviors. Developmental studies show that human infants have capabilities for interaction with others that fall under the heading of primary intersubjectivity.[32] Neonate imitation shows that infants, from the very start, are able to distinguish between inanimate objects and people and are attuned to the latter in a special way.[33] Infants are able to see bodily movement as goal-directed intentional movement, and to perceive other persons as intentional agents. Baldwin and colleagues, for example, have shown that infants at 10–11 months are able to parse some kinds of continuous action according to intentional boundaries.[34] The infant follows the other person's eyes, and perceives various movements of the head, the mouth, the hands, and more general body movements as meaningful, goal-directed movements. Such perceptions give the infant, by the end of the first year of life, a non-mentalizing understanding of the intentions, emotions, and dispositions of other persons.[35] If human faces are especially salient, even for the youngest infants, or if we continue to be capable of perceptually grasping the meaning of the other's expressions and intentional movements, such face-to-face interaction does not exhaust the possibilities of intersubjective understanding. Expressions, intonations, gestures, and movements, along with the bodies that manifest them, are not free floating; they are found *in the world*, and infants soon start to notice how others interact with the world. Around the age of 9–14 months infants go beyond the person-to-person

[32]   C. B. Trevarthen, 'Communication and Cooperation in Early infancy: A Description of Primary Intersubjectivity' *Before Speech*, M. Bullowa (ed.) (Cambridge: Cambridge University Press, 1970).
[33]   S. Gallagher and A. Meltzoff, 'The Earliest Sense of Self and Others: Merleau-Ponty and Recent Developmental Studies', *Philosophical Psychology* 9, 1996, 213–236.
[34]   D. A. Baldwin and J. A. Baird, 'Discerning Intentions in Dynamic Human Action' *Trends in Cognitive Science* 5, No. 4, 2001, 171–178; D. A. Baldwin, J. A. Baird, M. M. Saylor and M. A. Clark, 'Infants Parse Dynamic Action' *Child Development* 72, No. 3, 2001, 708–717.
[35]   T. Allison, Q. Puce, and G. McCarthy, 'Social Perception from Visual Cues: Role of the STS Region' *Trends in Cognitive Science* 4 No. 7, 2001, 267–278; D. A. Baldwin, 'Infants' Ability to Consult the Speaker for Clues to Word Reference' *Journal of Child Language* 20, 1993, 395–418; S. C. Johnson, 'The Recognition of Mentalistic Agents in Infancy' *Trends in Cognitive Science* 4, 2000, 22–28; S. Johnson, V. Slaughter and S. Carey, 'Whose Gaze Will Infants Follow? The Elicitation of Gaze-Following in 12-Month-Old Infants', *Developmental Science* 1, No. 2, 1998, 233–238.

immediacy of primary intersubjectivity, and enter into pragmatic *contexts* of shared attention in which they learn what things mean and what they are for.[36] Trevarthen and Hubley call this 'secondary intersubjectivity'.[37] Infants begin to perceive others as agents whose actions are framed in pragmatic contexts. It follows that there is not one uniform way in which we relate to others, but that our relations are mediated through the various pragmatic circumstances of our encounters. In this regard, to understand another person, we do not need to gain access to their hidden minds by some kind of inference; we are rather pulled into their world as we engage in what they are doing.

It is clear that although we do not leave primary and secondary intersubjective capabilities behind, these embodied, sensory-motor (emotion informed) interactions are not sufficient to address what are clearly new developments around the ages of 2, 3 and 4 years. A developing narrative competency during this time moves the process forward and transforms it. For narrative, language acquisition and the development of a more objective sense of self, autobiographical memory, and metacognitive abilities, are important, and narrative competency has its beginning around 2–4 years as we gain increasingly linguistic and nuanced understanding. Narrative competency operates in two ways to further our intersubjective understanding. First, through narrative practice, in the form of the stories that others tell us, and, with the help of others, we start to tell about ourselves, we gain access to folk psychological concepts. This is what Hutto (2004) calls the 'narrative practice hypothesis'.[38] Second, it is also possible to use narrative as a way to make sense of another person's actions without employing folk psychological concepts, but rather by framing their behaviors, actions, expressions in meaningful contexts. In this process, as McIntyre points out, 'It is because we live out narratives in our lives and because we understand our own lives in terms of narratives that we live out, that the form of

---

[36] W. Phillips, S. Baron-Cohen, and M. Rutter, 'The Role of Eye-Contact in the Detection of Goals: Evidence from Normal Toddlers, and Children with Autism or Mental Handicap', *Development and Psychopathology* 4, 1992, 375–383.

[37] C. Trevarthen, and P. Hubley, 'Secondary Intersubjectivity: Confidence, Confiding and Acts of Meaning in the First Year', *Action, Gesture and Symbol: The Emergence of Language,* A. Lock (ed.) (London: Academic Press, 1978), 183–229.

[38] D. D. Hutto, 'The Limits of Spectatorial Folk Psychology', *Mind and Language* 19, 2004, 548–573.

narrative is appropriate for understanding the actions of others'.[39] With narrative competency, then, we gain not only a more complex and extended sense of self, we gain a sophisticated understanding of others.

What do we lose when something goes wrong with narrative?

Narratives can fail either in regard to content or structure. On the one hand, the content of self-narrative is provided by autobiographical memory and our actions, but content is also shaped by expectations and plans. Without content, narratives are impoverished. The contribution of autobiographical memory to self-narrative content is significant, as is apparent from cases in which such content is lost, as in amnesia or Alzheimer's disease. Bruner points out that dysnarrativia (encountered for example in Korsakoff's syndrome or Alzheimer's disease) is destructive for the selfhood that is generated in narrative.[40] In addition, dysnarrativia involves the loss of the ability to understand others' behavior and their emotional experiences.

Narrative structure, on the other hand, can mean different things although it is generally related to how narrative gets generated. Per Aage Brandt, for example, understands structure as 'a textual architecture' where aspects of narrative structures depend on utterance-based local microstructures.[41] Lysaker and Lysaker suggest that narrative structure derives from an internal self-dialogue which generates the self: 'The self is inherently 'dialogial', or the product of ongoing conversations both within the individual and between the individual and others'.[42] James Phillips[43] equates narrative structure with the temporal structure implicit in narrative, but, similar to Roe and Davidson,[44] understands this as

[39] Op. cit. note 26, MacIntyre 1984, p. 212.

[40] J. Bruner, *Making Stories: Law, Literature, Life* (New York: Farrar, Straus and Giroux, 2002), 86 and 119; See also K. Young, and J. L. Saver, 'The Neurology of Narrative' *SubStance* 30, No. 1 and 2, 2001, 72–84.

[41] Op. cit. note 2.

[42] P. H. Lysaker, and J. T. Lysaker, 'Narrative Structure in Psychosis: Schizophrenia and Disruptions in the Dialogical Self', *Theory and Psychology* 12, No. 2, 2002, 207–220, 201.

[43] Op. cit. note 27.

[44] D. Roe. and L. Davidson, 'Self and Narrative in Schizophrenia: Time to Author a New Story', *Medical Humanities* 31, 2005, 89–94.

the ordinary plot structure: that a narrative has a beginning, middle, and end. I think Phillips is correct that narrative structure derives from the various kinds of temporality involved in narrative, but this structure is not necessarily equivalent to plot. Capabilities related to temporal integration and the linear ordering of events within a temporal framework are essential to the formation of the narrative perspective and to the sequential order that characterizes narrative. These aspects of temporal structure appear to be necessary conditions for capabilities that involve minimal self-reference, and episodic-autobiographical memory.

As I indicated above, the construction of narratives involves a perspectival A-series—the temporal position of the narrated events relative to the narrator, a perspective that is external to the narrative itself. That is, the narrated events may be in the past or the future, or may be happening now, relative to the narrator. Narrative competency also involves the ability to deal with a non-perspectival B-series—the internal order of events that are told in the narrative and that may or may not make up a plot. In addition, we noted that these temporal aspects also depend on a more basic time-consciousness, the coherent flow of experience which includes retentions and protentions and which structures the minimal self, including sense of agency.

Schizophrenic subjects often experience problems pertaining to temporal experience in ways that interfere with both internal and external temporal frameworks and the basic aspects of time-consciousness.

- Disruptions of the external A-series may be due to the fact that future time-perspective is curtailed in schizophrenia[45] and subjects act 'without concern for tomorrow.' One patient states: 'There is an absolute fixity around me. I have even less mobility for the future than I have for the present and the past. There is a kind of routine in me which does not allow me to envisage the future. The creative power in me is abolished. I see the future as a repetition of the past'.[46]

- Disruptions of the internal B-series are also apparent in schizophrenics who experience difficulties indexing events in

[45]   C. Dilling, and A. Rabin, 'Temporal Experience in Depressive States and Schizophrenia' *Journal of Consulting Psychology* 31, 1967, 604–608.
[46]   Quoted in E. Minkowski, *Lived Time: Phenomenological and Psychological Studies*, trans. N. Metzel, (Evanston: Northwestern University Press, 1933/1970), 277.

time, which is positively correlated to symptoms of auditory hallucinations, feelings of being influenced, and problems that involve distinguishing between self and non-self.[47]

- Reflecting possible disruptions of the more basic temporal flow of experience, some schizophrenic narratives are characterized by a derailing of thought; by constant tangents, the loss of goal, the loosening of associations, or the compression of a temporally extended story to a single gesture.[48]

Self-narratives of schizophrenic patients reflect general problems in the sequencing of events and self-placement in appropriate temporal frameworks. One patient during a lucid period reports:

I felt as if I had been put back, as if something of the past had returned, so to speak, toward me .... so that not only time repeated itself again but all that had happened for me during that time as well.... . In the middle of all this something happened which did not seem to belong there. Suddenly it was not only 11:00 again, but a time which has passed a long time before was there ... In the middle of time I was coming from the past toward myself.... . Before there was a before and after. Yet it isn't there now.... . [When someone visits and then leaves] it could very well have happened yesterday. I can no longer arrange it, in order to know where it belongs.[49]

Schizophrenics have difficulty planning and initiating action,[50] problems with temporal organization,[51] and experienced continuity,[52] and a variety of impairments of 'self-temporalization'.[53]

[47] F. T. Melges, 'Time and the Inner Future: a Temporal Approach to Psychiatric Disorders' (New York: Wiley, 1982); F. T. Melges, and A. M. Freeman, 'Temporal Disorganization and Inner-Outer Confusion in Acute Mental Illness' *American Journal of Psychiatry* 134, 1977, 874–877.

[48] J. Cutting, *Psychopathology and Modern Philosophy* (London: Forest Publishing Co, 1998).

[49] Op. cit. note 46, 284–286.

[50] S. Levin, 'Frontal Lobe Dysfunction in Schizophrenia–Eye Movement Impairments' *Journal of Psychiatric Research* 18, 1984, 27–55.

[51] R. A. DePue, M. D. Dubicki, and T. McCarthy, 'Differential Recovery of Intellectual, Associational, and Psychophysiological Functioning in Withdrawal and Active Schizophrenics', *Journal of Abnormal Psychology* 84, 1975, 325–330.

[52] E. Pöppel, 'Temporal Mechanisms in Perception' *International Review of Neurobiology* 37, 1994, 185–202.

[53] P. Bovet, and J. Parnas, 'Schizophrenic Delusions: A Phenomenological Approach', *Schizophrenia Bulletin* 19, 1993, 579–597, 584.

Basic retentional-protentional structures of experience are reflected in the neuropsychological concept of working memory, which involves the temporal integration of experience over very short periods of time. Studies of spatial and verbal tasks in schizophrenics show marked deficits of working memory[54] which sometimes manifest themselves as 'formal thought disorders'—a breakdown of the temporal organization of reasoning and speech,[55] 'cognitive dysmetria',[56] relatively slow speeds of cognitive processing.[57] Problems that some schizophrenics have in keeping track of recent actions,[58] and with respect to the sense of agency, may involve their inability to anticipate or sequence in working memory their own actions.[59] All of these problems can interfere with the formation of self-narratives. One patient reports: 'sometimes everything is so fragmented, when it should be so unified. A bird in the garden chirps, for example. I heard the bird, and I know that he chirps; but that it is a bird and that he chirps, these two things are separated from each other'.[60]

[54] See Vogeley et al., op. cit. note 22, for a review.

[55] J. M. Fuster, 'Commentary on "The Human Self Construct and Prefrontal Cortex in Schizophrenia" ' (Vogeley et al. op. cit. note 22)', *The Association for the Scientific Study of Consciousness: Electronic Seminar* (1999), (http://www.phil.vt.edu/assc/esem.html).

[56] N. C. Andreasen, S. Paradiso and D. S. O'Leary, 'Cognitive Dysmetria as an Integrative Theory of Schizophrenia: a Dysfunction in Cortical-Subcortical-Cerebellar Circuitry', *Schizophrenia Bulletin* 24, 1998, 203–218.

[57] S. Tauscher-Wisniewski, 'Cognitive Processing Speed Slows before Schizophrenia', Poster session, *Society of Biological Psychiatry*; reported by M. A. Moon, *Clinical Psychiatry News* 27, No. 7, 1999, 1; See J. M. Fuster, 'Network Memory', *Trends in Neuroscience* 20 (10), 1997, 451–458; and J. M. Fuster, 'The Prefrontal Cortex and Its Relation to Behavior' *Progress in Brain Research* 87, 1991, 201–211.

[58] J. Mlakar, J. Jensterle, and C. D. Frith, 'Central Monitoring Deficiency and Schizophrenic Symptoms' *Psychological Medicine* 24, 1994, 557–564.

[59] S. Gallagher, 'Self-Reference and Schizophrenia: A Cognitive Model of Immunity to Error Through Misidentification', *Exploring the Self: Philosophical and Psychopathological Perspectives on Self-experience*, D. Zahavi (ed.) (Amsterdam and Philadelphia: John Benjamins, 2000); and op. cit. note 22.

[60] Cited by Minkowski 1933, op. cit. note 46, 285.

Shaun Gallagher

We can see how narratives break down in the cases discussed by Phillips[61] and by Lysaker and Lysaker.[62] Phillips distinguishes three styles of schizophrenic self-narrative.

1. Impoverished and fragmented self-narrative
2. Impoverished because focused (on illness)
3. Flamboyant delusional narratives

Lysaker and Lysaker consider 1 and 3 but add a fourth:

4. Monological and rigid narrative with sustained delusions

Phillips describes a patient, Mr. B, as providing *impoverished and fragmented self-narratives* that are characterized as involving disordered and incomplete thoughts, interruptions of ongoing narrative 'with statements about how it all started,' a lack of a coherent sense of self, a minimal sense of future.[63] In effect, this kind of narrative demonstrates problems with all four capacities required for narrative competency:

- *temporal structure* (internal temporal disruptions and disorganization)
- *ipseity* (incoherent sense of self)
- *autobiographical memory* (impoverished content)
- *metacognition.*

I note here that problems with metacognition may involve either a failure to monitor one's experience,[64] or an inclination to over-monitor one's experience in a kind of hyper-reflection.[65] Mr. B seems to have problems with over-monitoring rather than a Frithian failure of monitoring, at least in regard to interrupting and sending the narrative back to 'how it all started.'

Phillips's patient Mrs. M. provides an example of someone who produces *impoverished because overly focused narrative*, and this

---

[61] Op. cit. note 27.

[62] Op. cit. note 42.

[63] Also see P. H. Lysaker, A. Wickett and L. Davis, 'Narrative Qualities in Schizophrenia: Associations with Impairments in Neurocognition and Negative Symptoms' *Journal of Nervous & Mental Disease* 193, No. 4, 2005, 244–249.

[64] C. D. Frith, *The Cognitive Neuropsychology of Schizophrenia.* (Hillsdale, NJ: Lawrence Erlbaum Associates, 1992).

[65] L. Sass, 'Schizophrenia, Self-Consciousness, and the Modern Mind', *Models of the Self*, S. Gallagher and J. Shear (eds.) (Exeter: Imprint Academic, 1999), 319–341.

again reflects a problem with metacognition involving a hyper-reflective concern for her illness and medication and what it does to her.

In the case of Phillips's patient Mr. S we find *flamboyant delusional narratives*—'He believed that his entire mental life was controlled by other people ... he would regularly misinterpret the actions and motivations of others, assuming that events or actions were intended for him that bore no relation to him'.[66] Although he had good autobiographical memory and his self-narratives reflected a coherent pattern, they were always presented in the passive voice and he identified with historical figures. His primary problems involved his sense of agency and self-identity.

Lysaker's patient C produces *monological and rigid narrative with sustained delusions*. He interpreted all events in terms of a delusional belief, i.e., that he was the subject of persecution by a former high-school teacher. 'C drove past provocative graffiti on the highway and saw a message from his persecutor.'[67] The narrative is fixed and absolute; to challenge it is perceived as further persecution organized by the teacher, and this simply becomes part of the narrative. In this regard new events in the subject's self-narrative are dominated by events (veridical or not) that are past. His self-narrative is nicely characterized by the same terms expressed by Minkowski's patient: absolute fixity and the lack of motivation that would enable him to envisage a future that would be different from the past, reflecting problems with temporal structure specifically in regard to the external, perspectival A-series.

On a more basic level problems with retentional-protentional structure can result in narrative disruptions known as clang associations. In the case of clang associations, schizophrenic subjects can lose their way and get ensnared in a current (present) aspect of language or the narrative itself; subjects are captured by semantically non-relevant aspects of the story and go off on extreme digressions. Clang associations are usually explained in terms of rhyming words—'whip', 'tip', 'lip'—where patients are more likely to connect words because of similarity of sound, rather than by meaning. This is something often seen in clinical interviews. Susan Duncan shows that it also occurs in gesture, where a particular iconic gesture will lead the patient into

---

[66] Op. cit. note 27, 330.
[67] Op. cit. note 42, 214.

digression—and she appeals to problems with protention (loss of a sense of where the narrative is going) to explain this.[68]

These various examples suggest that schizoprenic narratives reflect problems in the same capacities that give us narrative competency. The result is not simply disruptions in narrative structures and content but disruptions in the narrative self. There is also evidence to suggest that dysfunctions in narrative abilities in some schizophrenics have an effect on their ability to understand others. This is a complex issue that depends on how one conceives of the role of narrative versus mentalizing abilities in understanding others.[69] Frith and Corcoran, for example, conducted theory of mind (false belief) tests on schizophrenic patients by presenting stories and cartoon pictures (narratives are involved in the majority of false belief tests).[70] They were able to show that patients with paranoid delusions and those with negative symptoms or incoherence were impaired on questions concerning the mental states of others. For a good review of the complex issues associated with this question, see Brune's article.[71] No matter how we interpret the results of these tests, however, it is clear that schizophrenics often have problems understanding others, and at least one possible way to explain this is in terms of a failure of narrative competency.[72]

We can ask whether pathological disruptions in narrative simply reflect or also contribute to disruptions in the sense of self and/or

---

[68]   S. Duncan, 'Spatiomotor Imagery, Affect, and Time in Discourse', *Deuxième Congrès de l'International Society for Gesture Studies (ISGS): Interacting bodies*. (Lyon, France, 15–18 June 2005).

[69]   See S. Gallagher, and D. D. Hutto, 'Understanding Others Through Primary Interaction and Narrative Practice' *The Shared Mind: Perspectives on Intersubjectivity*, J. Zlatev, T. P. Racine, C. Sinha and E. Itkonen (eds) (Amsterdam: John Benjamins, in press); and S. Gallagher and D. Zahavi, *The Phenomenological Mind* (London: Routledge, forthcoming).

[70]   C. D. Frith and R. Corcoran, 'Exploring 'Theory of Mind' in People with Schizophrenia', *Psychological Medicine* 26, No. 3, 1996, 521–530.

[71]   M. Brune, ' "Theory of Mind" in Schizophrenia: a Review of the Literature', *Schizophrenia Bulletin* 31, No. 1, 2005, 21–42.

[72]   For the connection between narrative ability and false-belief tests, see N. R. Guajardo and A. Watson, 'Narrative Discourse and Theory of Mind Development', *The Journal of Genetic Psychology* 163, 2002, 305–325; and L. Abbeduto, K. Short-Meyerson, G. Benson and J. Dolish, 'Relationship between Theory of Mind and Language Ability in Children and Adolescents with Intellectual Disability', *Journal of Intellectual Disability Research* 48, No. 2, 2004, 150–159.

intersubjective processes. The answer appears to be both. On the one hand, it seems clear that in some cases something goes wrong at the metacognitive level and problems with ipseity are generated in the resulting narrative. As Stephens and Graham suggest, some aspects of self-agency are based on 'our proclivity for constructing self-referential narratives' which allow us to make sense of our behavior retrospectively.[73]

> [Normally] the subject's sense of agency regarding her thoughts ... depends on her belief that these mental episodes are expressions of her intentional states. That is, whether the subject regards an episode of thinking occurring in her psychological history as something she does, as her mental action, depends on whether she finds its occurrence explicable in terms of her theory or story of her own underlying intentional states.[74]

Our own self-narratives provide a coherence to our lives and if they are disrupted by inexplicable episodes, or failures in content or structure, the coherence of the narrative self is threatened. On the other hand, narratives may be veridical reports of what the subject actually experiences. Disruptions in first-order experience connected with self-agency and the perception of the actions of others may involve failures in neurological processes that ultimately get reflected in the self-narrative.[75]

Whether delusions are generated by problems with metacognition / metarepresentation,[76] the failure of some aspect of rational belief procedures—e.g., belief revision,[77] neurological disruptions of first-order experience,[78] or failure to register that one is

[73]   G. L. Stephens and G. Graham *When Self-Consciousness Breaks: Alien Voices and Inserted Thoughts* (Cambridge MA: MIT Press, 2000).

[74]   G. Graham and G. L. Stephens, 'Mind and Mine', *Philosophical Psychopathology*, G. Graham and G. L. Stephens (eds.) (Cambridge, MA: MIT Press, 1994), 91–109, 102.

[75]   See S. Gallagher, 'Philosophical Conceptions of the Self: Implications for Cognitive Science', *Trends in Cognitive Science* 4, 2000, 14–21; Gallagher 2003 (op. cit. note 11); and I. Gold and J. Hohwy, 'Rationality and Schizophrenic Delusion', *Mind & Language* 15, 2000, 146–167.

[76]   Op. cit. note 64.

[77]   G. Harman, *Change in View: Principles of Reasoning* (Cambridge, Mass.: MIT Press, G. 1986).

[78]   Op. cit. note 75: Gallagher 2000, and Gold and Hohwy 2000.

imagining rather than perceiving,[79] these various possibilities feed into, are sustained, and may be exaggerated by narrative.

Conclusions

The study of schizophrenic narratives throws light on the construction and mis-construction of self-narrative and the narrative self, but also cautions us to refrain from any quick generalizations. Not all schizophrenic narratives go wrong. For example, someone suffering from schizophrenic symptoms of thought insertion or delusions of control may correctly complain or describe these feelings in a coherent narrative. Furthermore, not everything about schizophrenic narratives goes wrong. Many of them may be well-formed and in good order, demonstrating a controlled metacognitive grasp on their experience. Sass cites a good example. A patient states:

> I get all mixed up so that I don't know myself. I feel like more than one person when this happens. I'm falling apart into bits ... I'm frightened to say a word in case everything goes fleeting from me so that there's nothing in my mind... . My head's full of thoughts, fears, hates, jealousies. My head can't grip them; I can't hold on to them. I'm behind the bridge of my nose – I mean, my consciousness is there. They're splitting open my head, oh, that's schizophrenic, isn't it? I don't know whether I have these thoughts or not.[80]

Just as it is important to understand that the logic of inserted thoughts requires that there be some thoughts that are not experienced as inserted (e.g., the patient's thought that a particular thought is inserted is not experienced as inserted), so examples of narratives from schizophrenic subjects suggest that it may be equally important to understand those things that don't go wrong in schizophrenic narrative.

---

[79]   G. Currie, 'Imagination, Hallucination and Delusion', *Mind and Language* 15, 2000, 168–183.
[80]   L. Sass, *The Paradoxes of Delusion: Wittgenstein, Schreber, and the Schizophrenic Mind* (Ithaca: Cornell University Press, 1995), 70.